LIBRARY MANUALS

Volume 12

A MANUAL OF LIBRARY ROUTINE

A MANUAL OF LIBRARY ROUTINE

W.E. DOUBLEDAY

LONDON AND NEW YORK

First published 1933 by George Allen & Unwin Ltd

This edition first published in 2022
by Routledge
4 Park Square, Milton Park, Abingdon, Oxon OX14 4RN

and by Routledge
605 Third Avenue, New York, NY 10017

Routledge is an imprint of the Taylor & Francis Group, an informa business

Copyright © 1933 by Taylor & Francis.

All rights reserved. No part of this book may be reprinted or reproduced or utilised in any form or by any electronic, mechanical, or other means, now known or hereafter invented, including photocopying and recording, or in any information storage or retrieval system, without permission in writing from the publishers.

Trademark notice: Product or corporate names may be trademarks or registered trademarks, and are used only for identification and explanation without intent to infringe.

British Library Cataloguing in Publication Data
A catalogue record for this book is available from the British Library

ISBN: 978-1-03-213109-2 (Set)
ISBN: 978-1-00-322771-7 (Set) (ebk)
ISBN: 978-1-03-215787-0 (Volume 12) (hbk)
ISBN: 978-1-03-215789-4 (Volume 12) (pbk)
ISBN: 978-1-00-324566-7 (Volume 12) (ebk)

DOI: 10.4324/9781003245667

Publisher's Note
The publisher has gone to great lengths to ensure the quality of this reprint but points out that some imperfections in the original copies may be apparent.

Disclaimer
The publisher has made every effort to trace copyright holders and would welcome correspondence from those they have been unable to trace.

A MANUAL OF
LIBRARY ROUTINE

by

W. E. DOUBLEDAY

LATE CHIEF LIBRARIAN OF THE HAMPSTEAD PUBLIC LIBRARIES;
LECTURER IN LIBRARY ROUTINE AND LIBRARY ECONOMY
AT THE SCHOOL OF LIBRARIANSHIP, UNIVERSITY
COLLEGE, LONDON

ILLUSTRATED

LONDON
GEORGE ALLEN & UNWIN LTD
AND THE LIBRARY ASSOCIATION
1933

FIRST PUBLISHED IN 1933

All rights reserved
PRINTED IN GREAT BRITAIN BY
UNWIN BROTHERS LTD., WOKING

GENERAL INTRODUCTION
TO THE SERIES

The publication of a systematic series of practical and authoritative Manuals of Library Work, which shall survey Library polity and practice in their latest aspects, is a requirement of which administrators, librarians, and students alike have long been conscious, and is much overdue.

In the Library world not the Great War alone, with its aftermath of new conditions, but also the Library Act of 1919, have marked the termination of one long epoch and the commencement of a new and yet more prosperous era. The removal of the crippling limitation of the penny rate at once paved the way for a renaissance of the Library Movement, and remarkable extensions and innovations, both in buildings and in service, have ensued. The great work of the Carnegie Trustees in fostering the development of urban Public Libraries has now been largely diverted into fresh channels, and County and Rural Library Systems now cover the country from Land's End to John-o'-Groats. The public demand and appreciation of Libraries have increased enormously, and, in response, old methods have been revised and new ones introduced. The evolution of Commercial and Technical Libraries and the development of Business and Works Libraries would amply suffice to indicate this spirit of progress, but, during the last decade or

A MANUAL OF LIBRARY ROUTINE

so, the entire field of Library service has been subjected to review and experiment, and little, either in administration or routine, remains entirely unchanged.

It will, therefore, be sufficiently obvious that the old textbooks relating to Library practice can no longer serve, and that there is a real need for new manuals, written by persons of experience and authority, and treating of the new conditions in a full and thoroughly practical manner. It is this void that the series of Library Manuals is designed to fill, and the fact that these volumes are to be issued by Messrs. George Allen and Unwin Ltd. in conjunction with the Library Association, should afford adequate proof of the qualifications of the authors to treat of the subjects upon which they will write. If sufficient support is forthcoming the series will be made comprehensive and complete.

The volumes will be supplied with bibliographical references throughout, and will be illustrated where necessary. No effort will be spared to make the series an essential tool for all those who are engaged in Library work, or who intend to embrace Librarianship as a profession. To students they will be invaluable. The uniform price of 10s. 6d. net will be adhered to so far as possible, so as to bring the Manuals within the reach of all.

Wm. E. DOUBLEDAY
General Editor

PREFACE

The term "routine" as applied to library work is capable of differing interpretations. Understood in its widest sense it would include much of administration, more or less of organization, book selection, classification, and cataloguing, together with those customary duties which have recurrently to be performed for the maintenance of service. A more narrow definition would restrict it to the manual and clerical processes associated with accessioning, preparing books for circulation, office-work, the supervision of rooms, the maintenance of shelf order, the registration of borrowers, and the mere counter work of issuing books to borrowers and receiving them back again. This *Manual* attempts to steer a course midway between these extremes. Major subjects can be adequately treated only in separate volumes, and in the following pages they are discussed particularly with reference to their routine aspects, but for the rest a wide survey is given of the methods in use at libraries of various categories. Municipal practice, naturally, looms large, but due attention is paid to the methods of university and special types of libraries.

Routine procedure varies considerably, for the technique is by no means fixed. Uniformity would imply perfection or stagnation, and whilst the former is ever the objective the latter is wisely avoided, or progress would cease. Every library adopts methods which are considered to be best adapted to its purposes. What is suitable for one might be undesirable for another. It is largely a matter of "adaptation to environment" and purpose. Collegiate systems differ quite as much as those of municipal libraries; county library methods from those of urban libraries; and even among libraries of the same kind variation is demanded by size, scope, and local conditions. It must, therefore, be clearly understood that there is not, nor can there be, any one single method which is best for all libraries: that system is the best which most efficiently and economically meets the requirements of each individual library. If the basic principles are mastered, and the object of each process grasped, difference in detail will not be perplexing.

Methods alternative in kind and degree are, accordingly, here described, and for this purpose many actual routine systems have been examined. To the librarians—too numerous to be specified—who have so generously and unhesitatingly afforded information my grateful thanks are tendered. I am under especial obligations to Mr. E. A. Savage for suggestions made for the improvement of the chapter on Classification, but Mr. Savage is not to be held responsible for any views expressed therein. I have also to thank the respective owners of the blocks for kind permission to use them in this book: acknowledgment of this courtesy is individually made upon each such illustration.

W. E. DOUBLEDAY

CONTENTS

CHAPTER		PAGE
	PREFACE	9
	LIST OF ILLUSTRATIONS	13
I.	SOME PRELIMINARY CONSIDERATIONS	15
II.	BOOK SELECTION AND ORDERING	23
III.	THE PREPARATION OF BOOKS FOR PUBLIC USE	42
IV.	ADMINISTRATIVE RECORDS	61
V.	CLASSIFICATION AND ITS PRACTICAL APPLICATIONS	80
VI.	CATALOGUES AND CATALOGUING	95
VII.	THE ADMISSION AND REGISTRATION OF BORROWERS	122
VIII.	BOOK ISSUE METHODS	145
IX.	REFERENCE LIBRARY ROUTINE, INCLUDING COMMERCIAL, TECHNICAL, AND SPECIAL LIBRARIES	162
X.	CHILDREN'S LIBRARIES, BRANCH LIBRARIES, AND DELIVERY AND DEPOSIT STATIONS	187
XI.	MAGAZINE AND READING ROOMS	207
XII.	UNIVERSITY, COLLEGIATE, AND SCHOOL LIBRARIES	223
XIII.	CO-OPERATIVE LIBRARY WORK: COUNTY AND RURAL LIBRARIES, REGIONAL CO-OPERATION, THE NATIONAL CENTRAL LIBRARY	246
XIV.	STOCKTAKING, WITHDRAWALS, AND REPLACEMENTS	269

CHAPTER		PAGE
XV.	BOOKBINDING: SPECIFICATIONS AND RECORDS	282
XVI.	FINANCE, COMMITTEE WORK, AND OFFICE ROUTINE	296
XVII.	SOME EXTENSION ACTIVITIES: LECTURES, PUBLICITY, BROADCASTING, CO-OPERATIVE WORK, HOSPITAL LIBRARIES, AND BOOKS FOR THE BLIND	322
	APPENDIX	
	SOME EXAMINATION QUESTIONS	337
	INDEX	343

ILLUSTRATIONS

PLATES

ISLAND STAFF ENCLOSURE, HAMPSTEAD CENTRAL LENDING LIBRARY	*Frontispiece*
	FACING PAGE
THE ELECTRIC STYLUS PEN IN USE	56
CARD CHARGING: A SORTING TRAY	145
CARD-CHARGING TRAYS, SHOWING GUIDES	152
MAGAZINE RACKS, HENDON PUBLIC LIBRARY	216
VERTICAL CABINET, WITH CORRESPONDENCE FOLDERS	312

SKETCHES IN THE TEXT

	PAGE
PROCESS-RECORDING STAMP	50
ACCESSION REGISTER CARD	75
SUMMARY STOCK-REGISTERS	78
MARKS USED IN PROOF CORRECTING	108
RATEPAYER'S APPLICATION VOUCHER	130
CHANGE OF ADDRESS NOTICE	142
OPEN-ACCESS CHARGING: BOOK-CARD	147
OPEN-ACCESS CHARGING: A "CHARGE"	148
REGIONAL CO-OPERATION: A LOOSE-LEAF UNION CATALOGUE ENTRY	259

By courtesy of Libraco, Ltd.]

ISLAND STAFF ENCLOSURE, HAMPSTEAD CENTRAL LENDING LIBRARY

A MANUAL OF LIBRARY ROUTINE

CHAPTER I

SOME PRELIMINARY CONSIDERATIONS

In a manual of library routine it cannot be too promptly or too strongly stated that method is essential for the satisfactory working of a library; but no system, however carefully devised, can be effective unless its details are faithfully performed. Some of these details may be mechanical in character and in themselves may appear to be unimportant, but their cumulative effect will be unmistakable, and the degree of accuracy and neatness with which minor processes are carried out will produce a marked result upon the quality of the service and the reputation of the library. Working methods should be carefully studied; their details should be comprehended, the rules and regulations—whether for the public or the staff—should be learnt, and the allotted duties should be discharged with good will, interest, and zeal. This, and this alone, is the royal road to success.

One of the fundamental qualities demanded by library service is accuracy. Quickness is desirable, but not at the expense of exactitude. Observation should be cultivated, and tactful initiative will usually be appreciated, while a lively interest taken in routine tasks will to a considerable extent relieve the monotony of recurrent work and dispel any tendency to perfunctory performance. Courtesy is, of course, assumed even although it may at times impose a strain upon patience, and in dealing with readers it is ever to be remembered that the library exists for their benefit. By far the greater number of borrowers are reasonable and agreeable enough to deal with, but if now and again a few individuals seem to be "difficult" there is then all the more reason for patience and tact upon the part of the staff. Rules and regulations may have to be enforced, but this should be done in as pleasant a manner as may be, and it is by no means impossible to combine firmness with politeness. Nothing irritates the public more than an undue display of officiousness, and this is a fault to which many youthful assistants appear to be peculiarly liable. *Fortiter in re, suaviter in modo* is still the golden rule.

Another qualification of sufficient importance to be singled out for mention is that of good and clear handwriting, and the assistant to whom this comes easily enjoys an initial advantage in comparison with those whose style is cramped, irregular, or even fanciful. The first essential in the writing of letters or figures is clearness, and the importance of this factor is continuous for, although modern methods of book charging may eliminate handwriting and the typewriter is employed for many clerical purposes, much handwork remains for

SOME PRELIMINARY CONSIDERATIONS

accessioning and many other daily processes, and it is necessary that it should be done with neatness and efficiency. Assistants whose calligraphy is indifferent should re-model their style in conformity with the plain round-hand which is compulsory in the Civil Service. Many municipal and other authorities now insist upon it, and it is usually included in the preliminary tests of candidates before the bestowal of appointments.

The handling of books

The life of books can be shortened or extended in accordance with the usage they receive, and it is necessary that they should be properly treated. A few practical hints as to the correct manner of handling them may be adventured here for the guidance of the inexpert.

As issued in cloth covers by publishers, books are but ill-adapted for heavy library wear, being "cased" and not "bound" in the technical sense of that term. Examination will show that the bodies of these volumes are lightly attached to their protective covers by strips of flimsy muslin-like material which pass round their backs and are glued, with or without the aid of projecting ends of the tapes to which the sections have been sewn, to the inside of the covers beneath the end-papers. This connecting material—called jaconet—may vary in quality and width, but its resistance to strain is limited, and if such books are tugged or lifted by their covers, the book and its cover will soon part company. Volumes specially bound for libraries are usually reinforced at this weak point by linen joints, but, even so, it would be injurious in the event to impose undue strain upon them. New and newly bound volumes need to be opened with care until the sewing becomes flexible. To open them wide, and especially with rapid action, is calculated to burst the stitches and cause the sections to "start," after which they will soon require re-binding. The correct treatment is first of all to open them gently, inserting a finger somewhere near the front and rear sections, and to "play" the pages by gentle movings to and fro. Other fingers should be slipped between the inner sections, and if the process of "playing" is repeated the book will be ready for use. The operation takes almost as long to read as to perform. It is perhaps needless to remind readers that books should never be pulled out from the shelves by their headbands. In modern bookbinding these convenient ridges are ornamental rather than useful, and in response to strain they will quickly sag and burst.

MAINTENANCE OF SHELF ORDER

Part of the daily routine will consist of the replacement of books upon their shelves, and the maintenance of shelf orderliness. In many libraries certain sections of the stock will be placed under the care of different assistants, who are held responsible for the restoration to their proper places of books returned by borrowers. It is important that

SOME PRELIMINARY CONSIDERATIONS

they should be correctly inserted, and the classification symbols or call numbers on the outside of each volume should make mistakes practically impossible except by careless placing. Any temptation to squeeze a book into an insufficient space must be resisted or it may be rendered shapeless by the pressure and the stitching be adversely affected. The shelves should be adjusted by re-arrangement of the books upon them until easy accommodation is obtained, and if the shelf guiding thus becomes disordered the guides must also be adjusted. Misplacement by readers is to be looked for and corrected by placing the books in their right positions, and if any volumes are discovered to be in bad condition they should be removed for examination. When the sections of a book once begin to work loose deterioration is rapid, and it is bad policy as well as poor economy to allow such books to circulate.

Book moving and dusting

Beginners should note that the backs of books are slightly thicker than their fore-edges are, owing to the ridges made in binding, and that while this is almost imperceptible in a single volume the effect when many volumes are concerned will be pronounced. Binder's cloths are smooth-surfaced and books are prone to slide unless lying evenly; if stacked in number upon their sides they will be apt to slip and fall with damaging effect. Assistants should never attempt to carry more books than they can safely and comfortably control, and the books should be carried with their backs outwards so that the thrust will be towards, and not away from, the body.

When dusting shelves the cloth should be damped just sufficiently to prevent the dust from flying, and when attending to the books themselves care should be taken not to rub the dirt *into* them. For reasons of hygiene and general convenience it is better that the books should be removed from the department and the dust lightly brushed or blown off either in the open or by an open window. The old-fashioned way was to eject the dust by knocking the books together at the risk of spoiling the bindings. The modern method is to use a library vacuum cleaner provided with special brushes and attachments so that the dust may be withdrawn by suction, or expelled by a forced draught. Under no circumstances should old leather-bound books be beaten together or they would promptly split at the joints.

SELF-EDUCATION

The most recent developments in library practice to date are, so far as the space allows, considered in the following chapters, and select reading lists are given for the use of readers desiring further information upon the different subjects. These bibliographies are by no means exclusive, and it would be easy to add to them. Mr. Cannons' encyclopaedic survey of professional periodical liter-

SOME PRELIMINARY CONSIDERATIONS

ature, covering all departments of library work[1] from 1876 onwards, is a quarry for the worker, and the Public Libraries Committee Report (1927), although it treats of librarianship from the point of view of administration and policy rather than that of practical routine, should be familiar to all who are interested in library work. The same may be said of the Annual Reports of the Carnegie United Kingdom Trustees. Those who wish to keep abreast of developments as they occur should consult the *Library Association Year Books* and the volumes of *The Year's Work in Librarianship* as issued, and they should also study the articles on routine work in the successive numbers of the *Library Association Record* and the other excellent professional journals as they are published.

SELECTED REFERENCES

BALDWIN (E. V.). Library Service. (A.L.A. Manual, 14.) 1931.
BROWN (J. D.). Manual of Library Economy, 4th edn., ed. and newly revised by W. C. Berwick Sayers. 1931. (Div. ii: Staff qualifications, duties, etc.)
COUTTS (H. T.). Special Rules and Regulations. (In *Open-Access Libraries*, pp. 179–90.) 1915.
DANA (J. C.). Library Primer. 1899. (Chs. xvii and xviii—Handwriting, care of books, etc.)
FLEXNER (J. M.). Circulation Work in Public Libraries. 1927. (Ch. ii—Contact with the public.)

---

[1] *Bibliography of Library Economy, 1876–1920*, by H. G. T. Cannons, 1927.

A MANUAL OF LIBRARY ROUTINE

HITCHLER (T.). The Successful Loan-desk Assistant. (In the *Lib. Journal*, xxxii, 1906, pp. 554–9; and in the *Wilson Bulletin*, ii, 1926, pp. 483–6.)

STEWART (J. D.). The Sheaf Catalogue. 1909. (Handwriting, etc.)

CHAPTER II

BOOK SELECTION AND ORDERING

Anyone can get together a quantity of books and dub it a library—and a library of sorts it would be. To the inexperienced the thing looks so easy that neither training nor experience is called for: all that is necessary is to look over the glowing advertisements of publishers and to order such volumes as engage the fancy. But it is not so easy as that. On the contrary, the wise choice of books, nicely balanced after exhaustive investigations into local requirements, proportioned with well-informed discretion, and judiciously purchased in the right editions, is one of the most difficult of all the tasks with which a librarian is confronted. There is no severer test of the value of a library than the quality of its books, and although a tolerably good book stock may possibly be acquired by the exercise of a moderate amount of educated effort, especially if backed by experience, such perfunctory work can never ensure success and no effort should be spared to achieve the best result.

Briefly stated, the whole problem is to acquire the largest stock of the most suitable books at the least cost for the greatest number of readers, and the very first lesson to be learned is that the stock must always be obtained by extremely careful selection and not by haphazard accumulation. Another point to bear in mind is that the cheapest editions are frequently the most expensive in the end. A wide knowledge of literature, familiarity with the particular needs of local readers, practical acquaintance with all sorts of bibliographical tools, patient research, and experience are all required for the work of book selection, and these qualifications must be systematically applied if satisfactory stock is to be acquired.

FORMING ORIGINAL BOOK STOCK

For libraries in course of establishment a careful survey of the district is a necessary preliminary, and it should be one of the first of considerations. In a manufacturing area the predominant industries will have to be specially catered for, and consultation with the industrial leaders will yield valuable information and induce a friendly feeling and co-operation. If there are colleges or technical or other training institutes, or large libraries within easy distance, these should be approached with a view to arranging for interchange of books, and to obviate the unnecessary duplication of special or expensive works. The mass-psychology of the local population should be carefully studied, and the librarian should inform himself to the fullest possible extent as to the nature of the demand which he will probably have to meet. Armed with this information, and bearing in mind the invaluable assistance to be derived from the National Central

BOOK SELECTION AND ORDERING

Library and by regional co-operation in supplying the needs of special students, he may set himself to the task of drawing up his lists of books.

Bibliographies and catalogues of selected libraries will be extremely useful for this work, but it must be remembered that published bibliographies are no sooner printed than they begin to fall out of date. There is no dearth of bibliographical aids, and the number of general, subject, and author bibliographies is so large as to call for expert knowledge in choosing them. Mr. Esdaile devotes two chapters[1] to this subject in his *Manual of Bibliography*, and gives a classified list of numerous works, and enhances its value considerably by the annotations he appends to the various entries. Of general bibliographies Brunet's *Manuel du Libraire* is useful for older books, but its latest supplement only comes up to 1880. The British Museum *Catalogue of Printed Books*, 1881–1905 (now being superseded by the new edition), carries on the good work, but its cost and size render it unsuitable for many libraries. Subject bibliographies of a general character are represented by Minto's *Classified and Annotated Guide to the Principal Works of Reference* and its *Supplement*, Mudge's *Guide to Reference Books*, Sonnenschein's *Readers' Guide* and the same compiler's *Best Books*, the *Subject Indexes of the Modern Works added to the Library* of the British Museum, the *Subject Catalogue*, with its supplements, of the London Library—all annotated except the last two

[1] Chapters ix and x—Bibliographies: some classes and examples.

catalogues, and the Library Association's *Books to Read*, for adolescent readers. As admirable specimens of special bibliographies *The Claim of Antiquity*, issued by the Councils of the Societies for the Promotion of Hellenic and Roman Studies, and the excellent little handbooks to special subjects, issued by the Leeds Public Library, may be mentioned, and the sectional lists of books occurring in Drury's *Book Selection*, will put the enquirer on the track of other useful guides.

Perhaps it may be thought desirable to invoke the aid of specialists. If this be done these experts should be informed as to the amount available for the purchase of the books concerning which their advice is sought, and if they can be induced to distinguish between elementary, intermediate, and advanced treatises, and to specify which they particularly recommend for general library use, the value of their assistance will be materially augmented. Usually their lists exceed the limits and must be reduced to manageable dimensions or the stock will be "out of perspective."

BALANCE OF STOCK

The book stock should be balanced in such a way that whilst all sections are represented no one division is exploited at the cost of others; but little or no attempt should be made to conform to academically standardized limitations. As a matter of fact the proportions vary considerably and justifiably in different libraries. University and special

BOOK SELECTION AND ORDERING

libraries will, for instance, have no need of current fiction, and on the other hand they must provide for their own peculiar necessities; even rate-supported libraries have to cater for differing communities, and their stocks exhibit such variations as to render averages of other libraries of little account. This having been stated, the following comparative table of proportions may be tentatively submitted as a sort of basis subject to all kinds of alterations in order to satisfy local requirements.

	Brown	*Walker*	*Williams*	*Dana*
	Per cent	Per cent.	Per cent.	Per cent.
General works	3	2	3	4
Philosophy	4	1·9	3	1
Religion	5	3·2	6	2
Sociology	7	5·5	6	9
Philology	4	1·2	2	1
Science	9	5·5	8	8
Useful arts	9	5·7	9	6
Fine arts	7	7·6	7	4
Literature	28	14·2	35	12
Prose fiction	—	34	—	20
History	8 ⎫			13 ⎫
Biography	8 ⎬	19·2	21	10 ⎬
Geography and Travel	8 ⎭			10 ⎭

The first three columns relate to British libraries and the last one to America. Brown's figures are taken from his *Manual*. Walker's are given in *A Primer of Librarianship* as the actual proportions of the Hendon Public Library; Williams' from his *Courses of Study in Library Science*, and Dana's from his *Library Primer*. There are sufficient divergencies in these percentages to show that proportional representation is far from being fixed, and the tendency of libraries towards specialization in certain subjects is of itself sufficient to account for this lack of uniformity.

So far only the number of books in each section of stock has been mentioned, but there is another way of planning it out, *viz.* allocating a proportion of the book fund to each of the divisions. Whichever way may be adopted there is one thing which must never be done: it would be sheer folly to attempt to represent each subdivision of any system of classification in a library. The requirements of ordinary readers should first be provided for; then those of advanced students to such a degree as the book vote may seem to warrant. The whole of the available amount should not be exhausted however carefully the lists are compiled and reviewed, for there will assuredly be oversights and a balance should be held in reserve for such omissions.

MAINTENANCE OF STOCK

The librarian who forms original stock has to work more or less in the dark, but in the maintenance of a library his task is easier, for the use of the books already in use can be tabulated and the demand is largely known.

Bibliographies will still be essential, but the new factor of keeping abreast of current publications enters into consideration and fresh sources of information must be tapped. Publishers' lists of

BOOK SELECTION AND ORDERING

announcements—usually appearing in early spring and late autumn—and press advertisements herald the deluge, but publishers are optimistic concerning their own books, and it must be recollected that it is their business to sell the books which they produce, and their claims cannot be accepted without investigation. Then come the reviews—good, bad, or indifferent, and confusing because of their discordant pronouncements. Ordinary journalistic notices of books are not usually very helpful to the librarian, but *The Times Literary Supplement*, the *Manchester Guardian*, at least two of the Sunday papers, and certain other English and Scottish papers, have established a high reputation for sound criticism. As a rule signed reviews are preferable to anonymous ones, for the reason that the status and characteristics of reviewers become known, but the rule is not rigid: for example, *The Times Supplement* reviews are not signed, but their value is unquestioned. Many of the weeklies, and not a few of the monthlies, devote considerable space to notices of books, and the professional journals of the library world. The *Library Association Record* (to a minor degree), the *Library Review*, the *Library World*, and the *Librarian* (to a still greater extent) single out for critical notice such of the latest publications as they consider worthy of notice by librarians. The *Bookman* and the *London Mercury* will suggest themselves as indispensable literary monthlies.

For scientific, technical, and other special subjects those representative organs which devote themselves to particular aspects should receive careful attention, for their reviews are generally well informed and highly competent. The *English Historical Review*, *Nature*, the *Church Quarterly Review*, the *Electrician*, and the *Architect*, all here suggested at random, may be cited by way of illustration. The *Book Review Digest* as an American publication naturally pays special, but by no means exclusive, attention to transatlantic publications, but it is especially useful inasmuch as it gives extracts or synopses of favourable *and* unfavourable reviews.

The *Publisher and Bookseller* and the *Publishers' Circular* are British trade weeklies each giving a list of the most recent publications with cumulative summaries at the end of every month, and appearing as volumes at the end of the year under the respective titles of *Whitaker's Cumulated Book List* and the *English Catalogue*. The latter is again cumulated in one alphabetical sequence every five years. For American books the *Cumulative Book Index* and *Publishers' Weekly* are indispensable. France has its counterparts in the weekly *Bibliographie de la France* and the annual *Catalogue mensuel de la libraire française*, and other countries are similarly provided.[1] It should be noted that these publications give bibliographical details only, and are not evaluative. Their function is to supply information as to authors, titles, format, price, publishers, and date and cost

---

[1] For details of foreign bibliographical periodicals, see Drury's *Order Work for Libraries*, pp. 38–40.

BOOK SELECTION AND ORDERING

of each publication. The *English Catalogue* goes back as far as 1835.

Much of the work of selection will devolve upon the librarian, but with so large a survey no single person could possibly cover the whole field. In some libraries the laudable practice of encouraging the staff to notify likely books is found, and assistants forward suggestions with brief notes and references for guidance.

THE PREPARATION OF BOOK LISTS

From sources such as the foregoing may book lists be drawn up at any time, and, as it will be necessary to refer to, or take out, individual items for that purpose, cards or paper slips of uniform size appear to be particularly suitable, for the process of addition and elimination will be perpetual. The cards should be filed in systematic order in a special drawer or cabinet tray. Thus, if later information suggests elimination any card may easily be withdrawn or additional ones may be inserted in their proper order. Extracts from reviews may usefully be pasted upon these cards and in this fashion a comparative conspectus is always at hand. Reviews should be dated and their sources specified.

The book vote for the year will limit the expenditure, and when drawing up lists the amount already spent must ever be borne in mind. To allocate the yearly amount into twelve equal portions, if monthly purchases are made, would be most unwise, for the spring and autumn seasons account for a very considerable proportion of the annual output of books; but some sort of regulated expenditure should be maintained. Possibly a block amount may be set aside for replacements, or for separate departments or branches. In university libraries there will probably be special funds to which purchases must be charged. It will therefore be necessary to keep a record of all these expenditures, and to adjust it as fresh commitments occur, to show both what has been spent and how much of the book vote remains available.

From the filed cards selections will be made at intervals, usually for submission to the committee, although some librarians are vested with plenary authority to purchase at discretion either within or without limitation—subject to subsequent report of the number of volumes bought and their cost. Every such list should be most carefully compiled with due regard to demand as reported from the counter or ascertained by examination of the issue-papers in books by the same authors or on kindred subjects. The records in which book issues are tabulated will be useful here, and the finer the sub-divisions the more precise will be the information yielded. Weak spots must be strengthened and new subjects added. Where there is choice of editions good type, at least a fair paper, and satisfactory stitching and binding should always have preference: pulpy paper and wire-stitched books should be avoided. Keen oversight upon popular books,

BOOK SELECTION AND ORDERING

especially fiction, will be necessary, or when the demand, often short-lived, declines the shelves may be cumbered with derelict books. Remember that money spent upon books that are indifferent or bad means so much less available for the purchase of good ones, and, whilst meeting reasonable demands so far as possible, be chary of frittering away the book vote upon works of ephemeral interest.

To this end each card should be critically reviewed before it is included in the list of prospective purchases, and, when the list has been drawn up and totalled, consider the wisdom of appropriating so much of the book vote at the present juncture. When the list is in final form it should be checked by the catalogue to prevent unintentional duplication, and the number and cost of the volumes should be ascertained, either as a whole or by classified sections: it is then ready for the committee.

THE BOOK LIST IN COMMITTEE

Where lists are circulated in advance of the meeting the chairman will "put" them *en bloc*, stating the number and cost of the volumes. If objections are upheld by a vote the librarian should at the time delete such items from his copy of the list and alter the figures correspondingly. If no such list has been circulated the librarian will read out particulars of each item—author, title, price, number of copies, and destination. Committee decisions will fall under one or other of the following four categories:

(*a*) Books unconditionally approved for purchase.
(*b*) Books approved for purchase at a reduced cost.
(*c*) Books deferred for further consideration.
(*d*) Books rejected.

The cards should be marked as decisions are reached, and should later be sorted into drawers labelled in accordance with those groupings. If sheet-lists are used cards should be written, at least for books approved or deferred, so that the file may be uniform and complete. Items deferred may require fuller information, and this should be supplied as opportunity permits. They will then be placed in the drawer as a separate group with the next batch of cards for the consideration of the committee.

BOOKS SUBMITTED ON APPROVAL

Many committees desire to have an opportunity of examining books before deciding for or against their purchase, and no bookseller will hesitate to send them for inspection. They should be checked off by their delivery notes, and then placed upon shelves and made accessible to the members several days preceding their meeting. If all the books which the librarian is proposing for purchase are so received, reading out the details may be omitted and only those not displayed need have their particulars read out. Where sheet-lists have been distributed the books awaiting examination are sometimes

BOOK SELECTION AND ORDERING

starred, and details of the others are read out. Should any volumes not be approved they ought to be returned with the utmost promptitude, and every precaution must be taken to ensure that they are received back by the bookseller in the same mint state as when sent out. Second-hand books should be similarly treated, and always the books should be protected by ample wrappings if they have to be returned by post or rail.

READERS' SUGGESTIONS

Most of the proposals for books will arise from the librarian and his staff (whose co-operation will be most helpful), but suggestions by outsiders should be encouraged and provision made, either by suggestion books or boxes, for their reception. If the former plan is preferred each page may well be headed with a request that publishers and prices should always be indicated if possible. Date, author, title, publisher, price, and the names and address of the proposer are the details required, and unless it is intended to leave an "open door" for ribald comments the book should be kept at the counter and be produced only upon request. The alternative is to affix a slotted box to a wall or fitting in some conspicuous position, with a supply of blank forms, or cards, close at hand. These, when filled up and signed, will be dropped through the slot, and will be protected from public reach.

Whether books or forms are used they should be examined at frequent intervals, the recommendations checked, and, if permissible, books suggested should be purchased forthwith at discretion. Otherwise the proposals may be submitted to the committee and decisions recorded thereon. Books (or other publications) when approved will be purchased in the normal way, and each item may have to be reduced to card form for filing and general purposes. Here, again, it is important that decisions shall be marked against each entry as they are reached, or uncertainty will ensue. As the books are received the persons who suggested them should be advised, and it is usual to allow them the first use of books, subject to a time-limit for claiming them, but fiction is, for obvious reasons, excluded from this privilege. A card, tactfully worded, and printed with alternative reasons—the relevant one being left and the others struck out—may be sent to proposers whose recommendations were rejected, but some libraries prefer to advise readers in a more general way of their regret that their suggestions were not approved.

ORDERING BOOKS

Each library will have its own method of ordering books, but a practice so common as to be almost universal is that of making carbon copies in duplicate or triplicate. In either case one copy will be kept upon the office file. If three are prepared the other two will be sent to the agent: one he may use as a delivery note or invoice, the other he will retain as a check upon full execution of the order. Unless he has been supplied with an official memorandum

BOOK SELECTION AND ORDERING

of the conditions of supply, or unless this running instruction is included in a contract, order forms should be printed with brief particulars, *e.g.* that books not delivered within a specified period, say fourteen days, are not to be supplied unless re-ordered; that reasons for non-delivery shall in each instance be notified, and that unless instructed to the contrary the latest editions shall always be sent.

Order forms carry an individual number for reference use and should be provided with columns for details of authors, titles, publishers, prices, and the number of copies in each case required. If £.S.D. columns are included the form returned by the bookseller may serve as an invoice, while a remarks column may be used for noting causes of non-delivery. Where books are chargeable to special accounts separate orders should be issued.

Before making out orders discrimination must be exercised, for not all the books approved for purchase will be obtained at published prices: some may be old books no longer in print, and others too expensive to be acquired in a hurry. The cards for such works should be filed apart in the hope of acquiring them by sending lists of desiderata to second-hand booksellers or by examining their catalogues as received. Those to be purchased forthwith will be set out on the order forms as described above, but it will be advisable to check the items or errors may occur. As this process is performed each card should be marked to show from whom and upon what date the item was ordered. The cards thus treated are placed in the "Books on order" file. The cards for books to be sought for or to be obtained at a reduced price may be sorted into a drawer marked "Second-hand," and this differential filing can be extended to cover all requirements. When the forms have been examined and signed by the responsible officer the order is ready for dispatch. Some authorities require that their finance officer shall be advised as to financial commitments as they occur. Where this regulation is in force it must be observed in the manner locally prescribed. For his own information the librarian should also record estimated or actual order amounts under the headings of the votes to which the orders relate.

ADJUSTING THE ORDER FILE

Cards are abstracted and slipped into the books as they are received and checked, for these contain information which will be wanted for accessioning, and they may subsequently be employed as process cards or for shelf-lists. Cards of volumes not received should be marked with the symbols[1] indicating reasons for non-delivery, and the date of these reports should be added, for what is relevant at one time may be inapplicable at another. If a book is being reprinted, or at the binder's, or is being procured, it may be restored to the "Books on order" drawer. Items reported as not traceable should be checked and corrected where necessary; but works reported "out of print" or for any other

[1] See pp. 44–5.

BOOK SELECTION AND ORDERING

reason not available for supply should be separately filed for re-ordering from another agent, or perhaps at second-hand. The file will need to be examined from time to time, and any items long overdue may well be reconsidered as the necessity for purchasing them may no longer exist.

THE NET BOOK SYSTEM

In estimating expenditure on books allowance must be made for the fact that, under certain conditions, libraries are no longer required to pay full prices for newly published books. Until 1900 booksellers were at liberty to allow such discount as they chose, but undercutting rendered the trade unprofitable and the "net" system was introduced for its protection. This arrangement stipulated that the full public price of books issued on net terms should be charged to all customers. Novels and school books were exempted from this restriction, which was a compulsory obligation upon the whole of the retail book trade, but during the Great War fiction was swept into the net, and libraries, which had enjoyed large discounts as compensation for the loss of preferential treatment in regard to other books, were placed in the position of ordinary retail buyers. Through the efforts of the Library Association the great service rendered by libraries in the dissemination of books has been officially recognized by the Publishers' Association and the Associated Booksellers, and in the capacity of "book agents" such libraries as obtain a licence for the purpose, and spend not less than £100 a year upon the acquisition of new books, are entitled to deduct a "commission" of 10 per cent. from all bills for newly issued books.[1]

SELECTED REFERENCES

BAKER (E. A.). Book Selection: Fundamental Principles and Applications. (In *Lib. Assn. Record*, xiii, 1911, pp. 17–29.)
BASCOM (E. L.). Book Selection. (A.L.A. Manual, 16.) 1930.
BOSTWICK (A. E.). The American Public Library. 4th edn. 1929. (Chs. xi–xii—Book selection and purchase.)
—— How Librarians Choose Books. (In *Library Essays*.) 1920.
BROWN (J. D.). Manual of Library Economy. 4th edn. 1931. (Div. ix—Book selection.)
DRURY, (F. K. W.). Book Selection, 1930.
—— Order Work for Libraries. 1930.
—— Selection and Acquisition of Books for Libraries. 1928.

---

[1] Licences are granted subject to the conditions that the libraries to which they are issued shall not otherwise accept discounts or commissions from suppliers of newly published books, and that where labelling and stamping are performed by book vendors the following charges shall be paid; for labelling and rubber stamping, ½d. per volume; for labelling, rubber stamping, and affixing pockets and preparing cards, 1d. per book. In cases where the materials (cards, labels, pockets, etc.) are supplied by the library the charges may be reduced by two-thirds. Second-hand books are not affected by this agreement. Forms of application for licences are obtainable from the Library Association, which will forward them, when filled up and officially signed, to the trade organization for approval and registration. Libraries may nominate their suppliers and change them, upon request, from time to time. Collegiate and other non-municipal libraries are eligible for licences if, under reasonable conditions, they are willing to admit outsiders to consult their books, with certain reservations, without charge throughout the usual library hours.

BOOK SELECTION AND ORDERING

McColvin (L. R.). Theory of Book Selection for Public Libraries. 1925.

Savage (E. A.). Plea for the Analytical Study of the Reading Habit. (In *Lib. Assn. Record*, n.s., ii, 1924, pp. 210–23.)

Sayers, (W. C. Berwick) and Stewart (J. D.). Book Selection and Ordering. (In *The Card Catalogue*, p. 66.)

Walker (J. E.). Book Selection. (In *Primer of Librarianship*, ch. ii.) 1931.

Warner (J.). Reference Library Methods. 1925. (Book selection, pp. 87–95.)

Wheatley (H. B.). How to Form a Library. 1902.

Wheeler (J. L.). The Library and the Community. 1924.

CHAPTER III

THE PREPARATION OF BOOKS FOR PUBLIC USE

(CHECKING OFF, COLLATING, STAMPING, PROCESS RECORDING, CUTTING, LABELLING, AND BOOK-NUMBERING PROCESSES)

When books are delivered it is necessary that they should be checked to ascertain whether the items charged for have been received, and also whether they correspond in all respects with the terms of the order upon which they have been supplied. It is most desirable that this should be done without loss of time and that the volumes should not be dispersed or allowed in any way to become mixed up with others; if this were to happen, it might be extremely difficult to collect them together again with any certainty of actual identity.

The documents required for this purpose are usually invoices, which afford details, sufficient for verification, of the various books delivered, the number of copies sent, and, in each instance if the books are newly issued, the published price. If the books are second-hand the published price may not be given or it may take a secondary place, the selling price being indicated in the cost columns. Occasionally, however, parcels may be accompanied only by delivery notes, which present similar information but serve no further purpose, whereas invoices are

PREPARATION OF BOOKS FOR PUBLIC USE

official records upon which payment will in due course be made. A growing practice is to issue orders in duplicate or triplicate form, one of the copies being returned with the books either as a delivery note or invoice. The advantage of this method is that the order form states such details as publisher, edition, series or format, which ordinary trade invoices do not attempt. All this information will be required from one source or another if a proper check is to be made, and if it does not occur in this manner it must be obtained from the order file from which the order itself was prepared.[1]

Checking off

The process of checking off is largely mechanical, but it calls for care. It can be performed by one individual, but it is better, at all events where large consignments are concerned, for one assistant to read out the order details and for another to see that the books agree therewith. It will facilitate progress if the books are arranged in alphabetical order at the outset. The assistant who calls out the items will probably have the order file before him and will abstract the cards concerned (if the file be composed of cards[2]) and insert them in the books as they are found to be correctly supplied. He should also place a tick against each such invoice item, or make a brief note in case of doubt or error. It is the duty of the other assistant not only to find the

[1] See p. 37.   [2] Order files are described in Chapter II.

volumes as their details are read out, but to see that they correspond in number and other respects with the details as specified on the order. Any books which do not comply with the specification should be laid aside for subsequent treatment; they may have to be returned and credited. If and when all have been satisfactorily accounted for the invoice may be initialled sheet by sheet by the responsible assistant, but this should only be done when the necessary corrections (if any) have been made, and the initials should be taken to mean that the assistant in question was responsible for making such adjustments. Whether the pricing out and casting up, or the deduction of allowance by discount or commission, should be attended to at this stage or later is a matter of purely local determination.

If the order be of any size it is improbable that the books will all be received in one batch. The supplier as a rule sends such copies as he has in stock and collects the rest from wholesalers or publishers. Some volumes may have to be imported, others may not be ready for publication, or for other reasons cannot be immediately supplied. The cause of non-delivery should be given by the bookseller, and this is customarily done by symbols which are common in the trade. A list of those most generally employed is given herewith:

    bdg.   Binding. (Available shortly.)
    c.t.   Cannot trace. (Details should be verified.)
    dis.   Discontinued. (Unobtainable.)
    i.p.   In preparation. (Not yet ready. See n.r. below.)

PREPARATION OF BOOKS FOR PUBLIC USE

n.d.   Not done. (n.d.u., not done up, is sometimes stated.)
n.k.   Not known. (Equivalent to c.t. as above.)
n.r.   Not ready. (Sometimes n.o., not out, is preferred.)
o.o.   On order. (Not in stock, but is being procured.)
o.p.   Out of print. (Unobtainable new.)
o.s.   Out of stock. (Similar to o.o., is being obtained.)
o.t.o.   Only to order. (Not procurable on approval.)
r.p.   Reprinting. (New edition ready shortly.)
s.h.   Second-hand. (In lieu of new copies.)

Such of the foregoing information as may be applicable should be supplied by the bookseller, either upon the returned copy of the order or in the form of an advice note, when delivering books. The order file should be marked accordingly and the cards of unprocurable items withdrawn, or the file will soon be in a state of confusion. The invoices will go to their file in the office or, alternatively, may accompany the books so that they may be provided with accession or other clue numbers for showing where the individual books have been stocked.

The next process is that of collation; not the bibliographical collation as described by Mr. Esdaile in his *Student's Manual of Bibliography* (pp. 215–44), but something simpler and more rapid. Some libraries do not trouble to collate lending-library books of any kind; others collate everything save fiction, and some collate every volume as it passes into stock. Whether it is wise to omit this examination altogether or to restrict it to special kinds of books is a matter of opinion.

A MANUAL OF LIBRARY ROUTINE

The object of routine collation is to ascertain whether the sections of individual books are complete, in proper sequence, and whether the books are otherwise in good condition. Books are, of course, printed upon sheets of various sizes, and these sheets when folded are known as sections, sometimes called "gatherings." Each sheet has a clue in the shape of a letter or a numeral printed at the foot of the first page of each folded section. This clue is technically termed a "signature," and it forms a convenient guide for both binding and collation, since the signatures follow in sequence, and any omission or departure from the proper order automatically calls for investigation. A section may have been omitted, duplicated, inserted upside-down, or a sheet from another book may accidentally have been included.

The sizes of books are governed in the first place by the dimensions of the printed sheets and, secondly, by the number of times the sheets have been folded, and these sizes are designated by their Latin names. Those folded into eight *leaves* or sixteen *pages* are called octavos; those which are folded into four leaves are known as quartos; and those having only two leaves are termed folios. The conventional symbols, frequently met with in advertisements and catalogues, are respectively 8vo, 4to, and fol. (or fo.). This *Manual*, for example, is a large crown octavo (la. cr. 8vo for short), and every sixteenth page has its progressive letter signature, as may be seen by reference to pages 17,

PREPARATION OF BOOKS FOR PUBLIC USE

33, 49, etc. It should be noted that the letters I and J and V and W are generally regarded as alternatives, and rarely, if ever, are both signatures used in the same volume. Not infrequently the first page of the text proper is marked with the signature A (or 1), and the prefatory matter—which is often the last to be put into type—is guided by Roman numerals, elasticity being thus provided for. Some bulky tomes, omnibus volumes for example, contain so many sections that the alphabet is overrun. In that case the later sections may have such double signatures as AA, BB, CC, and treble letters are not unknown; but when this size is reached a change of device is likely to be adopted, and signatures may appear as 2A, 2B, 3A, 3B, and so onwards. Small volumes such as duodecimos (12mos), and possibly 16mos and 24mos, are subject to special foldings.

If collation shows that these signatures are all in order it may be taken that the book is complete, but there are other factors requiring attention. Plates and maps (if any) should be checked by the list printed in the forefront of the volume; mechanical damage may have been suffered during the operations of printing or binding; and in one way or another pages may have become torn, soiled, or otherwise disfigured. If the printer has used too much ink the print is likely to be smudgy and there may be leaves stuck together—technically called "set-offs"—if pressed too soon. On the other hand, too little ink may have been used, with the inevitable result that the impressions are so faint as to be almost "blind" and undecipherable. Occasionally faulty imposition on the printing machine may produce bad "registering" and the print may stretch somewhat obliquely across the page, or the book covers may have been damaged through defective packing. All these possibilities should be explored, but, except when rare or costly books are involved, a more or less casual examination generally suffices. It is only fair to say that defects in production are relatively few.

When blemishes are found to be of such a character that volumes are not acceptable, the books so affected should be returned to the supplier, and if they have not been rendered unsaleable by stamps or other markings fresh copies will readily be supplied. If, however, collation has been omitted and a book has passed into stock, some delay will be inevitable, for the bookseller will have to send it to the publisher, and the latter will return it to the binder for correction, and three or four weeks may elapse before the volume finds its way back to the library. Books returned to vendors for this or any other reason must, of course, be entered in the registers provided for the purpose, and when the matter has been adjusted the entry must be cleared.

There is no rigid uniformity as to the order in which the various processes of preparing books for circulation is to be done, but it may well be that as soon as books are found to be physically perfect they should in some way be marked as library property.

PREPARATION OF BOOKS FOR PUBLIC USE

In libraries where collation is not part of the routine this marking can be done directly after checking off; in others it is performed at any convenient time. If the library has an embossing machine the covers may be stamped, and that may be regarded as sufficient for the time being and the stamping of the pages may be deferred until a later stage, perhaps when the books are being labelled.

The apparatus for embossing book covers is simple and effective, consisting of a steel die operated by a revolving handle which, when set in motion by a swing of the hand, rapidly descends by screw action and strikes the boards with sufficient force to make an indelible impression. The covers to be stamped are held on the striking bed, and it should be seen that they are so placed that the die will strike a central or such other position as may be preferred. The die itself should never be allowed to strike the metal base upon which the book is placed, or a blurred definition will gradually be produced, and when not in use a wedge of cardboard or blotting-paper should be inserted for it to rest upon. Incidentally it may be mentioned that the assistant who revolves the handle of this press should stand clear of its reach or a disagreeable blow may be received: if the finger-tips are not out of the limited range of the descending die more serious injury may result, but with ordinary caution accidents will easily be avoided.

Many libraries now find it convenient to maintain a record of the various processes through which books pass before becoming available for general use. This is called process checking or process recording, and it is achieved in various ways, cards (or slips) or stamped impressions in the books being available for choice. The degree of fullness attempted varies enormously, some providing for information in *précis* respecting each book from the time when it was first noted for consideration and through all the intermediate phases of its library history down to the time when it is discarded—from birth to death, so to speak. Others are less elaborate, requiring only such details as the classification number, accession number, and spaces for the initials of the assistant responsible for collation and for ticks to indicate whether the book has been catalogued or not.

A fuller record of this character is as follows:

Accsn. no.		Annotated by	
Classfn. no.		Stamped by	
Collated by		Cut by	
Catalogued by		Labelled by	
Card ctgd. by		Checked by	

In this sketch the words are expanded, but as the size of the stamp must be kept within narrow limits it is customary to adopt abbreviations: the impres-

PREPARATION OF BOOKS FOR PUBLIC USE

sion is thus more compact and it is easier to make good impressions. The checking alluded to (in the final division above) means that the book has been inspected to see that it is in all respects ready for placing upon the public shelves. There are probably fuller forms, but this seems fairly adequate and many libraries totally ignore the process record.

Process cards (or slips) are invariably fuller of detail, necessarily so because they are filed apart from the books to which they relate. Author, title, and publisher must be entered also, and in some instances the whole library history of each volume is here recorded. If the process record is stamped in the book there is no fear of it being lost, but there is often a real risk of the ink showing through to the other side of the page. Where cards are used there is an ever-present danger of them falling out of the books, in which they ought to be kept until all the preliminary stages are completed. To minimize this risk the book-card pocket should be pasted into the cover of the book now and the process card placed within it will be protected.

Cutting and labelling

Volumes produced with "bolts," or uncut edges, are agreeable enough to the book collector, and more than one essay has been written concerning the pleasures of the paper-knife, but to the librarian such books are an unmitigated nuisance. The edges have to be cut one at a time, and if by inadvertence one is overlooked there is more than an outside chance of the book coming back to the library with edges scalloped or pages torn across by readers who, having nothing more appropriate at hand, have severed the leaves by using a cigarette-holder, a hatpin, or a finger. The proper tool to use is a smooth-edged paper-knife, preferably of material other than metal, of medium thickness, and not too sharp or too pointed at the end.

Many kinds of paper are perfectly easy to cut, but those of a spongy or fibrous texture are often troublesome and must be very carefully treated or jagged edges will be produced. Perhaps the best way is to cut through the "bolts" with an even and steady motion, working from the bottom to the top of the pages, avoiding anything like a sawing action, and applying most of the strength to the pull rather than the push of each stroke of the knife. A very common fault is failure to cut right back to the spine (or back) of the book, and if this occurs the page will be torn when opened by readers. An objectionable practice favoured by a few publishers is to issue books whose top and side edges have been trimmed flush by the guillotine, but with some of the bottom folds uncut. To libraries this procedure is particularly obnoxious, and it ought not to be continued. The only course is to prefer other editions when possible and to maintain a watchful lookout for these offences, or mutilated pages will ensue.

Labelling is such a straightforward piece of work that little need be said about it save that it should be neatly done. The paste should not be too freely

PREPARATION OF BOOKS FOR PUBLIC USE

laid on or it will exude from the edges with disastrous effect, nor should it be too thin or the papers will peel off. Care must be taken that the whole surface to be laid down is covered with paste, or the edges will curl and tear. For manilla and other stout substances the paste itself should be of greater density than for thinner papers, and it is unwise to water down the paste as that detracts from its adhesive quality and promotes mildewing and decay. If it be seen that paste is exuding, a little blotting-paper will take it up, but if the books are of any particular intrinsic value no risk should be incurred, and a piece of clean paper should be laid over the pasted matter by way of precaution. There are some papers which have a pronounced tendency to buckle when moistened, and this cannot always be avoided, but it will minimize the risk if paste is not too thickly applied and if the label is affixed quickly. A pad of blotting or other absorbent paper placed over it, and a weight put on the top of the book when closed, will go far to produce a good result. The labels, or plates, commonly used include extracts from the library rules, date papers, book plates, and, in open-access libraries, the manilla pocket, which is generally placed at the left-hand bottom corner of the front or back cover of each volume. Each item will have its appointed position, and every label should be correctly placed. If they are laid down awry or "out of truth" the effect is very unpleasing.

Good paste may be purchased ready-made, but

it is cheap and easy to make, and it is an advantage to have fresh supplies at hand whenever wanted. Here is a satisfactory recipe—the quantity may, of course, be altered provided that the proportions are maintained: Take 1 lb. of flour and add to it half an ounce of powdered alum. Add enough cold water to make a thickish cream when well stirred, and see that any lumps are thoroughly broken up, either by fingers or a stick. Then add two pints of cold water, a few drops of oil of cloves, and let it be slowly heated until it reaches boiling-point, stirring being continuous until the required thickness is obtained. If this point is passed and the paste is too thick, it may at this juncture be thinned down with cold water, but not later. When made, the paste should be poured into jars or bottles, and it should be kept as airtight as possible until required for use.

BOOK-NUMBERING PROCESSES

Book numbering, that is the process of marking the classification or call numbers on the covers of books, is done in various ways. To write these details with a pen and ink is inadequate and can be justified only as a temporary expedient. Painting the numbers on with Chinese white is not bad if the paint does not smear, as it readily does, and it is not altogether easy to make good neat figures with this medium. Process white, although rather dearer, is superior, as it is "flatter," easier to work, has more body, and does not rub off easily if covered with a solution of shellac. A fine camel-hair brush is re-

PREPARATION OF BOOKS FOR PUBLIC USE

quired for this operation. Gummed labels are frequently used, and if they are moistened on both sides they will probably adhere so firmly as to defy removal, but the damping process may cause the ink to run.

The best way of numbering is to have the symbols burnished with gold-leaf. The apparatus is comparatively inexpensive, and the art of using it is easily acquired, whilst the advantage of having books permanently numbered at any time without delay is considerable. The average assistant can master the process with ease, but fine tooling, or even plain lettering if in quantity, is better left to expert binders.

The plant for this purpose should not cost more than a few pounds, and would have to include as a minimum the following items:

> One finisher's stove (for gas or electrical heating).
> Two sets of brass type with wooden handles.
> One finishing press.
> A gold-leaf cushion and a binder's knife.

The supplies for current use comprise gold-leaf, a piece of soft rubber, a small sponge, glaire, and a bit of rag for "cleaning off."

The stove is for heating the metal type, and if economy necessitates it an ordinary gas-ring may be adapted for the purpose. The flame comes under the inner part, where it strikes a circular plate upon which the metal ends of the type are heated whilst the wooden handles rest on the outer rim which is

By courtesy of the Woolstar Book Co. Ltd.]
THE ELECTRIC STYLUS PEN AND ITS METHOD OF USE

shaped to receive them. It is of the utmost importance that these tools be arranged and kept in their proper sequence or errors in numbering will be frequent. A little experience is necessary for judging the degree to which the brass types should be heated, for if they are too hot they will burn their way through the binding and the volume will be spoilt. On the other hand, if they are not sufficiently hot it will be impossible to get a satisfactory impression. Practice will reward intelligent observation, but a ready test is to hand. If a drop of water falling upon the metal hisses or flies off at the moment of contact, the "iron" is too hot for use, and should be touched upon a piece of wet sponge to cool it down.

Gold-leaf is almost incredibly thin metal and is liable to fly like gossamer. Great care and some little skill is necessary to lift one of these leaves from its book to the cushion where it is cut into squares by the broad-bladed knife, for a breath of air will cause it to shift and curl and may render it almost impossible to use. The correct method of transferring a sheet of gold-leaf is to place the knife beneath it and to lift it slowly and carefully into position, the book being held close to the cushion to minimize the risk of disarrangement. If the leaf does not readily lie flat on the pad, breathe upon it gently, and the flat surface which is essential will be obtained. The leaf should then be divided with gentle but firm strokes of the knife, and the requisite evenness of touch is soon acquired.

PREPARATION OF BOOKS FOR PUBLIC USE

Meanwhile, the books to be numbered are screwed up rigidly in the wooden clamping press, a note being taken of the numbers or other details which are to be burnished on to their backs, and the books must be arranged in that sequence. The portion of the binding which is to be treated is now painted over with glaire. Glaire is composed of the white of eggs mixed with half its quantity of vinegar, and it must be thoroughly well shaken and allowed to "settle" for some hours, preferably overnight, before being used. There is on the market a dried albumen, and a quarter of an ounce added to a quarter of a pint of water, left to soak for some hours, will serve equally well. In either instance the admixture soon becomes malodorous, especially if exposed to the air, and too much should not be made at one time, for it does not keep well. It should be applied only to that part of the binding where the letters or numerals are to show. If laid on too lavishly, or so as to cover more surface than is necessary, a bad effect will be permanently visible; if insufficiently covered, the gold-leaf will not be fixed, and a second application will be necessary. The glaire should be nearly dry before the leaf is placed upon it, and this is done by a wad of cotton-wool lightly touched with olive oil. It is to be remembered that glaire dries quickly, and too many books should, therefore, not be "glaired" at one time or the glutinous quality will have perished before the books are tooled.

At this stage the handle-letters are tested, and, if heated to the proper state, they are impressed, one at a time, upon the bindings, firm pressure being required. It is important to see that the correct symbol is being used, even though the tools are presumed to be arranged in their proper order on the stove, for mistakes are troublesome to repair. It is equally desirable to preserve alignment and to maintain proper spacing, and this can be achieved with reasonable care. If titles are to be burnished, individual lettering may be done, or a different kind of metal letters, without handles, may be screwed tightly into a metal case with a central handle (something akin to a rubber dating-stamp), but this calls for skilled treatment and should only be attempted by the inexpert as a matter of urgency.

The burnishing is now accomplished, but the final effect will not be apparent until that part of the gold-leaf which has not been burnt in has been cleaned off. The square of gold looks unpromising at the moment, but soft rubber will remove all the leaf which has not been permanently impressed. All that remains to be done is to check the lettering to see that it has been correctly done. If error occurs, it may be rectified by washing out the wrong symbols with a solution of ammonia, but in many cases the rough-and-ready way of soaking the gold with paste and then gently scraping it out with a match is adoped: the result is likely to show as a sort of scar, and errors should be prevented.

Numbering with an electric stylus is a recent method and has much to recommend it. It is simpler than gold burnishing, requires little in the way of

PREPARATION OF BOOKS FOR PUBLIC USE

outfit, and gives good results if done with care. The stylus is a pencil-like instrument with a pointed metal end resembling that of a stylograph. It is connected by a thin flex or insulated cord from its upper end to an electric point by means of a bayonet fitting which is fixed or removed precisely like an ordinary electric lamp. It is necessary that the voltage of the stylus should be that of the electric current, and the current is turned on and off by a tiny switch. The medium used for numbering takes the form of tape-like strips of paper one side of which is plain and the other charged with gold or Chinese white or its equivalent. The strip is placed face downwards over the back of the book and is held tightly in position, whilst with the other hand the writing or numbering is done. To be satisfactory, some skill in producing clear lettering is required, and bad writers should not attempt this method, but if the "library style" of writing can be achieved the result is excellent. It will be sufficiently obvious that when the current is "on" the stylo must be carefully handled or mishap may occur.

SELECTED REFERENCES

AMERICAN LIB. ASSN. BOOKBINDING COMMITTEE. Lettering on Library Books. 1919.
BROWN (J. D.). Manual of Library Economy. 4th edn. 1931. (pp. 201–5 and ch. xxii.)
CANNON (C. L.). Order and Accession Department. (A.L.A. Manual, 16.) 1930.

A MANUAL OF LIBRARY ROUTINE

DRURY (F. K. W.). Order Work for Libraries. 1930. (pp. 81–96, and ch. ix—Mechanical preparation of books.)

ESDAILE (A.). Student's Manual of Bibliography. 1931. (Collation, pp. 314–47.)

FAY (L. E.) and EATON (A. T.). Instruction in the Use of Books and Libraries. (Ch. iii—The Physical Book.)

JAST (L. S.). Accessioning: the Checking of Processes. (In *The Library*, i, 1899, pp. 152–63.)

McCULLOUGH (E. F.) and VAN BUREN (M.). Essentials in Lib. Administration. 1931. (Mechanical preparation of books, pp. 41–4.)

McKERROW (R. B.). Introduction to Bibliography for Literary Students. 1927. (pp. 145–53.)

ROEBUCK (G. E.) and THORNE (W. B.). Primer of Lib. Practice. 1914. (Book preparation, pp. 46–8.)

WARNER (J.) Reference Library Methods. 1928. (Book cutting, numbering, etc., pp. 118–22.)

WILLIAMS (I. A.). Elements of Book Collecting. 1927. (pp. 14–26.)

CHAPTER IV

ADMINISTRATIVE RECORDS

(INVOICE RECORDS, ROUTINE ACCESSION REGISTERS, DONATION BOOKS, ACCESSION REGISTERS, AND SUMMARY STATISTICS)

Routine methods vary in accordance with the requirements of the libraries to which they are applied. Municipal libraries find one form eminently satisfactory, while university and institutional libraries, with equal propriety, adopt other methods as being better adapted to their peculiar needs. These variations are nowhere more pronounced than in administrative records, which differ considerably in number, size, and scope.[1]

Invoice books, for example, are in many libraries regarded as being absolutely necessary, while in others they are dispensed with altogether. Routine books—not generally used—are held by some librarians to be most desirable, or even fundamental. Apart from the number of records employed, their contents are remarkable for diversity rather than uniformity. Local necessities and individual preferences account for these conditions, but if the following dominant principles are grasped, any

[1] "Many of the conventional library records are really not worth while, and particularly is this so in the case of recording books added."—*Small Municipal Libraries*, p. 101. At the present time the system of administrative records is under review in several libraries, with a view to reduction and simplification.

method of administrative recording will easily be mastered.

The general principle embodied in any satisfactory system of accessioning is that every book or other item acquired by purchase, gift, or exchange shall be permanently recorded, and the information so preserved shall in each instance be so complete that the history of each unit may be traced from its reception to its final withdrawal from stock.

This recording system must, in one volume or another, be sufficiently detailed as to enable any copy of a book to be replaced by another exactly similar (if procurable). It must reveal what books have been purchased, from whom, and at what cost. It must declare what donations have been received, with all necessary particulars of the donors. If books, etc., have been acquired by exchange—more frequent, perhaps, in collegiate libraries than in others —the facts relative to outgoing and incoming works must be recorded. The stock of each department or branch library must be fully detailed. Provision must be made for showing that all items accepted have actually passed into stock, and where they have been placed, and there must be a checking list for stocktaking use. All these may be comprehended within the definition of accessioning, and there are other records to be kept, such as binding records, withdrawal and replacement registers, overdue lists, and the necessary checks for the receipt of books and periodicals which have been placed on order, while in large library systems will be found a series

ADMINISTRATIVE RECORDS

of aggregate and summary records of various kinds. It is unlikely that the full range of records to be described will be found in any one library, and it is to be noted that whether the records are in the form of ledgers, cards, or loose-leaf sheets, the information required will be practically the same.

Registers

The following registers are, in one form or another, to be found in use at most libraries:

Invoice books (or files).
Donation records.
Routine accession records (sometimes).
Accession records (usually the fullest and main record).
Shelf-lists or Stock books.

Invoice books

Invoices are important official documents, and as the prime sources of information concerning purchases they must be treated with the most scrupulous respect. In one fashion or another they must be copied into a register, or duplicated, and be filed, for in municipal practice the originals pass to the council's finance officer, and elsewhere the treasurer becomes responsible for them. The last that a librarian usually sees of invoices is when they are submitted to his committee for approval.

Invoice books, into which are transcribed all the details occurring in the bills, are frequently but not invariably adopted for this purpose. There are several alternatives. Some libraries require suppliers to provide duplicate invoices with each delivery. In that case one copy is regarded as the official invoice, and is temporarily filed after being checked and prepared for submission for payment, the other being reserved for office use. Where process cards are employed, the required data will be copied upon them and the duplicate invoice will go upon the permanent file; but in libraries where process cards are not adopted these duplicate invoices may accompany the books so far as is necessary during the various stages of their preparation for use. The most common way of preserving bills is to arrange them in alphabetical order of vendors in a vertical or other file, separate folders being provided for the different agents, but numerical sequence is sometimes preferred.

More than one entry to a line should not be permitted in invoices, for modern practice demands that the accession number, or some other clue, shall be added to each item-entry as a link for tracing purposes. By this means it can easily be shown that purchases have been passed into stock and where they have been placed.

If invoice books are used, the entries therein should be exact transcripts of the invoices, with the addition of the names of suppliers, and of the order number or date. The clue number is also entered, and, to make the destination of each item easily traceable, the particular departmental register to which reference is directed must be specified. This indication is given by adding the initial letter of the

ADMINISTRATIVE RECORDS

particular register, or by some other recognized symbol, such as R4238 for a reference book to which that clue number has been applied, or CL9765 for one belonging to the central lending library. Each line in the invoice book bears a progressive number, and this number should be entered in the accession or other main register to make the linking up complete.

These connecting clues are perhaps not adopted to the extent they deserve in the various records, but if systematically done they are capable of saving much repetition in collateral registers, just as cross-references serve the same purpose in catalogues.

Donation records

Very little practical experience is needed to convince a librarian that all offers of gifts are not to be accepted. At the same time none should be rejected without careful examination, and refusal should always be tempered by tact. Except where the books offered are clearly desirable, the golden rule is to "look gift horses in the mouth,"[1] or a heterogeneous collection of faded divinity, out-of-date scientific works, school books devoid of educational value, torn, soiled, or imperfect copies—all unusable—will accumulate upon the shelves; but while it would be folly to close the door against future donations, it would be worse to accept without discrimination. Many donations bespeak their own

[1] See Dr. Baker's paper on "Gift Horses," *L. A. Record*, xi 1896), pp. 422–3.

desirability, but in the case of mixed parcels only the good should be selected, and the indifferent and bad rejected. Usually donors are quite willing that the library should reserve the right to accept for stock only such items as are found suitable and wanted, and to allow the librarian to dispose of the remainder at discretion. Hospitals, settlements, orphanages, and various other social organizations, even prisons (provided that detective stories are excluded!) will be glad to pick out books from this residuum, and the other undesirables may be sold as waste. If display objects are offered, similar care must be exercised or the public may mistake the museum for a mausoleum. It may be definitely laid down that, unless the library is to deteriorate in character, the same severe test as to desirability should be applied to gifts as to purchases: if a book is not likely to be of interest or value to readers it should not be stocked; if in doubt, accept, but only after due consideration.

All gifts must be acknowledged promptly and systematically, after which they should be registered in the appropriate record, and numbered as in the case of purchases. Probably there will be a donation plate to be pasted into one of the covers. Where collation of gifts is undertaken, this should be attended to at any early stage, and defects, if any, noted in the appropriate register—generally the accession register or stock book. In many libraries donations of all kinds are required to be submitted to the committee for formal inspection and accep-

ADMINISTRATIVE RECORDS

tance, and this retards the circulation of presented volumes for home reading.

The forms of acknowledgment vary. For recurrent official publications a printed postcard may suffice. Some libraries nicely graduate these forms to the value of the donation or the importance of the giver, sending formal sheets of acknowledgment for ordinary benefactions and ornately engraved ones for more important gifts. Whatever the form may be, it should be dispatched without delay, or tardiness may be construed as indifference. It is quite customary to forward a preliminary acknowledgment of receipt immediately upon the arrival of donations, conveying the librarian's thanks and stating that the offer will be laid before the committee at their next meeting. Such offers are recorded in a register and are reported, or displayed if actually received, for formal decision. Meanwhile the official form of acceptance and thanks may be prepared, for it seldom happens that committees interfere with the discretion of the librarian in this matter. At the meeting the list of donations offered or received is read out, and the prepared forms of thanks are signed by the chairman. In municipalities committees may approve gifts and report them to the council, when the town clerk will sign and send the acknowledgments as prepared by the librarian.

It is good policy to send with the formal acknowledgment a personal letter of appreciation, and the courtesy of this personal touch is generally appreciated by donors. Many libraries furnish the local newspapers with particulars of recent donations, and the publicity thus given may encourage others. At all events it advertises the fact that the library is open to receive donations, and it tends to keep it in public evidence.

Every library will have its donation register, usually in ledger form. This must be posted up as gifts come in, and the date, name, and address of the donors, details of the gift, destination, and identity number are the details usually recorded, together with a record of the date when submitted to the committee and a note of the official decision. If the record of donations is kept on cards, the entries are largely the same. In book form, entries must be chronological, but with cards the arrangement may be by the names of donors or any other sequence that may be preferred.

ACCESSION REGISTERS

The various items of information which have been stated as necessary for preservation in an efficient system of book registration are usually scattered in different registers, each one having its own objective, but one of these will be fuller than any of the others and will be regarded as the main record. This is generally the accession register, and it is found in widely differing forms. In one library it is a stoutly bound ledger; in another it is composed of cards; elsewhere it is compiled on the loose-leaf system. Each method has its peculiar advantages and drawbacks. Bound volumes offer the greatest protection

ADMINISTRATIVE RECORDS

against loss or misplacement of entries, but their absolute rigidity is proof against adjustment to change. The mobility of cards makes adjustment a simple matter, and the cards which are abstracted as volumes are discarded may be used for withdrawal records or other useful purposes; but cards have an unhappy knack of becoming misplaced or lost. Loose-leaf registers are less liable to accident than cards, and although precise shelf order cannot be maintained by this system, no such exactitude is required here, and the substitution of a newly revised page for an old one is the task of a minute or two. To make erasures and additions upon pages which are permanently bound is fatal to neatness and conduces neither to accuracy nor quick reference.

Accession registers, whatever their form may be, are usually, but not always, restricted to individual departments, exceptions from the rule being chiefly in the smallest libraries. Such special contents as maps, prints, manuscripts, local collections, and bequests advantageously have registers of their own. Entries may be expanded or condensed, but fullness of detail here renders it unnecessary to repeat all the particulars in cognate records, for the clue numbers act as guides, so that every particle of recorded information may be traced with little trouble. Unless a distinct register is devoted to pamphlets, these are not usually accessioned until bound up together into volumes.

Not many accession registers include a closely detailed class analysis of acquisitions but some have a fair amount of process recording, *e.g.* a column for the number of the proposal in the suggestion book, and others for marks relative to stamping, cutting, etc. To include overmuch either crowds the page or entails registers of such ponderous size as to make them inconvenient for use, and the present tendency is decidedly towards condensation.

The sequence in which the various phases of book preparation are performed is often determined by mere convenience, and if process marking is observed the order matters little; but accessioning is usually done at an early stage. For this operation each volume is accompanied by its process card, which is now being gradually filled with its recording details, or by the original or duplicate invoice, for it is from one or other of these sources that much of the matter now to be recorded must be obtained, and the cards and invoices have to be marked with their individual accession numbers for tracing back to this main register of information.

Entering books is simple enough, for the rulings will prescribe what facts are to be recorded. Acquisitions are accessioned in chronological order and each *volume* has its own numbered line of entry. A work in four volumes thus requires four lines progressively numbered, and duplicate copies, even though identical in all respects, must have separate numbers and individual lines. This is necessary inasmuch as each volume is a distinct item, and the accession number as recorded in each book must guide to particular copies or it has no tracing value. Whether

ADMINISTRATIVE RECORDS

newly acquired books shall be continuously entered as unbroken blocks as charged in upon invoices, or whether the previous numbers of any books which have been withdrawn from stock shall be filled up as vacancies occur, is a matter of opinion, and there are good arguments on either side. If the register is in card or sheet form there can be little objection to the latter method on physical grounds, but if it is attempted in permanently bound registers erasures and insertions will be troublesome.[1]

The argument for filling up numbers as they become vacant by withdrawals is that if this is not done trouble may arise in the charging system later on, and that a filled-up register reveals the whole stock numerically at a glance. As against this it is held that the charging risk is negligible, that the break in chronological sequence of acquisition is unfortunate, and that withdrawals can easily be counted off at any time, or a column for the insertion of the book number in the withdrawal register (or a note in the remarks column of the accession register)

---

[1] "Withdrawn numbers may be applied to any new books so as to prevent blanks in the sequence, as these may play havoc with the charging system later on."—Brown's *Manual*, 4th edn., p. 207.

"Never use an old accession number for a new book, even although the original book has disappeared from the library."—Dana's *Library Primer*, p. 77.

"Lost books have a way of turning up long after all hope of their recovery has been abandoned, and there is a risk of old and new books being entered to the same accession number in charging systems where accession numbers are used as clue numbers in open-access charging."

"Some . . . have adopted the practice of giving to a replacement the same number as the volume that it replaces and letting the original entry stand. This . . . is on the whole objectionable."—Bostwick's *American Public Library*, 4th edn., p. 200.

will clear this issue, and the more readily if a special tint of ink be reserved for the purpose.

As each volume is entered, the serial number—that is, the number of the line upon which the particular entry is made—is recorded in the book. The customary place for this purpose is somewhere on the verso of the title-page, where possibly an impression of the process stamp is now made, or already awaits this clue number. It must be remembered that if the paper is spongy the ink will run through unless carefully done, and in such case a modicum of ink upon the pen will suffice, or, better still in this case, an indelible-ink pencil may be used. This accession number is basic; "it is inseparable from the book while it lives, and dies with it. It represents the actual, material book, not the title; . . . it is used to ascertain certain facts about any particular book, such as the date on which it was added, its sources, and its cost. In case of loss it tells what sum the loser must be charged; in case of fire, the insurance adjustment is made by its records."[1] It is frequently the individual number by which each book is charged up in the issuing system, and it indicates in other registers where the main record of information about each book is to be found, thus enabling entries in them to be reduced to the merest proportions for identification. In gross it is the key to the value of the book stock, and it is from its figures that insurance amounts are obtained.

[1] *The American Public Library*, 4th edn., 1929, pp. 197-8.

ADMINISTRATIVE RECORDS

It serves a useful purpose if this number, in addition to its entry in the forefront of each volume, is also recorded in the margin or at the foot of some fixed page or pages. If the title-page is at any time missing, as sometimes happens, this additional entering guides to the main entry, so that full identification is possible. Some libraries write this second entry very inconspicuously so as to escape ordinary observation, and this upon occasion has served to establish identity in police courts when the aniline-ink stamp and the primary numbering behind the title-page have been erased by dishonest persons.

Where special accession registers are used for prints, manuscripts, etc., the initial letter of the register (in the above instance "P" or "M") is prefixed to the item number for differentiation. When writing the number upon such items as prints the number should never impinge upon the printed surface, and the same practice must be observed with regard to stamping. The margins or a blank verso should alone be used for these necessary markings.

If the accession record is in card form the process is precisely the same, but in this case, as there are no lines consecutively numbered ready to receive the entry; each card as it is written has the serial number boldly written in, and the cards are placed on file according to these numbers. Sheets are treated as pages, and immediately a sheet is filled, or even partially filled, it must be secured within its binding-case to prevent misplacement. If process cards are used, the appropriate record must be made as each book is entered. To allow call numbers, classification numbers, or any other form of entry to accumulate is highly dangerous and should never be permitted, and the accession numbers should be carried into their proper places upon invoices, shelf-lists, etc., without delay.

ACCESSIONING BY LOT

Block entries are sometimes attempted, perhaps more in American libraries than British, to economize effort and expedite recording. Under this scheme individual entries are abandoned; the invoice number is recorded, and the number of volumes is allowed for by count. If thirty volumes were to arrive in one delivery and with a single invoice, and the first blank line in the accession book was numbered 1571, the entry would be, in one line, 1571–1600. The books would be numbered according to this sequence, and for particulars respecting the various books reference would be made to the invoices concerned, the invoice numbers serving as the clue. It needs only a glance at accession registers and invoices to show that unless full details are insisted upon in invoices so used the information supplied will be inadequate; but it is held that invoices commonly supply sufficient information for tracing books, and that process or order cards, or bibliographies and publishers' catalogues, may be used as supplementary sources of information.

ADMINISTRATIVE RECORDS
ACCESSION CARD

```
Accsn. No.........    Date.........    Class No.......
Author ....................................................
Title ......................................................
Publisher ............    Price......    Net Cost.........
Place of publication .............         Date ............
Binding ............    Donor or Vendor ...............
Withdrawal Book No.......    Replact. Book No.......
Remarks  ................................................
                         O
```

The clerical work of accessioning demands accurate entry in the form locally prescribed, and the entries should be neatly and completely performed. To leave them imperfectly made is slovenly and dangerous, and they have a way of accumulating until gigantic proportions are reached, and too often the arrears are never caught up. This would be bad enough in any record, but it is fatal to efficiency in such a main record as the accession register. It is equally important that the individual book number should be entered in all the collateral records, or the broken link entirely destroys the value of the connecting chain.

When these individual tracing numbers have been determined by the accession register they should forthwith be marked upon the appropriate

A MANUAL OF LIBRARY ROUTINE

lines of the original and duplicate invoices or the transcripts in the invoice book, and when this is done the sooner the invoices are transferred to their proper file the better. If process cards are included in the routine, the clue number should now be entered there also, and when doing so it will be useful to note whether the processes have been marked thereon as having been attended to. The cards themselves should be placed in the books when the latter are entered in the register, and will accompany them throughout the successive operations of classification, cataloguing, and any remaining stages of preparation for stock.

The donation book will require the insertion of the accession number, and a like entry will in due course have to be made in the shelf-list (or stock book), and also upon the charging card for each volume, for the accession number is not infrequently adopted as the individual symbol of each volume in the charging system. The importance of this clue number is obvious, and the absolute necessity for accuracy should be equally apparent.

SUMMARY STATISTICS

In addition to the foregoing records, there are in operation various kinds of summary and aggregate returns, found sometimes in single libraries and more commonly in systems comprising departments and branches. They are analytical summaries of stock, and are made up from the accession or other main registers, their object being to reveal the

ADMINISTRATIVE RECORDS

divisions of the book stock at a glance. The sketch (page 78) illustrates the rulings of the "summary stock book" as used in a large city library.

It will be noticed that the Dewey classification is in force, and that in this particular instance the only departure from the main groupings is that relating to fiction. Rather more elaborate are the analyses in the "summary register of stock" (page 78).

The first line of each page brings forward the total as recorded at the foot of the preceding page. To obtain a comprehensive aggregate, the totals of each of these departmental records are from time to time added up and entered into a master register. This form of record is, of course, not a substitute for, but an addition to, the registers previously described.

This is really statistical work rather than accessioning, but it is directly supplementary to accession work, and is therefore mentioned here. Tabular work of this character is always exacting, and unless the greatest vigilance is continuously maintained figures will stray into the wrong columns with disastrous results. Fortunately the modern tendency is towards the reduction and simplification of records.

Shelf-lists (or stock books) will also be required, but these can be more appropriately dealt with in connection with stocktaking. They are accordingly described in Chapter XIV.

SUMMARY STOCK BOOK
Number of Volumes in the Library

Date	000	100	200	300	400	500	600	700	800	900	Fiction	Total	Addns. &c

SUMMARY REGISTER OF STOCK

Date	0	1	2	3	4	5	6	7	Music 8	Fiction	Juvenile Fiction	History	Biog.	Travel	£ s. d.	Total

ADMINISTRATIVE RECORDS

SELECTED REFERENCES

BOSTWICK (A. E.). The Amer. Pub. Library. 4th edn. 1929. (Accessioning, pp. 197–200.)

BROWN (J. D.). Manual of Lib. Economy. 4th edn. 1931. (Ch. xiv—Accsn. methods.)

CANNON (C. L.). Order and Accession Dept. (A.L.A. Manual, 17.) 1930.

DRURY (F. K. W.). Order Work for Libraries. 1930. (Ch. viii—Accsn. methods.)

JAST (L. S.). Accessions: the Checking of Processes. (In *The Library*, n.s., i, 1900, pp. 152–63.)

LIBRARY ASSN. Small Libraries. 1931. (Ch. ix—Records and statistics.)

PITT (S. A.). Practical Accsn. Work. (In *Lib. Assn. Record*, vii, 1905, pp. 68–71.)

RATHBONE (J. A.). The Shelf Department. (A.L.A. Manual, 20.) 1930.

VITZ (C.). Circulation Work. (A.L.A. Manual, 21.) 1927.

CHAPTER V

CLASSIFICATION AND ITS PRACTICAL APPLICATIONS

In the preparation of books for general use the processes of classification and cataloguing play a most significant part, and although there is no fixed stage for the former of these operations it should not be unduly delayed, for until class symbols are assigned accessioning cannot be begun and cataloguing cannot be completed.

Classification may be roughly defined as the grouping together of books in systematic order according to their subject-matter, exceptions being sometimes made in favour of form arrangement where prose fiction, poetry, drama, and general essays are concerned. In the Library of Congress Classification, for example, literature is arranged (1) by language, (2) by period, and (3) by alphabetical order of authors' names within the period. Thus the prose, poetry, biographies, and criticisms of an author are in one place, alphabetically under his name, within his period, and under his language. In open-access libraries it is absolutely essential that the books be shelved in logical and correlated sequence so that the literature of any subject may easily be found by readers: in closed libraries—reference departments for example—the knowledge that librarians have of their stock is much more

CLASSIFICATION AND ITS APPLICATIONS

comprehensive and precise when the books are classed.

Detailed consideration of the principles and theories of classification lie beyond the scope of these pages: it is with practical applications that this chapter has to deal. For adequate guidance in theoretical classification, and full discussion of its numerous codes, reference must be made to the standard textbooks, and it may safely be asserted that nothing in the nature of perfunctory study will be of much assistance to a classifier.

The general theory must first be grasped, and for this purpose Jevons' *Elementary Lessons in Logic* —especially chapters v, xii, and xxxii—the chapter on Classification in the same writer's *Principles of Science;* Fowler's *Elements of Deductive Logic*, chapter viii, or his *Elements of Inductive Logic*, pp. 52–89, are usually prescribed. The principles of bibliographical classification are authoritatively set forth by Mr. E. A. Savage in his *Manual* on this subject in *The Library Association Series*; by Mr. Sayers in his various treatises, and by Mr. E. C. Richardson in his *Classification: Theoretical and Practical.* Excellent epitomes, which should serve as introductions only, are the chapter by Mr. A. J. Hawkes in *A Primer of Librarianship*, Mr. Jast's article in Greenwood's *Library Year Book* (1900–1 edition), the section on Classification in Brown's *Manual of Library Economy*, Warner's *Reference Library Methods*, or Miss Bacon's booklet which forms a part of the American Library Association's

A MANUAL OF LIBRARY ROUTINE

Manual of Library Economy. When the foundations of success have thus been well and truly laid the next step for the practical worker is to master the scheme of classification which is locally in force: the introductory matter, as well as the tables, should be carefully studied and time spent upon digesting them at the outset will later on be amply repaid. It is an education in itself.

The popularity of the Dewey system is largely attributable to the simplicity of its pure notation and to its mnemonic appeal. The printed code also enjoys the advantage of a remarkably full index, but this factor may conceivably prove to be a drawback for it offers great temptations as a "short cut," and assistants who make a practice of turning to any index and using it to the exclusion of the tables will never make much progress. In the actual work of classifying, numbers should not be assigned without consulting both tables and index unless the correct placing is assuredly known.

CODES OF CLASSIFICATION

Every existing code has its peculiar shortcomings, and the Decimal system is by no means free of perplexities to the classifier. One recurrent trouble is that, while it fails to make obvious provision for some topics, it offers competitive places for others, and the distinctions are so fine that the placing becomes uncertain: one position may appear to be correct one day and an alternative upon another

CLASSIFICATION AND ITS APPLICATIONS

occasion. All that can be said is that the most careful and cultivated judgment must be exercised, and whenever a decision is made it should promptly be recorded in all copies of the working code so that consistency may be maintained. Novices should never attempt to make these decisions—their only safe course is to consult an experienced and responsible senior. Any departures from the printed code should be recorded in similar fashion.

When no provision appears to have been made for a topic the work in question may be placed in the nearest sub-division and an additional figure added for differentiation, the code being marked in the manner just described. The safer way is, however, to refer the query to the editor of the code. By so doing a new topic may perhaps be opened out to him: immediate response is invariably made to such enquiries, the new item will appear in the next edition of the code, and uniformity—so desirable in this matter—is rendered easy.

Another drawback is that, in order to obtain close classification, it is often necessary to employ a long string of decimal numbers, and the greater the number of symbols the more risk there is of error in using them. It is a moot point whether really fine classification should be undertaken or not in libraries of a general character, and practice differs. Large libraries and highly specialized stocks require it; some others take the view that, having regard to the certain growth of the book stock, it is expedient to adopt full classification at once, but many libraries are content to use the main class number with a general limit of two decimal figures.

The foregoing observations must not be regarded as in any way belittling Dewey; they are put forward merely because that particular system is most commonly adopted. Textbooks on classification reveal the fact that other codes also exhibit problems, and each has its own good qualities. Their notation is usually modified by the inclusion of letters denoting subjects, thus reducing the range of numerals to be employed. The principal systems are described in detail and discussed by Mr. Savage in his *Manual*, by Mr. Sayers in his various books on this subject, and in other treatises of a similar kind. In various volumes of the (American) *Library Journal*, Messrs. Dewey and Cutter describe their own codes, and Mr. J. C. M. Hanson, whose long and intimate association with the Library of Congress Classification well justifies his appearance as its protagonist, describes and advocates that system as suitable alike for popular, technical, and educational libraries, and especially for large collections. A memorandum drawn up by Mr. Jast for the Government-appointed Public Libraries Committee (1927 Report) submits that "the Decimal Classification, by virtue of the simplicity of its notation, the practical character of its headings, its publication in one handy volume with one inclusive subject-index, and its wide adoption, is recommended for general use in popular lending libraries and reference collections," but, he adds, "in large reference libraries either the Decimal or the Library of Congress scheme is recommended." The latter also enjoys the great advantage of a replete index in one volume with separate indexes for class sections. Professor A. F. C. Pollard, of the Imperial College of Science and Technology, unhesitatingly affirms that the Decimal system as expanded and revised by the Institut Internationale de Bibliographie, and which is now variously known as the "Universal Decimal Classification," or "Classification decimale universelle," is "the most perfect and at the same time the simplest and cheapest method of indexing bibliographical material which has ever been devised." It would not be difficult to cite opinions equally emphatic in favour of the superiority of the Library of Congress scheme, but the lure must be resisted. Whoever desires to be a thoroughly competent classifier will be well advised to study at least the main principles of alternative codes.

PRACTICAL APPLICATIONS

The practical application of any code will offer an unending series of problems. A few of these perplexities may be touched upon and some hints given to simplify the work.

Perhaps the very first thing to be noted is that books should not be judged from their title-pages. A long list of deceptive titles could easily be submitted in proof of this truism. The classic instance is Ruskin's *Notes on the Construction of Sheepfolds*, which, in reality, treats of church discipline; but another example may be offered to show the danger of presumption in times of literary "booms." Shortly after the publication of Stanley's *In Darkest Africa*, when all sorts of books about African travel were in considerable demand, there appeared a volume with the innocent-looking title of *Travels in the Interior*. One classifier committed the cardinal fault of taking it for granted that this was one of the spate and classed it as such only to find, after it has reached the shelves, that it related to the supposed adventures of a pill within the human system! Some books have fanciful and vague titles and need to be examined in detail to discover their specific subject; indeed, a large proportion of non-fictional publications will demand such investigation if crude and erratic placing is to be avoided. Sometimes the prefatory matter yields the desired information, or the list of contents may assist, but otherwise and unless some extraneous source removes obscurity, the volume itself must be examined. It frequently happens that either in the opening or closing pages the "argument" is set out or summarized.

If any book treats of more than one cognate topic, or views a composite subject from several angles, the dominant feature must be accepted for classification. In cataloguing the difficulty is met by entering under every subject-heading concerned, or by cross-references; but as a book can stand in one place only, it is important that the chosen position be the right one, and the predominant "characteristic" is the determining factor. The pre-

CLASSIFICATION AND ITS APPLICATIONS

dominant subject for classification will also be the main subject-heading for cataloguing. Where two or more subjects or persons are involved, and it appears impossible to distinguish between their relative significance, the one first named should be regarded as dominant, but sometimes a classifier may be unnecessarily baffled. The point may be illustrated by Middleton Murry's *Keats and Shakespeare*. The great Elizabethan stands supreme, but this fact should not mislead the classifier to place the work under his name, for the subject of the study is the influence of the older poet upon the younger. Keats is the real subject of this investigation. Similarly, a book upon the geology of London should be classed as geology, possibly with a topographical sub-division; and the flora of a district goes under botany. Pitfalls must always be guarded against, and that is equal to saying that a classifier must never relax his vigilance or grudge the time spent in making sure before disposing of difficult books.

ROUTINE USE OF CLASSIFICATION NUMBERS

As volumes receive their distinguishing numbers these symbols should be copied into such registers as have provision made for their reception. The accession register, the shelf-list (or stock book), and the process card or other form of that record, should be marked with this information, and it must also be copied on the verso of the title or in any other preferred position in each volume as it is classified. Any attempt to defer this task is to be combated,

A MANUAL OF LIBRARY ROUTINE

for accumulations of arrears are sometimes never cleared, and some American libraries have for that reason abandoned accession registers and adopted substitute methods. The book-cards used in charging systems must have this information, and the books themselves will be marked upon their backs for shelving convenience.

SHELF-ARRANGEMENT

So far as is practicable the stock should be arranged in unbroken sequence upon the shelves, but exceptions have sometimes to be allowed. For physical reasons it is frequently found necessary to have size grouping. Quartos and folios, including atlases, probably the whole of music, and all works of large size, cannot economically be placed with crown or demy octavos. To do so would be extremely wasteful of space, and the effect would not be pleasing. Demys are the largest size that will conveniently range with the average stock, and books of larger size are therefore grouped together in specially provided shelving, and wherever this occurs the books should be marked in the catalogue for shelf guidance, and the books themselves for permanent use. This marking can be easily achieved. Sometimes one asterisk denotes a quarto volume and two a folio, but more commonly the notation marks are preceded by the letter "o" for imperial octavos and quartos, and "f" for folios. Unless the catalogue entries are so indicated books will vainly be sought for in the general run of stock. In card

CLASSIFICATION AND ITS APPLICATIONS

or sheaf lists the mark can be quickly made by means of a rubber stamp stating that the book in question is specially placed.

Fiction, in open-access libraries, is very often arranged in ribbon-like fashion, one or more shelves deep, throughout the lending department. This plan brings the borrowers unwittingly into contact with non-fictional literature, but its real value lies in the fact that readers are thus distributed and congestion is thus reduced.

Children's books, where they have to be included in the general lending library, should always form a section separated from the rest, and a special corner or alcove, preferably near the entrance, is desirable. Children prefer to be together: they are thus brought under closer supervision, and are less likely to be in the way of other borrowers or to take out wrong books. Chavasse's *Handbook for Young Mothers*, innocently selected for home reading by a youthful entomologist, may be cited by way of moral!

Fixed location is an antiquarian method of shelving which should never be seen in a lending library, and is justifiable only where collections are immutably complete and permanently placed. Such collections are usually important bequests which have to be preserved intact and are found in cathedral libraries, large university or institutional libraries, or in the reference departments in municipal libraries. The books may be classified alphabetically, chronologically, or systematically by subject as cir-

A MANUAL OF LIBRARY ROUTINE

cumstances may control or suggest, but the bookcases, tiers, and shelves are each numbered distinctively, and these guiding marks must be recorded in the books and catalogues. Thus a book placed in the second bookcase in the first bay and fourth in order upon the third shelf would be marked 2134, or in some equivalent manner. It is clear that any such arrangement would be totally unsuitable for popular departments.

When all the preparatory stages have been accomplished and the books are ready for circulation they must be correctly placed upon the shelves according to the class symbols with which they are marked. Except perhaps in special sub-divisions there will almost certainly be a number of volumes bearing precisely the same classification marks. Books about birds, for instance, will be marked (if the Dewey code is used) 598·2, but there may be many books about birds. Even when the sub-division of subject has to some extent separated them, and however finely this partition is done there may still be books with the same symbols. Large and special libraries may adopt the Cutter author-marks as explained in the introduction to that code, but in general practice books with like symbols are arranged first by authors and then by titles, and it is by this method that the stock is kept in order upon the shelves, and that volumes are restored to their places as they are returned by readers or have been misplaced by careless borrowers. Strict sequence is fundamental to classification; constant revision of

CLASSIFICATION AND ITS APPLICATIONS

the shelves is one of the bread-and-butter tasks of library routine, and to fix responsibility and ensure that this work is regularly done it is common for sections to be allotted to junior members of the staff. It is educational work for it enables assistants to become closely acquainted with the stock and its classification. Its value in this respect is enhanced if the sections for which individual members of the staff are responsible are changed from time to time.

Main entries in catalogues may be marked with the classification symbols of every subject-heading under which the books appear. This work should be done as the books are catalogued, and the marks are made either at the foot or back of the cards or pages, so that whenever a volume is withdrawn from circulation *all* the entries may with certainty be removed by means of this clue.

Bookstacks, tiers, and shelves should be adequately guided by boldly printed summaries being placed at the ends of island cases, over the tops of bays, and labels for the shelves. Brevity of description is compulsory, and the class numbers should be added for guidance. If, as sometimes happens even in well-regulated libraries, batches of books become slightly out of position upon a shelf, the numbers act as a corrective for the public. It is easy to overdo notifications, and if they become too numerous or elaborate they will not be noticed by busy readers. Neatly stencilled or rubber-printed notices are admirable for this work, but hand-drawn lettering with the letters or symbols left in white upon a black background are most effective. Shelf guiding may be done by using printed slips which fit into countersunk spaces and may be adjusted to any required position. If these are protected by xylonite strips they will keep cleaner and last longer, but xylonite has a tendency to buckle and fall out, and it should be part of the duty of the staff to see that the labels, as well as the books, are kept in good order.

With a classified stock it is necessary to have one or more copies of the governing code—or a sufficient summary thereof—available for public reference. These may be affixed to sloping shelves, attached to the ends of bookstacks, or elsewhere, and are of great service to serious students. Messrs. Libraco, Ltd., publish at a low cost an index to the Dewey code reduced to a satisfactory minimum by the elimination of special entries and the retention of those most commonly in use. Cards upon which are set out in bold type the main divisions of that classification for display are procurable from all library agents: these are all useful guides for readers, but only so long as they are maintained with neatness and orderliness.

CLASSIFICATION IN INDICATOR LIBRARIES

One special application of classification marks remains to be noticed—their use in libraries where indicators are employed. Here each volume has its specific call number, and books are, or were, generally placed upon the shelves in the order of their

CLASSIFICATION AND ITS APPLICATIONS

accession or alphabetically by authors, main classes only being observed, each class being distinguished by a letter of the alphabet. In such libraries classification is usually relegated to the catalogue, and the shelves reflect the promiscuous class order of the indicator, the class letter and the individual number of each book in its class being all that is required for indicator charging. But this need not be so, for if scientific order is considered to be worth while it can easily be obtained by recording in each indicator block the appropriate classification symbols as shown in each volume. These symbols should be marked upon the back of each book in addition to the call number, and when a work is asked for the indicator will reveal its position upon the shelves. Sometimes an indicator serves merely to denote whether books are "in" or "out," and has nothing to do with charging, which is operated by the ordinary open-access method. In such libraries the books will, of course, be arranged in classified order, and systematic sequence upon the shelves is just as useful to the staff as to the public, for it displays the resources of a library on any given subject.

SELECTED REFERENCES

ARNETT (L. D., and E. T.), *edrs*. Readings in Library Science. 1931. (Theory and codes, with descriptions by Dewey, Cutter, and others, pp. 55–92.)

BACON (C.). Classification. (A.L.A. Manual, 18.) 1925.

BROWN (J. D.). Manual of Library Economy. 4th edn. 1931. (Ch. xiv—Classfn. and shelf-arrangement.)

A MANUAL OF LIBRARY ROUTINE

Coutts (H. T.). Classification and Shelf-Guides. (In *Open-Access Libraries*, by J. D. Stewart and others.) 1915.

Cutter (C. A.). Author Marks. (In *Expansive Classfn.*, p. 139.) 1893.

Hawkes (A. J.). Book Classification. (In *Primer of Librarianship*, ch. iii.) 1931.

Jast (L. S.). Library Classification. (In Greenwood's *Library Year Book*.) 1900.

Mann (M.). Introduction to the Cataloguing and Classification of Books. 1930.

Merrill (W. S.). Code for Classifiers: Principles Governing the Consistent Placing of Books in a System of Classification. 1928.

Pollard (A. F. C.). The Decimal Classification of the Institut Nationale de Bibliographie and its Importance as a Key to the World's Literature. (In the *Report of the Second A.S.L.I.B. Conference*.) 1926.

Richardson (E. C.). Classification: Theoretical and Practical. 2nd edn. 1912.

Sayers (W. C. Berwick). Canons of Classification applied to the "Subject," the "Expansive," and the "Decimal," and the Lib. of Congress Classifications. 1925.

—— Grammar of Classification. (*Library Assn.*) 1924.

—— Introduction to Library Classification. 3rd edn. 1930.

—— Manual of Classification for Librarians and Bibliographers. 1926.

Stewart (J. D.). Guiding in an Open-Access Library. (In *Library World*, ix, p. 208.)

Wilson (M.). School Library Management. 1919. (pp. 36–51).

CHAPTER VI

CATALOGUES AND CATALOGUING

There are many forms of catalogues. Some are printed, some typewritten, and others are written by hand throughout. For widespread circulation lists are printed; for restricted use copies may be produced in quantity by the cyclostyle, while card and sheaf catalogues are usually typed, although handscript is occasionally preferred. Cataloguing may be bibliographically full or reduced to the most economical proportions—as financial restriction often dictates. Catalogues may be author lists, classified by subjects, or in one of the dictionary forms, that is, either in one continuous alphabetical sequence throughout, or may be alphabetic-classed—a compromise between, and a combination of, the subject and dictionary styles. In the last case alphabetical arrangement is sustained throughout, the subjects being grouped under main headings followed by their sub-divisions with reference thereto from minor headings in lieu of detailed entries there. The librarian will issue instructions for the guidance of the cataloguing staff, and, whilst it is eminently desirable to have uniformity of scope and method for the central and branch lending departments, fuller treatment may well be applied to books preserved in reference libraries or in lists prepared for special purposes. The local regulations in all these respects must be completely understood before the first catalogue entry is made.

ESSENTIALS FOR SUCCESS

Responsible cataloguing should never be undertaken by assistants who have not been specially trained for this exacting work. Rule-of-thumb methods may possibly be permitted in some of the minor aspects of routine, but here they would be worse than useless. A thorough comprehension of the cataloguing code in operation must form the groundwork of successful cataloguing, and this must be reinforced by a general knowledge which should be wide even if not always deep, for the selection of the most suitable headings, and the selection of books to appear under them, is anything but simple work. Where works in foreign languages are concerned they should be referred, either wholly or for checking, to someone who is familiar with the language in question: to presume upon a "cataloguing knowledge" of such languages is merely asking for trouble and may entail ridicule.

The main essential for successful cataloguing is, then, a trained and adequate knowledge; but this is not always enough, for the most complete and academic equipment may easily be ruined by indifferent application, and it is extraordinary how errors creep in if vigilance is in any way relaxed. The routine of cataloguing demands unbroken attention, exactitude of transliteration, minute observation throughout, and, last but not least, uniformity. Want of concentration begets inaccuracy; lack of observation causes wrong entries and headings, and inconsistency bewilders readers, who cannot be expected to follow the workings of an inconstant cataloguer's mind. One of the commonest faults is inattention to the correct spelling of names, the usual form being assumed when the title-page shows that it is departed from. Even ordinary words are sometimes incorrectly transcribed, and the meaning may thus be entirely reversed: the omission of the letter "t" from the word immortal once nearly led to an action for libel. Dates and figures offer a ready trap for the careless cataloguer, and there are numerous ways in which bad cataloguing may be achieved.

Errors may arise either from slovenly workmanship or from sheer fatigue of eye or hand. In many cases the defect is so obvious that the correct form is not altogether obscured, but vagaries in treatment are a more serious blemish inasmuch as they are less easily perceived during revision of the manuscript, and, once introduced, may persist despite all efforts to reduce the material to perfection. In each detail the same method should be followed, and, important as this canon always is, it is nowhere more essential than in the grouping of books under subject-headings and in the employment of cross-references. As already noted, a book will suggest an eminently suitable heading one day, and a variant equally excellent at another time, and steps must be taken to see that both are not used. Many headings are practically synonymous, and unless some method be adopted for guidance it will be impossible to preserve that consistency which is so supremely necessary. One heading should be chosen and it should be adhered to, and references should be made to it from its variants. There will repeatedly be temptation to depart from the rule on the ground of expediency, but this lure must be strenuously resisted.

For the maintenance of this uniformity a list of subject-headings is an essential tool. If it is in printed form it should be interleaved or have wide margins for notes, and the forms selected for use should be underlined. If a printed list is not available a card list should be compiled, and the variants entered on each card for cross-referencing. Alternatively, or even as a supplementary guide, a good catalogue may be used for example and its methods followed, note being made of any departures from its system.

Cross-references are a fruitful source of error. They may be used too sparingly or they may be redundant. One of the most annoying of mistakes is for a reference to be given to a heading not employed. As a rule this comes of relying too mechanically upon a standard list of headings instead of noting the items as they crop up during cataloguing and using the list as a check. Avoidance of this *faux pas* can only be ensured by a complete examination of every reference before the "copy" goes to the printer. This is one of the examples of the necessity for that persistent attention without which no really good catalogue can be produced.

Forms of catalogues

This is not the place in which to describe the various codes or the practice of cataloguing. That has been done, with numerous illustrative examples, in the *Manual* by Messrs. Quinn and Acomb.[1] The British Museum and many of the larger university and institutional libraries have their own rules, but the code most commonly in use is that which was drawn up jointly by the British and American Library Associations in 1908, known as the *Anglo-American Code*. As is the case with the Decimal Classification, local departures from these instructions are frequently made. The main principles are observed, but entries are often condensed, especially for printed lists of lending-library books, and there is diversity of usage in respect of personal titles of honour. The Anglo-American code recommends that the "blood name" be used, but, after all, the convenience of the public is the prime objective in a detail of this kind, and as a rule the general reader remembers the title (usually the last title held) and forgets, if he ever knew, the family name. All divergencies from the official code should be clearly indicated in the office copies so that the staff may know precisely what they are expected to do. If this and the similar marking of printed lists of subject-

[1] In *The Library Association Series*, vol. v.

headings are properly attended to consistency will be facilitated. Constant use will familiarize an observant cataloguer with the requirements of his catalogue, and the working rules should be committed to memory before cataloguing is commenced.

Catalogues, printed, typewritten, or handwritten, may be in the form of an ordinary printed volume, card catalogues, sheaf catalogues, or in placard style. The dictionary form is the simplest for general understanding, but it offers many pitfalls to cataloguers owing to the recurrent inducement to exceed the limits of specific entry and the exacting duty of giving proper cross-references. The problem of alphabetization is also a real trouble, for it is amazing how this simple task produces irregularities. Every entry should be carefully compared with the volume catalogued before it is accepted as correct; a model catalogue, or earlier editions of the one in hand, should be used as a test of general and detail treatment, and mistakes in classification symbols and textual literals should be looked for and corrected. If this is not done at the moment of cataloguing it may never be done at all.

THE MECHANICAL PREPARATION OF CATALOGUES

Paper slips, or cards, of uniform size, or, alternatively, sheets of paper which have subsequently to be divided into separate entries, are utilized for the "copy" of printed catalogues. If the former are employed the classification symbols appearing at the head of each card will serve as the guide for the arrangement of subject entries, and the first words of author and title entries for other items. Where sheets are employed class numbers or other guiding marks should be made at the extreme fore-edge of each entry. They will have to be detached subsequently, but for sorting purposes they are indispensable. For a subject catalogue additional entries must be prepared for the author and subject indexes which follow the main body of the catalogue, and it is advisable to mark at the time of cataloguing any slips of which the ultimate arrangement might otherwise be doubtful.

Some libraries which publish catalogues or bulletins make a practice of preparing the printer's slips when the original card or sheaf catalogue entries are made, and these data are preserved for use when wanted. They should be sorted into groups according to kind as the work proceeds, although the detailed sorting may be deferred for final adjustment. If cards or slips of uniform size are used they should immediately be placed in groups which are tied up or held together by elastic bands to allow of insertions and revision when required for printing. The final stage of preparation for the press is that of numbering each item consecutively as a check upon incompleteness when the slips arrive back from the printer's with the proofs. When sheets are cut up into strips there will be irregularity of size, and a different procedure should be adopted. The strips should be placed in stout envelopes, sorted by their first letters, numerals, or catchwords, into whatever degree of fineness is desired. Each envelope should have its contents indicated, and several of these may be accommodated in one of the cardboard boxes in which 5 in. × 3 in. cards are usually delivered. Every box should be labelled for ease of reference.

The unequal narrowness of these strips makes it impracticable for them to be treated like cards, and they are therefore pasted down upon sheets large enough to leave ample margins for headings and guiding marks. Certain weekly periodicals lend themselves admirably for this purpose, and the surface should be pasted over and the slips laid down in the order in which they are to be printed. Arranging them in order is not so easy as might be expected. It is inadvisable to lay out too many at a time, partly because a small number stands a better chance of careful scrutiny than a large quantity, and also because there is less risk of loss. Slips once laid out should be pasted up immediately checking is completed.

It has already been pointed out that simple alphabetization is elusive, and the importance of correctly supplying cross-references has been emphasized. Now—before pasting up—is the time for minute scrutiny. Nothing should be taken for granted. For the headings a previous edition (if any) of the catalogue, or a marked copy of a printed list of subject-headings, may be followed, and constant reference must be made in doubtful cases to ensure that entries are being properly placed. Eye-

CATALOGUES AND CATALOGUING

strain may cause irregularities in arrangement to escape attention, and someone who has not been engaged upon this particular piece of work should be called in to look over the batches of arranged slips. When finally approved the catchwords or other temporary guiding marks may be snipped off from the fore-edges, and the slips will be ready for laying down.

When the slips have been transferred to the pasted sheets they should be pressed firmly down either by blotting-paper, which is absorbent, or by any spare sheet of paper, avoiding smears. Care must be taken to see that any paste exuding from the slips or in the margins is removed or the sheets will stick together. Spongy paper should be avoided for it absorbs much paste, takes a long time to dry, and has an incurable tendency to blister. The sheets when pasted should be numbered progressively, laid out to dry, and then placed in turn upon the file of accumulating "copy," face downwards to maintain order, and preserved in a box or drawer for security.

Before it goes to the printer the material has to be marked for press. The contract specification will determine the general style and the various founts of type to be used. The conventional marks of the trade should be employed; *e.g.* words to be set in italics should be underlined; those for Clarendon type should have a wavy line placed beneath them. Large printing houses have their own code of practice, and general instructions may be given upon the alternatives presented in their schedules which are submitted before the work of printing commences. Thus it may be understood that entries not specially marked upon the "copy" are to be set in the type specified for the bulk of the work. Departures from this standard fount, *e.g.* those for sub-headings or annotations, may be indicated by vertical strokes in the margin, but the printer must be advised at the outset as to the meaning of each such indication. When an understanding has been established the printer should be asked to submit a trial proof, and this, set from the actual copy, must be meticulously scrutinized, for upon it the whole of the production will be based. Some libraries prefer to use inks or pencils of distinctive colours to denote types, but, generally speaking, it makes for smooth and accurate working if the printer's suggestions in this matter are adopted.

When this marking for press has been completed there remains yet another important task, that of editing the material. The script must be examined from end to end. Item by item the entries need to be scanned with eagle eye. Indistinct writing or lapses in spelling or typing may have to be cleared, punctuation adjusted, sequence checked, indents marked, consistency enforced, and every cross-reference tested. No effort should be spared to render the "copy" accurate and clear in all respects, for alteration when the matter is in type is costly, and opens out fresh possibility of error with little or no opportunity for correction. Now, if the list is in class

CATALOGUES AND CATALOGUING

form and the symbols are known, or when the proof is dealt with if page-references have to be given, the index items should be made and checked, and any preliminary matter, such as lists of abbreviations occurring in the catalogue, must be prepared.

Proof reading

Most printing specifications stipulate for the delivery of proof in equal quantities at stated intervals of time, and when it arrives it must be treated with the same care as that lavished upon the production of the "copy," which will come back with it. In ordinary bookwork a single proof in paged form is customary, but in catalogue work there is usually a galley proof, probably a revise in that shape, and finally a proof in pages.

Proof reading is done by two persons better than one, the junior to read carefully and slowly from the manuscript, spelling out unusual or doubtful words, the other to check the letterpress and to make any alterations that may be required. Every character should be regarded as a potential error, and numerals call for especial care, for if passed over now they will be apt to pass unnoticed until the mistake is pointed out by some victimized reader. Corrections should be made in the margins of the proofs, and the exact type matter to be altered must also be marked in the text itself. The recognized signs for proof marking are illustrated by the accompanying specimen pages (107–9), taken by permission from Mr. Stanley Unwin's *Truth about Publishing*, but if occasion arises for any marking not thus covered it should be explicitly indicated in a terse marginal note.

If a revise in galley form is supplied it must be read with the first proof, and this is a task which the cataloguer should perform alone, keeping a sharp look-out for errors previously unnoticed and checking by the original proof to see that the corrections there marked have been duly made. It is not yet too late to insert additional entries, but additions must be made in the clearest possible manner so that the printer may know beyond all doubt what the fresh matter is, how it is to be set, and precisely where it is to go in. Any corrections which may have escaped the attention of the printer, or be wrongly made, should be re-marked, and since printers accept responsibility for their own mistakes alone and will charge author's corrections as "extras," to be paid for by the library, it may be desirable to show by encircling or some other device those alterations for which liability is admitted.

The final proof will come as "paged revise." The printed matter has now been divided into pages, and, if necessary, set in double columns. This revise is, in fact, an advance section of the book as it is intended to be printed off. Obviously it would be unwise at this stage to interpolate fresh matter or to disturb the type in any way unless through sheer necessity. Even the advisability of adjusting minute errors is questionable since it would entail unlock-

CATALOGUES AND CATALOGUING
PROOF CORRECTING
Marks used in the Correction of Proofs
(See next page)

The caret mark; make correction indicated in margin.
Let the cancelled word, dotted underneath, remain.
Change to small capitals word underlined.
Change to italic letters word underlined.
Change to lower-case letter (small letter).
Transpose as marked.
Delete (take out).
Insert apostrophe.
Insert comma.
Insert semicolon.
Insert period.
Change to capital letter.
Make no break in the reading.
Remove space and close up.
Insert hyphen.
Insert one-em dash.
A space to be pushed down.
Wrong fount; change to proper fount.
Make a paragraph here.
Insert a space here.
Delete character indicated and close up.
Unevenly spaced; correct spacing.
A letter inverted; reverse.
Change to roman letters those underlined.
Lines to be straightened.
Indent one em.
Broken letter.

A MANUAL OF LIBRARY ROUTINE
PROOF CORRECTING
Proof showing Corrections

It is not possible even were I competent to attempt such a task, to give in a chapter any thing approaching a complete account of the numerous and highly technical processes such as paper making, block-making, printing and binding, which are employed in the making of a book. Nor is it necessary, because there exist popular hand books and learned treatises on all these subjects from which the reader can get more expert and detailed information than I could impart. All that will be attempted here is to put authors in a position to follow intelligently those parts of the processes with which they are likely to come in contact. It will probably simplify matters if we take each process separately though in practice several of them *are* often being dealt with concurrently

Printing. In an earlier chapter we discussed the process known as " casting off ' a manuscript, i.e. counting the number of words in it and calculating, after due making allowance for such variable factors as " small type,' etc., how many pages the book will make if printed in such and such a style. but we did not stop to consider a question which arises still earlier, viz. the choice of a printer. To the uninitiated, any printer is a potential book printer, but this more the case than that any tailor is competent to make a lady's costume.

Either a printer is a Book printer or he is not a book books printer the commercial printer who has occasionally printed a book (probably a local directory

CATALOGUES AND CATALOGUING
PROOF CORRECTING
THE OPPOSITE PAGE CORRECTED

It is not possible, even were I competent to attempt such a task, to give in a chapter anything approaching a complete account of the numerous and highly technical processes, such as paper-making, block-making, printing, and binding, which are employed in the making of a book. Nor is it *necessary*, because there exist popular handbooks and learned treatises on all these subjects from which the reader can get more expert and detailed information than I could impart. All that will be attempted here is to put authors in a position to follow intelligently those parts of the processes with which they are likely to come in contact.

It will probably simplify matters if we take each process separately, though in practice several of them are often being dealt with concurrently.

PRINTING.—In an earlier chapter we discussed the process known as "casting off" a manuscript, i.e. counting the number of words in it and calculating, after making due allowance for such variable factors as "small type," etc., how many pages the book will make if printed in such and such a style. But we did not stop to consider a question which arises still earlier, viz. the choice of a printer. To the uninitiated, any printer is a potential book printer, but this is no more the case than that any tailor is competent to make a lady's costume. Either a printer is a book printer or he is not a book printer; the commercial printer who has occasionally printed a book (probably a local directory or a glorified catalogue) is a person to be avoided.

ing the "formes" and upsetting the pages. Such alterations would, unless admittedly due to the printer, involve an additional charge for correction, and these costs have a disconcerting way of mounting up beyond all expectation. But there is another reason for hesitation, for as this is the *final* proof, and, failing a special arrangement, no further opportunity will be given for checking, there is a possibility of introducing one error while correcting the other. Such things have happened! At this late stage insertions are better made in the form of a supplement under a suitable heading.

A fresh cause for concern comes with this final revise—that of checking the headlines, page numbers, and turnovers. Careful printers make few errors in these matters, but it would never do to permit assumption to take the place of investigation, and the heading of every page or column, the pagination, and each broken entry which is continued in the next column or, maybe, upon the next page, must be subjected to scrutiny. Broken entries are, to say the least, unsightly, and should be avoided whenever possible, and at the outset the printer should be advised to that effect so that by a little spacing out they may be obviated. When the paged revise has been returned to the printer the section is struck off and the machine is cleared for the next piece of work.

The compilation of preliminary matter is the last to be undertaken, and for this purpose its printed pages are usually marked with Roman numerals.

CATALOGUES AND CATALOGUING

The matter for inclusion here is largely explanatory and official, and is administrative work; but lists of abbreviations, keys of the classification used, and other data collected from the body of the catalogue, must be put into shape for publication, and the letterpress to be printed upon the covers must also be prepared and sent to press.

Although the foregoing recommendations relate more particularly to the preparation of catalogues printed in dictionary form, they also apply to a very considerable extent to other varieties, and cover all sorts of lists, such as bulletins and short subject-lists, whether issued by municipal, collegiate, or other libraries.

Catalogues, printed or other, for children's departments follow the same lines of preparation, but with the difference that they should be simplified to the last degree, and scientific and technical terms should be judiciously replaced by more familiar words. In chapter x (The catalogue and how to make it) of his *Manual of Children's Libraries*, Mr. W. C. Berwick Sayers discusses this subject in all its aspects.

Subject-catalogues present special features for consideration. Here the entries are collected by main subjects corresponding to the chief divisions in classification codes, and are then arranged into subsections, each with its own appropriate heading, and the classification symbols as inserted in each volume by the classifier provide the guidance necessary for this detail sorting. Main headings should be marked upon the printer's "copy" for type sufficiently bold, and sub-headings for something rather less conspicuous, in the manner already described. The material for author- and subject-indexes (which are sometimes combined) will, as previously stated, be accumulated either from the manuscript as the books are catalogued or from the proofs as they are read, and it is sound policy to make a generous provision of alternative subject entries. Since the sequence in classified lists is governed by the code of classification and its symbols are permanent while page numerals change with every new edition, index references should be to sectional headings, as denoted by class numbers, rather than to pages.

CARD AND SHEAF CATALOGUES

Every library seeks to provide for public use an up-to-date catalogue of its books, but in these days when access to the shelves is so generally permitted in libraries, comprehensive printed catalogues are rarely attempted—at all events in libraries for popular use. They are costly to produce, and are no sooner issued than they begin to be incomplete by reason of fresh additions to stock, and as the shelves display the books, the need for printed catalogues is minimized: the catalogue for circulation in the homes of borrowers has therefore given place to the card or sheaf catalogue for consultation in the library.

In the United States card cataloguing is largely a matter of purchasing, at a nominal price, such printed cards as are wanted from the library of

CATALOGUES AND CATALOGUING

Congress,[1] and writing or typing thereon the subject-headings for duplicates of the unit card. Berlin offers assistance in co-operative cataloguing, but, although the National Central Library maintains a union catalogue of Metropolitan libraries for its own use, we have nothing comparable with the American system, and each library has yet to prepare its own card catalogues. Perhaps in time to come this wasteful practice will be overcome.

Handwriting, unless it is particularly clear and uniform, should not be permitted in the preparation of catalogues in card or sheaf form. Typewritten entries are to be preferred, but the ribbons must be of the "record" variety, not "copying": the latter smudge and fade; the former are cleaner and more durable, and it should be remembered that black ink is read more easily than violet, especially in artificial light. It is far from economical to use ribbons which fail to yield a sharp impression. For handwork the catalogue-cards and the loose-leaf pages of sheaf catalogues should be ruled with two vertical lines near the left edge to serve as starting-points and for indents, but the typewriter makes such aids to uniformity superfluous, and in addition to producing perfectly legible results it allows more than one cataloguer to assist in the work without exhibiting any variation in appearance. Cards showing corrections should be scrapped; it is better to rewrite them than to make a display of patchwork

[1] For an account of this system, see W. W. Bishop's *Practical Handbook of Modern Library Cataloguing*, chap. v.

which can never look nice and may possibly be confusing.

In preparing card catalogues it is always desirable to confine an entry to a single card, and the necessity for compressing the record is outweighed by the alternative necessity of having to turn over two or more cards to complete the reading of the entry. In view of the drawback, inherent in the card system, that one reader may obstruct the access of others to several drawers of the cabinet, it is advisable to catalogue books under variant headings, thus obviating cross-references to drawers which may not at the moment be available. This practice tends, of course, to increase the bulk of the catalogue, and size is an important consideration, but title entries are not invariably regarded as necessary, and the thinner cards which are now being employed offer compensation in that respect.

Subject-headings should be typed on the left-hand top side of each card in the boldest type at the cataloguer's command, and the classification marks will stand out better if instead of being placed at the extremity of the last line of the entry they are shown either above or below the entry on the right-hand side of the card. Annotations, if supplied, should appear in smaller type beneath the actual entry, but sometimes they occur as cuttings to be pasted on. If from non-library sources, acknowledgment of origin should be made.

Analytical entries should be written upon cards with printed notes that "This entry relates only to

CATALOGUES AND CATALOGUING

a portion of a book." Although laborious to compile, these analyses repay the trouble they give, for they reveal the resources of the library in a surprising way and frequently give information on subjects concerning which no monographs exist. The work of preparation will be lightened if entries are restricted to topics not adequately represented by special volumes, or to authors and subjects to which such cards bring information of special value. Libraries with a large stock of books may have little need for "analyticals," but smaller institutions will find them of great service.

Union catalogues, in which are brought together entries of the whole stock of the central and branch libraries, are an ideal not always attained: their cost, labour, and size all operate against them, but such a master-catalogue should be compiled whenever possible for use at the central library. If a book delivery system forms part of the library service it is almost imperative for such a comprehensive list to be there, although it may be impracticable at the branches, and, in any case, the knowledge thus afforded would be useful to the public and the staff alike. Where a union catalogue is provided it is desirable that the central stock be catalogued on white cards, and that of each branch on cards of distinctive tints. The coloured cards should also have a printed indication that the book referred to is stocked at the library so indicated. These cards are then filed with those relating to the local stock in the cabinet for public use.

The arrangement of cards in the trays or drawers may appear to the uninitiated to be a very simple affair, but in reality it is anything but that. It is a task which calls for the same knowledge and care as the preparation of "copy" for publication, and the insertion of cards is not a job for junior assistants. Half the battle consists in the provision and proper placing of guide cards; the other half is the difficulty of arranging the cards with absolute correctness behind the guides. Probably an insufficient number of guides is generally allowed, but from the point of view of the public too many can scarcely be given. Main headings may have guides whose projecting tabs extend over almost the whole length of the upper edge of the cards; sub-headings are shown in less bold style, in "thirds," "halves," or "fifths," running obliquely through the range of cards to which they apply.

The order in which these sub-headings shall appear may be alphabetical, chronological, or scientific and logical. The alphabetical arrangement is most generally used, but when it is departed from a card should be placed immediately after the main heading to explain the order in which the sub-sections are set. This is proved by experience to be desirable even although the guide cards give the same information, for it shows the scheme and contents at a single glance. In some libraries specially printed cards are inserted at intervals to explain the general method of the catalogue, and it attracts attention if these cards are of a distinctive colour.

CATALOGUES AND CATALOGUING

Sheaf catalogues are compiled in almost precisely the same way as cards, except that a page may contain several entries and may be written upon the back of a leaf as well as the front for the saving of space, whereas cards are almost invariably confined to single entries, and entries are never allowed to overrun a single side. Guiding is done by sunk "thumb indexes" for general purposes and by coloured pages for detail aid. When leaves are inserted it is important to see that the cover is securely refastened, or they will sag and work loose. In card cabinets the drawers need to be boldly labelled as to their contents; in sheaf catalogues the back of each volume must be similarly marked. A fair portion of the inner margin of each page is covered by the protective fastening, and it is a safeguard, covering risk by the tearing out of a page, if the accession number of each book catalogued upon the page is recorded on that margin, for the margin usually remains even though the body of the page has gone.

A feature that should be common to both these forms of catalogue is the marking, either at the base in front or somewhere upon the back of each entry, the symbols which indicate all the headings under which the book has been catalogued. When books pass out of stock and the cards or leaves are withdrawn the supplementary entries are thus indicated and the clearance may thus be made complete.

Card and sheaf catalogues are subject to much handling and in time show signs of wear. It is one of the functions of the cataloguer to see that soiled or defaced entries are replaced by clean and perfect ones. Sheaf catalogues may be placed upon the shelves near the books to which they apply, and where this is done it becomes necessary to see, by constant replacement, that the volumes are maintained in their proper position. The alternative method of display is to group them together in a special place.

PLACARD CATALOGUES

Placard catalogues are simply typed or written lists arranged in any approved order and framed; they are usually hung upon a wall or other fixture for general use. Short entries are almost all that can be attempted here, and single lines are desirable. If written out on slips a fair copy should be made upon sheets to fit the columns of the frame, and the frames may have movable backs to permit of ready interchange. Another method is to write the entries on slips of card uniform in size and to slip these into columnar slots, but this is not always satisfactory in practice as the slips have a pronounced tendency to bulge and become disorderly. Placard lists should never be large: if they extend to any considerable dimensions a card or sheaf catalogue ought to be considered.

TOPICAL AND OTHER DISPLAY LISTS

Topical and special display lists are a useful adjunct which should not be overlooked. The choice

CATALOGUES AND CATALOGUING

of books for this purpose should be selective rather than comprehensive, and the selection should be made by an experienced member of the staff. Entries should be typed when possible with a catchy title in outstanding type near the head, and a standing description displayed over that. These headings should be stencilled or done with rubber type of outstanding boldness to attract attention. It is fatal to public interest if these ephemeral lists are allowed to remain displayed too long: novelty and the quality of being right up to date are essential for success.

Special lists are sometimes exhibited to indicate the books which have recently been placed into stock. A less well-known method of conveying this information is to place the cards of such books in a special drawer of the card cabinet, the drawer being marked "New books." A guide card denoting the current month occupies the forefront, and the cards are ranged behind it in catalogue order as the books are stocked. The cards of the previous month may perhaps be allowed to remain behind its appropriate monthly guide, but then they are carried into the general body of the catalogue, and the freshness of this special drawer is preserved.

There are various mechanical contrivances which may be employed for the reproduction of special lists which cannot well be printed. The cyclostyle admirably lends itself to this use, and almost any number of sheets may be run off by competent workers. The typewriter for this purpose should have a good key-drive to cut through the waxed surface of the stencil, and the stencil itself must be carefully handled so that it is not allowed to crease and crack. By this means lists of books can easily be prepared for distribution in debating societies, schools, or at lectures, and one of the prime objects of municipal life—"economy with efficiency" is achieved.

SELECTED REFERENCES

BISHOP (W. W.). Practical Handbook of Modern Library Cataloguing. 2nd edn. 1924.
BROWN (J. D.). Manual of Lib. Economy. 4th edn. 1931. (Div. 1—Cataloguing methods.)
CLEVELAND PUBLIC LIBRARY. Filing Rules for the arrangement of Dictionary Catalogues. 1922.
CUTTER (C. A.). Rules for a Dictionary Catalogue. 4th edn. 1924.
—— Why and How a Dictionary Catalogue is made. (In *Library Journal*, xv.)
FEGAN (E. S.). School Libraries. 1924. (Section vi—Cataloguing.)
LINDERFELDT (K. A.). Eclectic Card Catalogue Rules. 1890.
London Library Subject-Index. 1909. (See notes in its preface.)
PEACOCK (B. M.). School and Librarian's Handbook, with Notes on Rural Libraries. 1920. (Section v—The catalogue.)
PHILIP (A. J.). The Production of the Printed Catalogue. 1910.
QUINN (J. H.) and ACOMB (H. W.). Manual of Cataloguing and Indexing. 1933.
SAVAGE (E. A.). Manual of Descriptive Annotation for Library Catalogues. 1906.

CATALOGUES AND CATALOGUING

Sayers (W. C. Berwick). Manual of Children's Libraries. 1932. (Ch. x—The catalogue and how to make it.)
—— and Stewart (J. D.). The Card Catalogue: a Practical Manual. 1913.
Stewart (J. D.). The Sheaf Catalogue: the Compilation of Manuscript Catalogues. 1909.

CHAPTER VII

THE ADMISSION AND REGISTRATION OF BORROWERS

The term "registration," as used in library work, is generally understood to cover all the routine associated with the admission of borrowers—the examination, acceptance, or rejection of applications for membership; the making out and filing of lending-library tickets; the preservation of voucher forms; and the various methods of registering borrowers. The processes about to be described relate to lending departments alone, and only to such libraries as the public have the right to use. Reference issue work follows a different routine, and collegiate and institutional practice, even when books are taken away from the library building, are akin to reference work.

Varieties of borrowers and tickets

The categories of persons to whom tickets are issued in municipal lending libraries may be summarized as follows:

1. Ratepayers.
2. Non-ratepayers locally resident.
3. Non-resident persons employed within the library area.
4. Teachers and students at local schools or colleges, whether locally resident or not.

THE ADMISSION OF BORROWERS

5. Non-residents, either with or without payment, including those holding privilege tickets.
6. Deposit borrowers, usually temporary residents.
7. Children.

The kind and number of tickets to which borrowers are entitled differ in accordance with the local regulations, but the increasing tendency is towards greater liberality. Most libraries permit each registered borrower to have one general ticket which is available for books of any kind, and also a supplementary ticket which is not available for works of prose fiction, and it is now extremely common to issue a third ticket the use of which is restricted to musical scores. Special tickets are often issued, at the discretion of the librarian, for the loan of additional volumes for educational and professional purposes. Tickets are usually coloured by kinds to aid in detecting validity of use.

Ratepayer borrowers

Almost invariably a ratepayer is allowed to act as his own guarantor. He is required to give his full name and address upon the voucher form provided for the purpose. His occupation may be requested—for report purposes—and occasionally the applicant's age is demanded, but this is now generally restricted to users of the children's department. Features containing elements of practical service are the business address and the applicant's telephone number; but these details are rarely found in this country, although the former would be of value for the recovery of books lost through unnotified changes of address by borrowers. All ratepayers are not locally resident, for some absentees have property votes within the library district and their names occur in the printed list of voters, which is the standard by which ratepayer applications are tested. Residents in flats and other compounding householders will appear (if qualified) in the voters' list, and the routine of examining is to see in the first place that each voucher is correctly filled up, and then, by reference to the official roll, to discover whether the applicant is entitled to sign for himself (and others) or not.

If the name is not found in the burgess roll it does not necessarily follow that the signatory is not a ratepayer within the meaning of the regulations, for a qualifying period must follow occupation before a vote is granted. If a rate or rent receipt can be produced that should be sufficient, but in any case of dispute or doubt the rate department of the local authority should be rung up or written to and the matter thus determined. All claims thus admitted should be entered into the official register to obviate future complications.

Non-ratepayer borrowers

Non-ratepayer applicants are usually required to have their applications countersigned by ratepayers who guarantee the library against loss or damage accruing through misuse of the library by the persons

THE ADMISSION OF BORROWERS

for whom they thus become responsible. The acceptability of these guarantors is ascertained by reference to the list of voters, as just described. Some libraries entirely dispense with these guarantees and allow locally resident non-ratepayers to fill up forms for their own tickets, checking their *bona fides* by reference to the current local directory or by posting a card of enquiry to the address given upon the form of application. Where guarantors are required the applicant signs on one side and the sponsor upon the other.

Non-resident borrowers

Non-resident teachers or students fill up voucher forms which are signed by the principal or secretary of the school or college which accepts liability. Applications from persons who are employed, but not resident, within the library area are authorized by the signature of an officially recognized representative of the employers who undertake the responsibilities of guarantors.

The fifth and sixth classes of applicants demand special treatment, for with them enters the new factor of money paid either as a subscription to be retained or as a deposit to be repaid. In each instance a formal receipt will have to be given, and some little book-keeping must be done.

Non-residents may be permitted to use the lending department of a municipal library either gratuitously or upon payment. The former is granted by special permission; the latter is regulated by local rule, and unless the vouchers and tickets are specially printed they must be distinctively marked. No subscription tickets should be issued until the money is paid. There may be specially printed receipts, progressively numbered, or the receipt may take the form of a numbered page from a counterfoil book, the record being made in duplicate—one for preservation, the other to be given to the borrower. To prevent the use of time-expired tickets a time register should be kept. This may be a dated card-file, or a diary entry for a year ahead, and a point should be made of advising each subscriber a fortnight in advance of the expiry of his ticket so that renewal may be effected without inconvenience or break.

PRIVILEGE TICKETS

Privilege tickets, where in operation, are granted at the discretion of the librarian, to whom all applications should be referred. They may be restricted to a single issue or for a limited period, to individual readers who establish their *bona fides*, or to persons registered as students at classes or lectures delivered within the library building or elsewhere. They are usually free from payment, although the Public Libraries Act, 1892, made it legal to impose a charge for the use of such tickets at seaside resorts. Holders of these tickets may be required to fill up application forms like other non-ratepayers, but are not called upon to provide guarantors; ordinary library tickets can be made to

THE ADMISSION OF BORROWERS

serve this use if specially marked. One way of doing this is to make a stroke obliquely across the face of the ticket to denote that it is a privilege ticket; another method is to stamp it with the word "Privilege," and the reverse side is endorsed with the limits of its use. Additional tickets requested for special purposes by registered borrowers are frequently issued at discretion, and marked copies of original tickets are required for this purpose. Sometimes adjoining or distant libraries agree to honour the tickets issued by each other. The chief routine aspect of this service consists of the careful observance, when making a claim for overdues or damage, of the library to which the defaulting borrower belongs. If this is not done, the holder of the local ticket bearing the same number may be applied to in error: a glance at the ticket should suffice to obviate any such mistake. Unless a first application for the return of such books and the payment of fines incurred elicits a satisfactory response, the borrower's local library should be advised and the "charge" should remain in the overdue file until the transaction is cleared.

Deposit borrowers

Deposit borrowers are persons who, while desiring tickets of membership, are not themselves ratepayers and cannot or will not procure guarantors. Often they are transient residents without local connections. They pay a deposit, which in different places may vary from 5s. to £1, and are then entitled to receive a ticket. A receipt must be given for every deposit, and a record of each receipt must be made. The receipt itself may conveniently be written out upon a page of the counterfoil receipt book which is commonly employed for such items as are not covered by printed receipts, and a carbon duplicate remains in the book when the other copy, bearing the same number, has been handed to the depositor. If this receipt is produced when the return of the amount is demanded, reference will be made easy; if not, the name index or a ledger record will suffice for clearance. The record must be cancelled, and a receipt obtained and entered in the petty cash book, for the amount will be repaid from that source.

These tickets should be subject to the customary time limit, and to prevent fraudulent use by non-residents the address should be verified. Verification should also be made if renewal of a ticket is requested, for the borrower may have removed from the library area.

Children's tickets

Children's tickets are in a category of their own, being issued upon the recommendation of a parent, guardian, or school teacher. The routine of this department is described in detail by Mr. Sayers in his *Manual of Children's Libraries*; here it need only be remarked that in many respects it closely conforms to the procedure for adults. By arrangement, schools will receive supplies of application forms for

THE ADMISSION OF BORROWERS

distribution through teachers, and the school stamp, implimented by the initials of the head, is regarded as adequate. Teachers should not be expected to assume financial liability, and, indeed, everything possible should be done to secure and retain their active good-will by troubling them as little as possible. Applications in respect of overdue or damaged books should first be made to the parent or guardian, and a messenger sent to the homes of defaulting children is very effective. Only when these attempts have proved abortive should the assistance of teachers be invoked. Offenders may have their tickets suspended, and headmasters may be advised of such cases so that they may, if they think fit, admonish the culprits.

Application forms

Application vouchers for all sorts of borrowers are now largely standardized, and take the form of printed cards of catalogue size, with blanks left for applicants to fill in. If now and again the old style of printed sheets be encountered, the routine treatment is the same. A specimen voucher as used for ratepayers' applications appears overleaf.

Reception of applications

It will be observed that here (as in the case of other varieties of voucher forms) provision is made for the issue of three kinds of tickets—ordinary, supplementary, and music—and borrowers are requested to strike out any not required. A variant

A MANUAL OF LIBRARY ROUTINE

method is to have the three types of tickets specified upon separate lines and to invite readers to initial

---

PUBLIC LIBRARIES

Ticket No..........

RATEPAYER'S APPLICATION VOUCHER

I, the undersigned, being a Ratepayer of the Borough of .... hereby make application for a Ticket entitling me to borrow books from the Lending Departments; and I hereby undertake to replace, or pay the value of, any book belonging to the .... Borough Council which shall be lost or injured by me, and to pay all fines, and all expenses in recovering the same, in accordance with the Rules, by which I agree to abide.

NAME IN FULL.............
(If a Lady, state whether Mrs. or Miss)

ADDRESS.............

DATE.............

N.B.—An additional ticket, available for Non-fiction only, and a further ticket, available for Music only, may be obtained upon signing the following request:

I desire to receive a Non-fiction Ticket
and/or
Music Ticket
(Strike out words not required.)

.... Signature.

WRITE LEGIBLY IN INK.   O   DO NOT FOLD THIS CARD.

---

each kind required. As forms are handed in, they should, in the presence of the applicant, be scanned

THE ADMISSION OF BORROWERS

for obvious defects. If omissions have occurred, they should now be filled in; handwriting may be undecipherable and should be made clear; or the form may have been filled up with pencil, which is undesirable, although a distinguished judge once ruled that if a signature was made with an indelible-ink pencil it was inviolate! This cursory inspection may save annoyance to borrowers and, in the long run, the time of the staff.

By rule a period of three days may be claimed for the examination of forms and the preparation of tickets, but this should not be rigorously enforced, and where circumstances permit it is advisable to issue tickets forthwith. Some libraries allow provisional tickets upon which books may be borrowed upon the presentation of filled-up forms of application. These tickets are available for one issue only, and at the first opportunity are replaced by the proper tickets, or, in the event of the applications being found to be out of order for any reason, are destroyed and fresh forms given to readers when the books so borrowed are returned for exchange. Applications received by post should be filed systematically, and it will conduce to safety if this is done without delay.

EXAMINATION OF APPLICATIONS

The method of testing applications has already been described, but two final checks are desirable before tickets are written out. The borrowers' register should be consulted to see that applicants are not receiving more tickets than they are entitled to, and the "black list" should be referred to in order to prevent the issue of fresh tickets to defaulters. If any amounts thus found to be due are now paid, the records should be adjusted and tickets may be issued; otherwise such applications must be refused.

Rejected applications

When applications have to be rejected, the reason should be stamped or written upon them, and the forms should then be filed under name sequence at the enquiry desk or counter. If, when the applicant calls, the defect is found to be capable of immediate rectification, the ticket may be made out or a provisional one permitted. Occasionally the checking list may be shown to be defective, and in such instances a special effort ought to be made to meet the borrower's convenience and the check-list should be put right. Some libraries include in their routine the posting of a form advising applicants of the rejection of their forms and the reason therefor, and where this is done a fresh voucher should be enclosed. Others prefer to explain the circumstances when the applicant calls, and a provisional ticket disposes of any temporary difficulty.

Issue of tickets

As applications are found to be in order, the tickets are written out. The blank line at the top of the form has the borrower's full name (in inverted order), indicated in block letters for the sake of clearness. The next vacant number is then inserted at the other end of the line, and the voucher is ready for registering. The tickets are then made out in accordance with the kinds specified as desired, and as the voucher card carries only one number, this particular number is copied on to whatever tickets are issued to the borrower. Care must be taken that the name, address, number, and date are correctly copied from the voucher as the tickets are written, and, when this operation has been checked, the forms are sorted into their file and the tickets are placed in trays or drawers in alphabetical sequence to await the borrower's call. A copy of the rules should then be handed to each new borrower, and, if the borrower desires, the card catalogue, the classified arrangement of the books upon the shelves, and other matters of public interest should be explained to him; but these good offices should not be pressed unduly: some borrowers resent it as interference.

Registering borrowers

Tickets are issued for a limited period, generally two years. By reason of death, removal, or other causes, they are constantly lapsing, and it is a moot point whether the numbers so voided should be applied to newly issued tickets or whether tickets should be progressively numbered until a maximum is reached, when a fresh commencement is made. Advocates of the former method record admissions chronologically in a book register provided with numbered lines and yearly columns in which the names of borrowers and the date of their tickets are entered.[1] As tickets lapse a coloured tick is placed against their holders' names to denote that the numbers are available for new borrowers, and when tickets are renewed the name and date are continued in the next column. Where it is preferred that a borrower should retain his original number so long as his membership remains unbroken this system is admirable, but many libraries adopt the other method. If tickets are valid for two years, they are progressively numbered for a period of three or four years, thus allowing ample time for clearance so that duplicate numbers may not occur, and then a return is made to number one. Lapsed tickets can be filed for counting off for statistical purposes, or may be recorded in a register. Either method can be worked successfully.

Centralized registration

Borrowers' tickets are generally coloured according to their purpose, one tint being employed for ordinary tickets, another for supplementary, and a third for those restricted to musical scores, and in some instances a further scheme of tints is used to differentiate between libraries comprehended within the library system. When only one library is affected no trouble arises, but where there are many branches

[1] Described and illustrated in Brown's *Manual of Library Economy*. 4th edn., p. 353.

THE ADMISSION OF BORROWERS

a "colour problem" emerges, for the range of suitable tints is not illimitable. Where each branch makes out its own tickets the difficulty is met by using the same distinguishing tints throughout and printing the initial letter of the name of each library immediately before the borrower's number. Borrowers are now almost universally allowed to use their tickets at the different libraries as they may prefer from time to time, and it is inevitable that charging trays will frequently contain tickets with the same numbers, with some risk of confusion. Some effective method of differentiation is therefore most desirable, and modern practice solves the difficulty by having *all* applications for membership examined, and all tickets made out, at the central library. The risk of duplicating numbers is thus eliminated.

Where this method is adopted, application forms are remitted daily to the central library, and although this may entail the three days' delay as provided for by rule, no inconvenience will be occasioned if provisional tickets are allowed. It expedites matters if rubber stamps are used to denote commonly recurrent reasons for rejection, and forms which are marked as unacceptable, together with such tickets as have been prepared, should be returned with the utmost promptitude to the library from which they were received. But before this is done the tickets must, of course, be registered by arranging the numbered vouchers in their correct order in the file.

A MANUAL OF LIBRARY ROUTINE

The advantage of having all tickets made out at one library is by no means restricted to the avoidance of duplicate numbers. It imposes a check upon any attempt by readers to obtain more books than they are entitled to by acquiring a supply of tickets from more than one library. It is also an effective way of defeating defaulters who, having had their tickets suspended at one library, seek compensation by getting tickets at another, leaving the onus of detection to the staff. If centralized issue of tickets is not in force, this malpractice can be checked if each library advises the others of its defaulters. Such evasions may not be common, but that is no reason why the rules should be defied with impunity, and the labour of interchanging this information will not be excessive.

Forms of registers

Until recently it might safely have been stated that libraries maintained a double register of borrowers, one arranged by names, the other by numbers, but modern practice tends to eliminate the latter, although in libraries where the ticket numbers enter into the charging system both of the forms must be retained. The vouchers themselves usually form the name-index. All that is necessary is to sort them into alphabetical order and to insert new ones as they appear, carrying in a sufficient number of guide cards to facilitate reference. Where numerical registers are in operation, they assume

THE ADMISSION OF BORROWERS

ledger form with the lines successively numbered. The essential details for entry are: (1) the running number, (2) full name in inverted order, (3) address, and (4) date. Sometimes additional columns are included to cover the various kinds of tickets issued to each borrower, but elsewhere independent records are maintained for supplementary and other special tickets.

Supplementary registers

Optional registers relate to guarantors and to streets. Whether they are undertaken or not is entirely a matter for local decision; many libraries dispense with both, but each has its peculiar use.

Guarantors, like non-ratepayers, sometimes default by refusing to discharge their liabilities, and it is undesirable that such persons should be allowed to become responsible for additional borrowers. Occasionally a limit is placed upon the number of persons whom any one burgess may guarantee, and in either event some form of check is required for the guidance of the assistant who examines applications. Serious defaults are recorded in the "black list," with the date, a brief note of the offence, and the amount of payment due; but it would be cumbrous if reference had in every case to be made to this register, and something more expeditious must be provided. Quite a satisfactory way is to mark the burgess list with the number of the page in the "black list," and thus the facts are readily disclosed.

Where the right of guarantee is limited, the ticket numbers may be entered against the guarantor's name in the same list, and if ink of a different colour is used for this purpose there will be no confusion.

Street registers serve two purposes. In the first place they reveal the distribution of borrowers street by street, and so attract official attention to areas which may be considered for a publicity campaign. Secondly—and this is perhaps the more important reason of the two—they offer local information which may be of service when cases of infectious diseases occur. But for this important information a specially compiled register is not essential, nor is the name or the address of the patient by itself sufficient. This subject is discussed in a later paragraph of this chapter, but here it may be pointed out that if a street register is not compiled its object may be achieved by marking a copy of the local directory as part of the routine of preparing tickets. Otherwise a copy of the rules should be posted to each address upon the officially supplied list of infectious cases as soon as that information is received. The risk may be *nil*, but it is due to the community that every safeguard shall be exploited, and it reassures the public to know that their welfare is so well looked after.

Unclaimed and unused tickets

The ticket file must be overhauled from time to time, for some tickets are never claimed, and others

THE ADMISSION OF BORROWERS

are handed back for storage until required again and appear to be forgotten. If these are allowed to accumulate indefinitely the file will become congested, and a card or circular is therefore sent to laggard borrowers advising them that their tickets await their call. Time-expired tickets should be destroyed at sight, but it is unsafe to cancel long deposited tickets until their limit of availability is attained. Each ticket bears the date of its expiry, and assistants should remind their holders in time for renewal. An automatic reminder is sometimes obtained by using distinctive colours for cards, the colour being changed each calendar year; but colour schemes may be overdone.

TICKET RENEWALS

The renewal of time-expired tickets is a matter of divergent practice. Most libraries require the original procedure to be repeated, on the ground that the duration of guarantee must be limited. Moreover, it is desirable that the qualification of guarantors shall be tested at intervals of time: they may have died or have removed from the district. The residential qualification of borrowers also demands verification. If, however, such repeated routine is dispensed with and borrowers are allowed to continue the use of their tickets by written or verbal request, the style of register described on page 134, which is ruled for such continuous marking, is eminently suitable, and a cross or other symbol will denote the extended life of the tickets.

WITHDRAWAL OF GUARANTEES

When guarantors intimate that they wish to be no longer responsible for the use of tickets issued upon their recommendation, they should be promptly advised that their responsibility will cease as soon as any books borrowed in connection with those tickets have been returned and any liabilities incurred therewith have been discharged. As such books are brought in their borrowers should be told that a fresh guarantor will be required, but, except in the case of untrustworthy individuals, a provisional ticket should be permitted and a fresh voucher given. Where the charging system allows, a "stop slip" should be inserted to prevent the further use of tickets so affected, but elsewhere a note should be posted up in a private part of the staff enclosure, and assistants must be vigilant to see that due effect is given to it. The original vouchers must be cancelled, with a brief note and the date, or a special card may be written and placed immediately behind the voucher or even attached to it.

LOST TICKETS

Borrowers are required to give immediate notice of the loss of their tickets—for the use of which they are held responsible. Note is taken of the name and address, and the date of notification is added, and this record is either displayed for staff use at the issue desk or is filed for reference. Few libraries

THE ADMISSION OF BORROWERS

now care to make out fresh tickets without delay or to issue temporary tickets, and an interval of time is very properly claimed for the interception of tickets improperly tendered for use and for the overdue trays and ticket files to be searched on the offchance of discovery there. At the end of this period a duplicate, boldly so marked, may be issued. It should be a replica of the original, and it is reasonable for a small charge to be made for it. The original voucher card should be endorsed accordingly, and, unless it is customary to mark these vouchers with details of defaults, the "black list" should be consulted to prevent the evasion of penalties. When it is discovered that lost tickets are obsolete, a new form should be supplied, and a provisional ticket may be allowed.

Surrendered tickets

The procedure when tickets are returned as no longer required for use is extremely simple. The original application voucher is marked as cancelled and the tickets themselves are filed for statistical purposes or destroyed. If filed, they should carry a cancelling mark to prevent them from straying into use. If destroyed, the entry in any cognate record should be voided so that the number thus vacated may be applied to a new ticket.

Changes of address

Invariably the rules prescribe that changes of address by borrowers shall promptly be notified in writing to the librarian, and a form is usually provided for this purpose. Preferably it should be of a size that will fit into a crown octavo book, and the wording need be but brief, as follows:

CHANGE OF ADDRESS NOTICE

> In accordance with rule ...... I hereby notify
> that I ....
> late of ....
> have now removed to ....
> ....
> Ticket number ....
> Date .... 193 .

As these intimations are received the register should be corrected by crossing out the old address and entering the new one. Unless these notices are preserved, it will be advisable to mark vouchers with the date of notification of change.

INFECTIOUS DISEASES

Medical officers are always willing to send confidential information of all cases of notifiable disease occurring within the district, and it is of importance that this information should be acted upon without delay, for it is supplied with a view to preventing the

THE ADMISSION OF BORROWERS

spread of infection through the use of books. Whether books act as a vehicle of infection or not is doubtful, but no library can afford to run the semblance of risk, and its obvious duty is to take all steps to arrest the circulation of any books which have either been handled by victims of such diseases or have come within the danger zone. The local medical officer will, in the performance of his normal duty, take possession of library books found in infected premises, and will either destroy them or return them, disinfected, to the library in due course. He should furnish particulars of books so treated, and the volumes should then be checked off in the charging system and the tickets filed pending the receipt of official advice of a clean bill of health. Details of destroyed books must be noted in the shelf-list and other registers, and replacement copies obtained if required.

In order to promote safety, a printed or other communication should be forwarded to each of the addresses noted on the doctor's letter of advice, stating that the borrower's ticket is temporarily suspended and that any library books there should be handed to the representatives of the medical officer of health. Occasionally, however, books are brought back with the information of illness before the official report has been received, and provision must be made for this contingency. A zinc-lined airtight box charged with disinfectants (which the medical officer will supply or suggest) should be ready to receive such rarities, and the doctor should be advised. It may be as well for the assistant who has handled any such book to wash his hands with disinfectants without delay. This may sound portentous; in reality the risk is slight, but it should not be ignored.

SELECTED REFERENCES.

AMERICAN LIBRARY ASSN. Survey of Libraries in the United States. Vols. 2 and 3. 1927.

BROWN (J.D.). Manual of Library Economy. 4th edn. 1931. (Ch. xxiv—Registration of borrowers.)

DANA (J. C.), *edr.* The Work of Registration, the Desk. (In *Modern American Library Economy.*) 1908.

FLEXNER (J. M.). Circulation Work in Public Libraries. 1927. (Ch. iii—Registration of borrowers.)

RAE (W. S. C.). Public Library Administration. 1913. (pp. 78–86—Registration of borrowers.)

ROEBUCK (G. E.) and THORNE (W. B.). Primer of Lib. Practice. 1914. (pp. 50–3.)

SAVAGE (E. A.). Union Register of Borrowers. (In *Lib. Assn. Record*, v. 307–12.)

SAYERS (W. C. BERWICK). Manual of Children's Libraries. 1932. (Ch. xii.)

VITZ (C.). Circulation Work. (A.L.A. Manual, 31.) 1927.

By courtesy of Libraco, Ltd.

CARD CHARGING: A SORTING TRAY

CHAPTER VIII

BOOK ISSUE METHODS

Whenever books are issued a record must be made and preserved so that they may be traced for due return. "Charging" is the library term for this process of entering to or charging up against borrowers the volumes which are lent to them, and it is accomplished in a variety of ways.

Any efficient charging system should show—

(1) what, and how many, books are issued from day to day;
(2) by whom they were borrowed; and
(3) the date by which they are due for return.

Different kinds of libraries attach varying importance to each of these factors. In collegiate libraries and in reference departments generally the whereabouts of the books is of prime importance, and a book record is adopted; in institutional and subscription libraries it is considered more important to know what books individual members have at any time, and a personal record is maintained; but in municipal and other busy libraries, where speedy service is imperative and loan periods are limited, the time record is pre-eminent, and this consideration dictates the method of charging. While it is perfectly true that "there is no one system which is best for all types" of service, the fact that card charging is now so widely employed speaks for itself.

In words which could hardly be bettered Brown's *Manual* states that "the fundamental idea of all card systems of charging is that each book or volume shall be represented by a movable card, which can be stored in various ways when the book is on the shelf, and used to register or charge the book, when issued, to its borrower." There are in common use two different ways of "storing" these movable cards—one known as "the book-card in pocket system" and the other as "the book-card in tray" method, and each of these will have to be described.

Each item of the charging equipment will have its proper place, and unless orderly arrangement is observed there will be confusion and a slowed-down service. Every day before opening-time it should be the routine duty of someone to see that the date-stamp is correctly set, that the "charges" of the previous day are arranged in the trays, counted up, and entered in the issue register; that the regulation amount of loose cash for change is deposited in the till, the receipt books checked and placed ready for use, the newly made-out tickets or rejected vouchers filed in order at the enquiry desk, and any staff notices duly posted up. The work of keeping books in order upon the shelves is recurrent throughout the day, but the early morning before the public enter offers a special opportunity for so doing, and it should be taken advantage of to the fullest extent.

In most municipal libraries a uniform period of

BOOK ISSUE METHODS

fourteen days (exclusive of the day of issue) is now allowed for reading, although exception is often made for new books which are known to be in great demand. The convenience of readers is consulted

```
┌─────────────────────────┐
│   17846        942      │
│  ───────────────────    │
│     Green, J. R.        │
│  ───────────────────    │
│   Short History         │
│  ───────────────────    │
│          of England     │
│  ═══════════════════    │
│   │    │    │    │      │
│   │    │    │    │      │
│   │    │    │    │      │
│   │    │    │    │      │
│   │    │    │    │      │
└─────────────────────────┘
```

MANILLA BOOK CARD

if the date of return, rather than that of issue, is marked upon the date-paper, and when setting the date in the rubber stamp care should be taken to make allowance for public holidays or other occasions when the department will be closed. Wherever two different loan periods are in operation distinctive date-stamps will facilitate accuracy, and to this end they are better kept apart at the counter.

```
┌─────────────────────────────┐
│   17846          942        │
│   Green, J. R.              │
│   Short History             │
│            of England       │
├─────────────────────────────┤
│ No. B861.3      ╲           │
│   Brown, Ada     ╲          │
│   17, Long Rd.    ╲         │
│ Expires 25 Apr. 1931         │
├─────────────────────────────┤
│         PUBLIC LIBRARIES    │
│  Available at any Lending   │
│  Library for ANY kind of    │
│           book.             │
│  Notify change of address   │
│         without delay.      │
│  Readers should consult the │
│  Card Catalogues, as all    │
│  books are not shown on     │
│       the open shelves.     │
│  This Ticket is NOT TRANS-  │
│  FERABLE and the person     │
│  named above is responsible │
│  for books borrowed upon it.│
└─────────────────────────────┘
```

A "Charge"

The accompanying sketches show first a book-card and then the card conjoined with a borrower's

BOOK ISSUE METHODS

ticket; the two items placed together constitute a "charge."

The numerals at the head of the card on the left-hand side denote the book's accession number—the identity clue by which books are often charged and traced; those on the right-hand side are classification numbers. Upon the lines immediately below are entered brief particulars of the author and title; the lower space is for recording dates of issue (or return), but for the sake of speed this feature is often omitted, it being considered that the stamped date-paper in the book affords all necessary information as to frequency of use. The borrower's ticket explains itself, bearing as it does the borrower's number, name, address, and the period of the validity of the ticket. The book-cards, tinted according to the main classes of the book stock, are prepared as the books pass into stock. In the "book-card in pocket" system they are slipped into pockets which are pasted upon the inside of the book cover, where they remain until the books are borrowed. If the "book-card in tray" method is in use, these cards are sorted into sequence and filed in trays, from which they have to be extracted when a volume is issued and in which they must be correctly replaced as the books are returned. The former is the quicker plan, but the latter enjoys the advantage of serving as an indicator, and if books are permanently or temporarily withdrawn for repair or any other reason the book-card may be marked, and the staff can find by referring to this file which books are "in" and which are "out." Old book-cards should be promptly replaced by fresh ones as the date columns are filled up or if they become disfigured or soiled, and for record purposes the issues should be counted up and recorded upon the new ones where the cards are so dated.

Extracts from the rules are usually pasted upon the book cover facing the date-sheet, and it is advisable that the accession number should in every instance be plainly written thereon. As books are returned by readers this number should be compared with that on the book-card. Thus errors are checked and rectified.

CARD-CHARGING PROCESSES

Book charging is a simple process. A borrower having chosen a book from the shelves, brings it to the charging counter and tenders it with his ticket. The book-card is removed from its pocket (or taken from the tray) and inserted in the pouch-ticket or coupled with the ticket by a loose pocket, the date is stamped upon the date-sheet in the book, and so far as the reader is concerned the transaction is completed. If convenient, the "charge" may then be placed in its proper sequence in the charging tray, but it frequently happens that this cannot then be done. In such case it may be put into a sorting tray, in which "charges" are grouped into main classes by the colour of their book-cards, or they may be dropped through a slot in the counter into a drawer below. At intervals, as work permits, the

BOOK ISSUE METHODS

tray or drawer must be thinned out by withdrawing "charges," sorting them into precise order, and placing them in the trays on the "discharge" counter, where they will await the return of the books to which they relate. The order of arrangement in these trays varies in different libraries. Perhaps the most common sequence is that of the accession numbers in class groups, with or without Cutter author-marks, with poetry and fiction sorted alphabetically by authors and then titles. Sometimes the arrangement is merely by authors throughout; but, whatever the method may be, the charges must be accurately arranged behind (or, in some libraries, before) projecting date-guides, so that they may be found when wanted with the least delay. Each day's issues follow that of the preceding day, and the trays containing them are ranged side by side. As books are brought back by borrowers these "charges" are thinned out, and the trays will require to be adjusted by closing up. At the end of the fortnight the remaining "charges" disclose themselves as overdues; fine-guides are inserted in accordance with dates, and these guides will require adjustment as the fines increase.

Discharging is equally simple. As each book is received back the date-sheet guides to the tray in which the "charge" is filed, and the accession (or other clue) number indicates its sequence. Now is the time to glance at the number on the book-card and upon the cover to see that they tally. If the book is not overdue the ticket is handed to the

By courtesy of Libraco, Ltd.] CARD-CHARGING TRAYS, SHOWING GUIDES

borrower and the book-card is restored to the pocket inside the book, or into the "book-card in file" tray if so required. If the book is overdue, the fine must be levied and a receipt given. Time may not allow of a detailed inspection of all the books as they are brought back, but some show of examination should be made by a hasty turning over of the leaves, and special books should either be examined or placed aside for that purpose before re-issue. Chamber music, for example, usually has the piano score bound in, and the other orchestral scores enclosed within the covering portfolio, the number of parts being indicated on the binding; these should invariably be checked in the presence of the borrower, both at the time of issue and that of return.

Sheet and ledger charging

Card charging is now so widely adopted that little need be said of the forms which it has superseded. In commercial libraries a personal ledger account may be desirable, but it is of little service in other spheres. A system much superior for ordinary library work, and one which combines simplicity with cheapness, is that of charging by daily entries on sheets or ledgers. Here the date appears at the head of each column-group, columns being provided for the progressive number, the call number, the borrower's ticket number, and, occasionally, for the date of return. Fifty lines to a page is convenient for calculation. The date and the progressive issue number are entered upon the date-

BOOK ISSUE METHODS

paper which each volume carries, and the borrower shows his ticket both as evidence of registration and to reveal its number. These clues are referred to when the books are brought back, and it is easy to find the charging entry and either cross it out or record the date of return. Entries not so cleared indicate overdues. The borrower always retains possession of his ticket. In various forms this principle is embodied in the charging systems of many colleges and schools, and, despite the fact that only one assistant can use a page at any time, it is not unsuited for service in deposit stations or other small libraries where book issues are not large or speed essential.

BOOK RENEWALS

Renewal of books for a further period of reading is generally provided for by rule, and the process of renewal is done in different ways. New books—especially fiction—and other books likely to be in popular demand, are often excluded from this privilege for a time, and they should be marked upon their date-sheets or elsewhere for staff information. Renewal is in other cases optional at the discretion of the librarian, and if any book is known to be required by other readers it should not be re-issued to its holder. When books are brought to the library no complications arise: the date is freshly stamped upon the sheet in the volume and the charge is removed from its old position for inclusion in the day's issues. Here the question of the desirability of non-renewal may occur, and, to prevent constant re-issue of the same book to a single reader without indication of these re-entries, renewal dates should be stamped with ink of a special colour; the position will then always be apparent.

Applications for renewal may come by post or telephone, and special forms are sometimes inserted in books requesting readers to fill in the headed lines specifying the name of the author, the title of the book, the date last stamped upon the date-sheet, and (sometimes) the call or accession number, with the name and address of the applicant. If the request is made by telephone these details should be taken down and verified by repetition, or sound distortion may lead to error. Where the matter cannot be attended to forthwith, the memoranda should be filed and the file cleared each day. If a fine is due, a slip stating the fact and amount should be inserted in the "charge," and the postcards or notes should be filed in case of date dispute.

Methods of adjusting the charges in the issue trays when books are not brought back for renewal vary. The date marked in such books when returned will, of course, be that of the original issue, and the assistant will, naturally, refer to the tray for that date and will demand a fine unless some provision is made to indicate the fact of renewal. If the "charges" are left in their first position the renewal date may be stamped upon the book-card or a slip denoting renewal may be inserted, or a narrow card slip bearing the letter "R" may take its place; but

BOOK ISSUE METHODS

if the "charges" are removed to a later tray it will be necessary to place a guide in the positions so vacated. Failing this, a separate file may be kept for renewals, and to this tray reference will be made upon declaration that the book had been renewed.

Many libraries allow, under special purposes, at the time of issue, an extension of the time allowed for reading. In these cases the time-limit is marked upon the date-sheet in the book and the "charge" is placed behind a guide of corresponding date either in the ordinary charging trays or in a special tray. Until this guide comes into normal use there may be some risk of accidental misplacement, but if these odd charges are wedged behind angle-blocks this liability will be reduced.

Special loans of books

Teachers and others are usually permitted for special purposes to take out books in excess of the customary number. Full records of these extra issues must be made, and the simplest plan is to provide temporary tickets and to charge the books in the ordinary manner.

Book reservation

In very many libraries readers may bespeak the next use of books which are in circulation, but modern fiction is excluded from this privilege. The general practice is to register details of the book and the name and address of the applicant upon a voucher card, and to request the borrower to address a postcard to himself, for which he pays a penny. Before accepting applications it will be well to see that the book is not upon the shelves, that it has not been withdrawn from stock, and the file of book applications should be consulted to ascertain how many times the particular work is already booked up. Sometimes there is a limit to such bookings, and in that case new applications must not be accepted; even if otherwise, the borrower may not care to wait for a period which may extend to several months.

The voucher cards, filled up so far as is possible at this stage, are filed in classified order either accompanied by the postcards or not. If not, the latter should be separately arranged under the names of applicants. If the library maintains a *book record*—which rarely happens in a municipal lending department—it is easy to stop the books as they come back. The alternative is to examine the trays until the desired "charge" is found, and then to insert a card slip, perhaps with the letter "B," which will guide to the file of bespoken book application vouchers. This search is not so laborious as may be thought, for the guides and the distinctive colouring of the book-cards are of considerable assistance to the searcher. The book is laid aside, and a postcard is sent to the borrower, stating that the volume is available and will be reserved for two days (or whatever other time the regulations prescribe), and that unless claimed within that time the book will pass to the next applicant. If this happens, the borrower next upon the waiting list will be advised; but if there is no such other applicant the book goes back into stock. Some borrowers may wish to be advised by telephone, and in case of such request the telephone number should be entered upon the postcard or voucher when reservation is booked. Some libraries require that the advice postcard shall be produced when the book is claimed.

Issue recording

As the day's "charges" are sorted into the trays they should be counted up and a more or less detailed analysis made of the issues. Division by main classes, with additional columns for music, perhaps history, biography, and geography (including travel), and certainly for prose fiction, is all that is commonly attempted; but some libraries prefer minute subdivisions which show to a fine degree the use made of topics. For main classes the coloured book-cards are a sufficient guide, but for anything beyond that detailed examination is required. "Charges" are accordingly sorted out first by main classes and then by classification (or accession) numbers. Sectional totals will be entered in their appropriate columns in the issue register. The final column is for the day's gross total, and the figures must be accurately recorded or the cross and long tots will not agree when the month's returns are made up.

The register of issues is usually in the form of a folio volume, and other statistics often appear in the lower portion of the page. Such, for example, are the number and kind of borrowers' tickets issued during the month, percentage of the issues, the corresponding figures for the previous year, the year's cumulative figures to date, and such other details as may be deemed worth while to note. If no separate register is kept for aggregated figures where branch libraries exist, their statistics may be recorded here, as also should those of the reference and children's departments, the figures being given in bulk, not detail, for each branch or department will have its own detailed records. Where there are many branches or departments a master-record will be essential, and thus a comprehensive survey is obtained.

Overdue books

Card charging automatically declares such books as have not been returned within the time allowed for reading, and they must be systematically followed up. Sheet charging shows overdues by uncleared entries on the various pages. In card-charging systems the date guides indicate that any remaining "charges" are overdue; in ledgers or sheets the pages must be most carefully scrutinized at regular intervals or oversights will occur. Columns which are entirely cleared should be run through with a vertical stroke, the others must be kept under surveillance. Indicators are now so outmoded as to require little notice. In the Cotgreave frames, guidance is afforded by the colour scheme of its cards or slides. The four colours employed are

BOOK ISSUE METHODS

exclusively used in weekly turns, and each Monday morning before the department opens the indicator must be searched and the book numbers taken when the "charges" are marked with the colour about to be used again.

Overdue books may have to be written for, but if this procedure is deferred for a time many books will be returned during the interval and the necessity for applications diminished. The length of this intervening period varies in different places, but it should not be unduly protracted or the fines will mount up disconcertingly. The form of notice sent to borrowers also differs, but folded circulars are superseding postcards as they offer some little privacy. The wording embodies a reminder that the specified book is overdue, that a fine (indicated) has been incurred, and that failure to return the book will increase the penalty.

The date and details of the application will be entered in an overdue register, in which the amount of the fine due on the date of entry will be recorded. There will almost certainly be columns ruled in which details of any second or third application are entered. The second request draws attention to the fact that the previous application was unsuccessful, and it specifies the amount of the increased fine. If a third application becomes necessary, it will probably be more strongly worded, and it may contain an intimation that unless the book is returned and the fines paid within a given time application will be made to the guarantor or the matter reported to the committee. These notices are advantageously printed upon papers of different tints, so that recipients will know that they are freshly sent. If the defaulter has no guarantor to whom application may be made, his ticket may be suspended, he will be entered in the "black list" of defaulters, and may perhaps be sued in the county court.

But postal applications do not exhaust the library efforts. If these prove abortive, a messenger should be sent to collect the books at all events, and if possible the fines. He should be provided with a detailed record abstracted from the overdue book, so that he may know exactly where to go and what to demand. Where borrowers have changed their address, he may discover that to which they have removed, or perhaps a business address. If a book is recovered without the fine, note should be taken for the use of the librarian; but whenever a fine is paid a formal receipt must be given from the stock carried by the messenger. In the event of no recovery or information being forthcoming, the fact must be recorded with the reason for the failure, and the whole report submitted to the member of the staff who is in charge of the overdues. He will enter the details in the remarks column of the overdues, and in the defaulters' register. The card should then be extracted from the overdue file, and the book may be written off as lost.

BOOK ISSUE METHODS

SELECTED REFERENCES

Brown (J. D.). Manual of Library Economy. 4th edn. 1931. (Ch. xxxv—Book issue records.)
Flexner (J. M.). Circulation Work in American Public Libraries. 1927.
Library Assn. Small Municipal Libraries. 1931. (pp. 92–100.)
Primer of Librarianship: ed. by W. E. Doubleday. 1931. Chs. vi–viii.)
Rae (W. S. O.). Pub. Lib. Administration. 1913. (pp. 13–18.)
Roebuck (G. E.) and Thorne (W. B.). Primer of Library Practice. 1914. (pp. 53–64.)
Stewart (J. D.) and others. Open-Access Libraries. 1915. (Ch. viii.)
Vitz (C.). Circulation Work. (A.L.A. Manual, 21) 1927.

CHAPTER IX

REFERENCE LIBRARY ROUTINE

(GENERAL REFERENCE DEPARTMENTS, COMMERCIAL AND TECHNICAL, AND SPECIAL LIBRARIES)

The scope and purpose of lending and reference departments are dissimilar, and their routine methods differ accordingly. In the former the book stock is of a more general character than in the latter: it includes a fair proportion of purely recreative reading, and the books are taken away—hence the necessity for verifying the *bona fides* of applicants for library tickets. In the latter the books are of a more special character: contemporary fiction and other light literature of the day have here no place; the books are provided for purposes of study or for strictly utilitarian purposes; they are often large and costly, frequently in long sets, and they are intended for use within the library building. In municipal reference libraries there are no registered borrowers; their resources are open to all without the intervention of guarantors or references of any kind, and it will be obvious that a charging system which is admirably suitable for the one department would be unworkable in the other. Each has to adapt itself to its own particular requirements.

REFERENCE LIBRARY ROUTINE

BOOK CHARGING

In municipal, and some other, reference libraries the system of charging is extremely simple. The time factor—predominant in lending departments—scarcely applies except in the case of universities, and there time records are sometimes maintained as a supplementary check, and the same may be said of readers' records. Institutional and subscription libraries may require to know how many and what books any member has at any given time, and some collegiate libraries also provide this information; but the outstanding requirement is to know where the books are at any moment, and the charging system is usually based upon this consideration. An application slip, duly filled up by the reader and marked by the staff, is placed upon the shelf in the place from which the books are taken, affords the necessary clue for tracing the whereabouts of borrowed books, and this, in brief, is the method customarily adopted.

These application forms vary in size and shape and in the amount of detail to be supplied, particularly by the staff; but they inevitably require each reader to specify the author and title of the works requested, and the number of volumes desired when the work is in more than one volume. In large libraries the number of the table at which the reader is working may also have to be indicated, so that the books may be taken there without having to search for the person who has applied for them. As a rule application forms are oblong in shape, mostly about eight inches long, with headed spaces at the right-hand side for the press mark, date, and the initials of the assistants who issue and replace the books. Occasionally the time of application and of issue has also to be marked upon the form, presumably as an incentive to quick service; but whether this feature is included or not, rapidity of issue is always to be striven for—a slow supply irritates readers and creates a bad reputation.

Any number of volumes of the same work may be issued upon a single form, but as it is impossible to place one slip in two places at the same time, a separate application must be handed in for each different work required. If a borrower who has asked for a certain number of volumes of a work or set of books afterwards requires additional volumes, the original voucher will suffice, but in such cases the reader should be invited to alter the figures and should initial the amendment.

The catalogue provided for public use, in whatever form it may be, will be referred to by readers who are familiar with the library, but strangers often display reluctance to consult it, and prefer to ask for guidance from the staff. This guidance should be cheerfully given. Sometimes no little patience, and perhaps a little tact, may be demanded of the staff, and it should never be refused; indeed, readers should be encouraged to make their requirements known, and every possible effort should be made to satisfy their needs. At the same time it may be

REFERENCE LIBRARY ROUTINE

advisable to instruct the reader in the use of the catalogue as a matter of convenience to himself, but this should not be unduly pressed. Some people seem to be constitutionally unable to comprehend either a library catalogue or a railway time-table, and they must be helped. If, therefore, forms are imperfectly filled in, or if a verbal request is preferred for assistance before the application can be written out, the desired first aid should be rendered. The first requisite is that when application forms are handed in they shall be scanned to see that they are signed and sufficiently detailed for use.

Whether readers are required to sign an attendance register upon entering the department or not is a matter of administration; but if that be the rule it will be necessary to maintain sufficient oversight to secure its observance, and forms should not be accepted from applicants until the book has been signed.

These preliminaries being attended to, the assistant takes the form to the bookshelves, procures the specified volumes, initials the slip which he inserts upon the shelf, and delivers the volumes to the reader. If the books are already in use, the form upon which they have been issued will indicate the fact, and the applicant should have the inoperative application returned to him. Possibly there may be other books treating of the same subject, and if that be so the reader should be informed and allowed to examine such works as he may desire; he may thus be enabled to carry on for a while until the other works are freed for his use. When the forms have been accepted, initialled, and books placed in the hands of the readers, the actual charging process is complete.

DISCHARGING

Most application forms bear an instruction to readers to the effect that the books which have been supplied to them must be returned to the counter when done with, and must not be left upon the tables. The rule is not invariably honoured, and the general surveillance should include careful watch to prevent such neglects, and defaulting readers should be reminded of the regulations. Generally, however, the books are duly returned to the staff, and in some libraries the original forms of application, or a duplicate or a special receipt, are given by way of acquittance from responsibility in respect of their use.

In at least one great municipal reference library the application forms are in two sections divided by a vertical line of perforation for easy separation. One part goes up on the shelf from which a book is taken, and the other is filed at the desk and is slipped into the returned book to which it refers and remains there until the book is replaced. Then the two halves come together again; they are compared to see that everything is in order, and the check is thus made absolute. Whatever may be the kind of form employed, it will be necessary to compare the books with the application details, and when this is done and the volumes restored to their shelf place the

REFERENCE LIBRARY ROUTINE

forms should be initialled so as to fix responsibility for correct replacement.

The rules of the library will no doubt prescribe that such things as the use of ink, tracing, etc., shall not be permitted, and the regulation must be rigidly enforced. It will be well always, but more particularly when rare or valuable publications are concerned, to make sure by investigation that they have not been misused, but unless this is consistently done it will be difficult to assign responsibility for damage unless the occurrence was observed at the time of occurrence. If proper examination cannot be made when the books are returned to the desk, a rapid turning over of the leaves will be better than nothing. Most libraries possess some items—books, maps, manuscripts, prints, etc.—which it would be difficult or costly to replace, and the use of these is often restricted to particular tables well within the oversight of the staff. These are indicated in some way for staff guidance, frequently by a coloured tab or private mark on the back of the binding or by a symbol within the book, and such items, at least, must be examined in the presence of the person who has just used them.

If the books have date-sheets, the date of issue must be stamped or written there before the discharging is completed. These dates are merely records of frequency of use; they serve no other purpose, and are gradually being abandoned as unnecessary: a library book-plate often takes their place.

A MANUAL OF LIBRARY ROUTINE

SHELF ORDER

One of the first requirements in reference library routine is the maintenance of absolute order upon the bookshelves. A book misplaced is practically lost. If any volume is not in its proper place it should be accounted for in such a way that its whereabouts is known. It is bad library form to delay delivery of books because a search has to be made, and, *per contra*, expeditious service is an advertisement of efficiency. It is important, therefore, that in replacing books on the shelves there should be no confusion, and that books which look alike shall not be mistaken for each other. The slips should be examined and compared with the books as the latter are re-shelved, and if this is properly done errors will not occur. Volumes which are neither in the possession of readers nor upon the shelves should be represented there by special slips, so that information may be given to applicants to whom they cannot be supplied. Thus, if a book is at the binder's, the slip (usually of larger size than ordinary application slips, and of a different colour for each standard reason) should state the author's name, title of the work, when it was sent for repair, and the location mark. If a book is withdrawn for re-cataloguing or other administrative purpose, a slip of another tint would be used and the reason for temporary withdrawal stated; if the book has been issued for home reading, a different slip would indicate the details, and the slips inserted in place

REFERENCE LIBRARY ROUTINE

of the absent volumes serve as ready indicators. Thus the books are either upon the shelves or the reason for their absence is discovered at a glance; any unexplained gaps should be investigated as they are noticed.

Very many libraries use application slips which are alike in every respect save that they are printed upon paper of different tints. One may be white and the other coloured, and these are used on alternate days. This simple device automatically shows whether the books were issued during the current day or on the previous day, and when white forms are in use the presence on the shelves of coloured slips denotes overdues. Particulars of any missing volumes should be jotted down, and the books themselves must be found or accounted for. Where a duplicate slip or a part of any double form of application is filed at the counter, the fact that books have not been replaced on the shelves declares itself, for as the original slips are cleared the forms are transferred from the books-in-use file to that of books-returned, and any residuum relates to volumes which have not found their way back to their permanent place, and denotes that their replacement is outstanding. It is one of the recurrent tasks of reference assistants to examine the shelves and see that books are promptly replaced. If books have to be brought from stores there is an additional prospect of misplacement, for any tendency to delay the replacing of books in remote parts of the building will be a prolific source of trouble. The reference librarian should keep a record of such borrowings and require the return of the vouchers as evidence of the completion of the routine; otherwise the books may lie about, undiscoverable if wanted, and the issues may not be recorded. Here again the duplicate or counterpart form serves as a check, but the stores should be inspected daily both to clear overdue forms and to see that the stock is otherwise in order.

OPEN-SHELVES

So far account has been taken only of those works of reference for which forms of application have to be filled up, but most reference departments permit free access to a portion of the stock. Encyclopaedias, gazetteers, atlases, dictionaries of various categories, and other books for ready reference may form the bulk or the whole of this section, but it is by no means unusual for a much more liberal selection of books to be placed upon the shelves which are available to all-comers without formality. This freedom of use is rarely abused, but as the risk is ever present the staff must maintain unobtrusive oversight to prevent misuse.

For more than one reason the rules usually stipulate that books taken from the open-shelves in this department shall be left upon the tables when finished with. Few readers would replace them correctly if asked to do so, for they have little or no knowledge of schemes of classification and books would probably be slipped into the first shelf-gap observed. Moreover, it is by the number of volumes collected from the tables and replaced by the staff that the circulation of these books is computed, and the presence of assistants moving from table to table in the performance of this duty helps to secure the observance of regulations and the proper use of books.

Special loans

Under special circumstances borrowers have often been allowed to have works of reference for home reading, and this privilege has latterly been extended to a generous degree. If special cause can be shown for such use, permission is not reasonably withheld, but encyclopaedias, dictionaries, and works in constant demand are always excepted from this concession. If the person preferring such a request is registered as a borrower at the lending library, the matter is simplified: he is known, and he has a ticket which may be held at the library as a pledge for the due return of books so lent, or particulars may be noted from the ticket and the books specially required may be entered to his ticket number. Whether the charging shall be done by special entry in the departmental diary or kept upon the file at the reference desk in the form of a dated memorandum is a matter of local preference, but a time-limit is invariably set, and the record should be so devised that the date of return is not likely to be overlooked. These loans are not often numerous enough to require a special charging system, and perhaps the best plan is to preserve the signed application forms upon the issue file until they are cleared by return, and to make a note in the library diary under the date of return. By this means the matter can hardly escape attention, and application should be promptly made for any works not brought back to time. As books thus lent are always liable to recall if wanted by other readers, it is desirable that in every instance applications shall bear the telephone numbers of readers, so that, in case of urgency, the books may be recoverable immediately; but this difficulty may often be solved by offering to disappointed applicants other works on the subject in which they are interested at the time.

USE OF LENDING-LIBRARY BOOKS

Small libraries are often unable to make separate provision of reference books beyond such works as dictionaries and encyclopaedias. For the rest they have to rely upon the stock of the lending department, and these books, excepting current fiction, are available as works of reference. Even in larger libraries this inter-departmental service is desirable and is frequently most useful, and printed catalogues or lists of lending-library books are frequently displayed for the use of reference readers.

The only point of routine involved is that of charging, and since the volumes are used in the reference department they should be regarded as reference issues and should be counted accordingly. The simplest method is to take the reference appli-

REFERENCE LIBRARY ROUTINE

cation slip, properly signed and filled up, into the lending library, fold and insert the slip together with the book-card in a coupling pocket, and place this charge in the tray containing the day's issues, or in the sorting tray if one is in use. The slip will proclaim the fact that it is not a normal charge and thus prevent the issue being counted twice over, and the tray is a convenient receptacle which must in due time be cleared, so that books not returned are self-evident. It is due to the department from which the book is fetched that it shall have some such clue, but to prevent oversight a record should also be kept in the reference department, and this may be either a duplicate or a memorandum as explained above for books obtained from a store-room. As soon as these books are brought back to the reference desk they should be returned to the department concerned, and the record of loan preserved there during the absence of the book should be cancelled.

STUDENTS' ROOMS

Some of the larger libraries make special provision for research workers and other students to whom quietness and ample table accommodation are essential. In such cases tickets are made out for applicants to whom this privilege is conceded, and evidence of *bona fides* and a satisfactory reason for the grant of such tickets are usually required. The tickets may be permanent or restricted to a specified period, and they have to be shown before admission into the room. Forms of application are filled up in the customary way, and the books are taken into the room by the staff. To prevent unauthorized access the door of the room may be fitted with a self-fastening lock of the night-latch variety, which can be operated easily from the inside but requires to be unlocked by a key on the outside. Readers are requested to return their books to the staff when they have finished with them, and the other procedure follows the normal routine of the reference department.

LOCAL COLLECTIONS

Every library strives to procure and preserve items of local interest, and the net for this purpose cannot be flung too wide. Books by local authors, or treating of the district, or published locally, pamphlets, minutes of the local public authorities, those of local societies of all kinds, deeds and ancient manuscripts, local maps, prints, portraits, election addresses, films and gramophone records of local interest—anything and everything in fact relating to the district should be acquired as opportunity occurs. Nothing, however ephemeral it may seem to be at the moment, is too insignificant for preservation. Local newspapers and Church magazines, calendars and programmes of local educational or other institutions, photographs, and even picture postcards—all are of potential value to future historians, and should be sedulously sought for and

REFERENCE LIBRARY ROUTINE

carefully classified and preserved. Deeds and other manuscripts of past days may be obtained by gift or purchase, or even as permanent loans; sale catalogues of historic houses or estates, and the illustrative plans which usually accompany them, are desiderata to be sought for and, when acquired, made accessible for use. Their treatment varies in different libraries. Large libraries may have separate accession registers for such items as manuscripts or prints; smaller ones may enter everything either in one register restricted to the local collection, or even in the general register, but however that may be, each item should be accessioned and should carry the accession number for tracing purposes. If more than one register is employed, the particular one to which the clue number refers should be indicated by its number of initial letter. All items should be stamped in some way to render them unsaleable. Whether they all are to be catalogued or not is a matter for local decision, but the desirability of cataloguing is as obvious as is their classification. The local collection is invariably preserved intact and apart from the general stock, and the fact of inclusion in this special collection should be notified in catalogues by the addition of the letter "L" before the classification marks.

Pamphlets

Many items in these local collections will be in pamphlet form, nor is this troublesome kind of publication confined to that section of the stock. Any unbound publication of more than two pages (for one page constitutes a broadside) and less than a maximum of, say, fifty pages may be regarded as a pamphlet. Frequently these are of temporary value only and, unless of local interest, will not be worth permanent preservation. Others, for one reason or another, will go into permanent stock, preferably (but not invariably) catalogued. The routine difficulty is the problem of their preservation. To bind each one separately is neither desirable nor practical. Obviously they cannot be shelved individually like books. The common plan is to place them in dust-proof cardboard cases in classified order, and either to place the boxes, duly labelled, upon the shelves with the books on kindred topics, or to arrange them in a separate sequence at the end of each class section. In this case the pamphlets should be protected by manilla or other stiff covers into which they may easily be sewn; if this be not done the leaves will curl and the pages become dusty or frayed. The alternative is to group them together by kind and have them bound up into volumes, but this is fatal to close classification and should only be adopted in very special instances where finality may be assumed. Vertical filing may be resorted to, but in view of the fact of their permanent preservation boxes are probably the most suitable method of filing them. Like books, the boxes vary in size, and they may be shelved with the octavos, quartos, or folios, as occasion may require.

REFERENCE LIBRARY ROUTINE

Maps

Many ways of storing maps have been tried, but the only feature upon which there is uniformity of view is that—like prints—they should be preserved flat. Large, shallow drawers, with covering boards to keep them down, are frequently used, and the drawers are descriptively or numerically labelled, and each map and its catalogue entry is marked accordingly. If classification numbers are employed, this method is fluid enough, but anything in the nature of fixed location will prove troublesome. The British Museum plan of cutting large maps into sections of uniform size, mounting them on linen, and folding them for preservation in cardboard boxes, has, of course, much to commend it. As the application forms for maps, pamphlets, prints, etc., would not be visible in the same easy way in drawers as they are when exposed on shelves, a desk record of all such borrowings should be kept, and this file should be cleared each successive day. The compound form, by which one portion of the application slip is filed at the desk and the other is placed in the position from which the item in question has been taken, solves this problem in most satisfactory fashion.

Prints

Engravings and other prints are best mounted on cards or stout paper of graded standard sizes and filed in boxes. That the latter should be as dustproof as possible goes without saying. The prints should be sorted out according to their kind, so as to bring all of one subject together, each item should be accessioned and individually numbered, and blind-die stamping, or perforating dies, are decidedly to be preferred to ink stamps. Care should be taken that the engraved or printed surface is not disfigured by these official stamps or dies, and the accession numbers, class symbols, or other official details should be placed well at the foot of the mount or upon the verso, so as not to distract the eye unreasonably.

COMMERCIAL AND TECHNICAL LIBRARIES

Commercial and Technical Libraries are a modern development of reference library work, sometimes forming a separate department within the main library building and sometimes housed in the heart of the industrial area of the district. Although they may be found combined their objectives are distinct, since technical libraries are chiefly concerned with production and commercial libraries with distribution. The former are therefore intended for manufacturers, inventors, and strictly technical users, while the latter are organized mainly for merchants, exporters, and others who are engaged in the marketing of goods. The common aim is to procure and make available without delay all sorts of printed information for the promotion of technical knowledge and the advancement of local trade and industries. This information must be up to date; it

REFERENCE LIBRARY ROUTINE

must be as complete as possible, with a view to local interests; and it must be so arranged as to be accessible to users with rapidity and ease.

Within the compass of a few paragraphs it would be impossible to convey any adequate idea of the working of these departments, but the subject cannot be entirely ignored in a chapter on reference library routine. The stock but partially resembles that in a normal public library. Books, indeed, may play a comparatively minor part in the supply of material, but such as are stocked must be invariably the best and latest editions regardless of cost. Works of quick reference, such as encyclopaedias, atlases, dictionaries, guides to foreign languages, on mercantile law, gazetteers, and a sufficient number of trade and other directories, may be cited as indications of the character of the books required, and they have to be extensively supplemented by such things as telegraph codes, all kinds of transport information, consular and market reports, rates of exchange in foreign countries, shipping information and maritime regulations, freightage, customs tariffs, manufacturers' and other trade catalogues, and all kinds of cognate publications, official and other, likely to be of service for the promotion of home and overseas commerce. All must be scrupulously maintained in up-to-date condition. No small part of the function of these departments is to procure and prepare for reference a liberal supply of technical and commercial periodicals, British and foreign, for manufacturers and merchants must have the very latest information, and this is frequently found in newspapers and other journals. Unless these publications are narrowly limited to special aspects, the various articles will have to be cut out, mounted, annotated as to source and date, and then classified and placed so that readers will know where to find them. Service must be accelerated in every possible way.

Books are placed upon open-shelves in classified order, and the classification must be close. Large-scale maps are best mounted on spring rollers. Articles excised from journals, mounted newspaper cuttings, perhaps some trade lists and other small items, are sorted into folders according to kind, and are deposited in vertical files which are duly labelled and always available to the public. Books and other permanent stock are card-catalogued, but the more ephemeral items need not be catalogued at all; they come and go with rapidity, and close classification renders cataloguing superfluous, although perhaps an index card may be made to guide from the catalogue to the file. The file itself is always under revision, for it is as important to remove old articles as to insert new ones, and this involves educated discrimination and perpetual care such as method only can secure. Subject to obviously special considerations, the routine is largely as in ordinary reference libraries. Mr. Pitt's *Manual of Commercial and Technical Libraries* will be found an adequate guide to every aspect of these departments for special research, and Mr. Halsall's chapter in the

REFERENCE LIBRARY ROUTINE

Primer of Librarianship offers a competent survey in brief.

WORKS AND BUSINESS LIBRARIES

Works and Business Libraries are a further refinement of reference work. They are established and maintained by business firms for their own use, and readers are restricted to members or employees of the respective firms. In many ways they conform to the style of commercial and technical libraries: their resources include much current literature of a nature peculiar to the special requirements of each individual library; their methods are largely the same, but books and periodicals may be removed for use by qualified persons. It may be part of the librarian's duty to look for and supply journals, or particular information to certain persons, and he should be so familiar with the material under his charge as to be capable of advising at any time as to sources of knowledge. In effect these libraries are private technical libraries, but they differ from the latter, as above described, in that they are in scope particular rather than general, and that material may be taken away and a suitable charging system will therefore have to be employed. Mr. Headicar's short chapter in the *Primer of Librarianship* describes the salient factors with details of their organization and management.

INFORMATION DESKS

It is not every library, however, which needs or can maintain a commercial or technical department, and by way of substitute in medium-sized and smaller libraries enquiry desks in the reference library have been instituted. Their chief use will probably be found to lie in advising readers concerning sources of information or explaining the catalogue and the system of classification of books upon the open-shelves. All sorts of local and general information, commercial intelligence, railway, and other time-table and directory details will be enquired for from day to day, and advice on the best books for consultation on different subjects will constantly be requested. The range of enquiries is sure to be wide, and the staff must be competent and willing to act as "guide, counsellor, and friend" to all legitimate enquirers. The "short cuts" to information—such as encyclopaedias, gazetteers, and dictionaries of various kinds—should be kept near the desk, as also may bibliographies and serviceable library catalogues, for these are common working tools for the staff. With these aids the assistants ought to make themselves familiar, and they should also be well acquainted with all the library book stock. It will be a great help for future use if, as difficult enquiries are met, a note is taken of the sources in which the information was discovered, and if compiled as a private card catalogue it will always be ready for easy reference. No enquirer should be permitted to depart unsatisfied, and if, after consultation with other members of the staff, it is agreed that the library does not possess the required information, the reader should be informed

REFERENCE LIBRARY ROUTINE

of the resources of the National Central Library and of the possibility of procuring the loan of the book in that way or by regional co-operation, and the offer to obtain such books should be made. These investigations educate assistants by widening their knowledge; they also reveal weaknesses in the stock, and a memorandum of desiderata thus disclosed should be made at the time for the information of the librarian. Where there is no special enquiry desk the work devolves upon the departmental staff, and enquiries are made at the counter.

General work

One of the ordinary duties of the reference staff is the maintenance of the stock in proper condition. Obsolete books should be noted for replacement, binding and repairs must be regularly attended to, and dust should not be allowed to accumulate or the books will speedily become soiled and unattractive. The daily and monthly statistics will require prompt attention, and general supervision of readers must be maintained. For the reason that books do not leave the department, save under special circumstances, stocktaking is regarded as of minor importance, and in many libraries it is undertaken only at lengthy intervals of time, but the open-shelves should be examined and the books there checked systematically and often. If the number of these books is not large, this check should be a daily operation; in larger libraries it should be done, section by section, as frequently as pressure of work permits, and careful watch must be kept for leaves turned down, and also, alas! for mutilations. When damage is discovered, the ill-treated books should be withdrawn from open access and a close oversight instituted on books of a similar character.

One other matter remains for mention—that of the amount of attention to be bestowed upon individual readers. Some persons are shy to make their requirements known, and they must be patiently helped. The vast majority of readers are perfectly reasonable, but now and again there are some who appear to think that the rules which others should observe do not apply to them. Others are not content to be informed as to the best books for their particular needs, but actually demand that the search for detail information shall be done for them! Tact and patience and unvarying courtesy find their place here, but there must be some limit to willingness. It is the reader's part to sift the material supplied, and although time may be freely devoted to enquirers, it is better to attempt to educate readers into helping themselves than to be cajoled or bullied into performing research work which, once done as a favour, is very likely to be demanded later as a right.

REFERENCE LIBRARY ROUTINE

SELECTED REFERENCES

Reference Libraries.

Baker (E. A.). The Public Library. 1924. (Ref. Libraries, pp. 44–55.)
—— (*Edr.*). The Uses of Libraries. New and rev. edn. 1930.
Ballinger (Sir J.). The Reference Library. (In *Library*, ix, 1908, pp. 353–69.)
Bostwick (A. E.). The American Public Library. 4th edn. 1929. (Ch. v—Reading and reference rooms.)
Brown (J. D.). Manual of Library Economy. 4th edn. 1931. (Div. ix and pp. 183–7.)
Johnson (C.). Care of Documents and Management of Archives. 1919.
McCombs (C. F.). The Reference Department. (A.L.A. Manual, 8.) 1929.
Pamphlets and Minor Library Material: clippings, broadsides, prints, etc. (A.L.A. Manual, 22.). 1927.
Pollitt (W.). The Duty of the Public Librarian in relation to Local Literature and Bibliography. (In *Lib. Assn. Record*, xvi, 1914, pp. 119–26.)
Powell (W.). The Reference Library. (In *Lib. Assn. Record*, new ser., ii, 1924, pp. 77–86.)
Roebuck (G. E.) and Thorne (W. B.). Primer of Library Practice. 1914. (Ref. Departments, pp. 64–6.)
Warner (J.). Reference Libraries. (In *Primer of Librarianship*, ch. v.) 1931.
—— Reference Library Methods. 1928.

Commercial, Technical, and Special Libraries.

Association of Special Libraries and Information Bureaux. Reports of Proceedings of Conferences. V. 1. 1924, to date.
Halsall (G.). Commercial and Technical Libraries. (In *Primer of Librarianship*, ch. xv.) 1931.

A MANUAL OF LIBRARY ROUTINE

HEADICAR (B. M.). Business Libraries. (In *Primer of Librarianship*, ch. xvi.) 1931.

JOHNSON (R. H.). Special Libraries. (A.L.A. Manual, 6.) 1915.

KRAUSE (L. B.). The Business Library: What it Is and What it Does. 1919.

NOWELL (C.). Commercial and Technical Literature in the Smaller Public Libraries. (In *Lib. Assn. Record*, new ser., vi, pp. 81–99.)

RIDLEY (A. F.). Special Libraries and Information Bureaux. (In *Lib. Assn. Record*, new ser., iii, 1925, pp. 242–55.)

CHAPTER X

CHILDREN'S LIBRARIES, BRANCH LIBRARIES, AND DELIVERY AND DEPOSIT STATIONS

A separate department should, when possible, be provided for the use of children, and it should comprise at least a lending library and a reading-room, preferably distinct, with an entrance apart from that for adults. This is generally achieved at central libraries and often at larger branches, but it is often impossible to provide such separate accommodation in the smaller branches. Even there, however, it will, *in default of anything better*, be advisable to set aside a special portion of the lending department for the accommodation of children's books, for young folk are gregarious, and it consorts with the general convenience if they are restricted to a "children's corner."

So far as methods of book acquisition, charging, and suchlike routine are concerned, there is little difference between adult and junior libraries, but there is some dissimilarity in organization, for the tables, chairs, and bookshelves have to be adapted to readers of small stature, and all arrangements should be simplified to the last degree. There is a difference, too, in the form and methods concerning applications for tickets, for here the new factor of teachers' recommendations and of contact with schools occurs. The whole subject is discussed in detail by Mr. Sayers in his *Manual of Children's Libraries*, and the same authority presents a general conspectus of the work in his chapter on "Children's Library Work" in the *Primer of Librarianship*.

THE LENDING DEPARTMENT

Only books which are very clearly printed should be placed in junior libraries, and before suggesting editions the children's librarian should make sure that the type will not strain the eyesight of youthful readers. A similar solicitude should be exercised with regard to the format and general "get-up" of books, for many of them are deplorably produced. Printed upon a spongy paper to bulk out the size, and often badly sewn, they appear to be designed for a short and merry life, and a low price may prove to be a delusion and a snare. Such publications, and all wire-stitched books, should be sedulously avoided. For these and similar reasons, personal examination, either in book-shops or at the library to which the books are forwarded on approval, should be insisted upon, and a list should be compiled of editions which are found to be especially suitable for purchase. It is part of the duty of the children's librarian to suggest acquisitions, and here, even more perhaps than elsewhere, reliance is generously accorded to such recommendations, for children have many idiosyncrasies, and their librarian will be better acquainted with their peculiar requirements than any more detached person can possibly be. When stocked,

CHILDREN'S AND BRANCH LIBRARIES

careful oversight must be maintained or the books will be thoughtlessly mishandled, and borrowers—especially new ones—should be taught to treat them with care, if not respect. Dirty or mutilated volumes should not be retained in circulation—they offer a bad example which children will be apt to follow. A high standard should be set by the library, and the borrowers must be educated to observe it, for it is only thus that the right use of books when in readers' homes can be promoted. The strongest possible binding should be given to books for which a reasonably long period of use may be expected.

Books are divided into two distinct sections—those which may be taken away by readers, and those which may only be read in the room. If these two classes are shelved in different rooms the division is clear, but if not the volumes should be marked by labels or other devices so that the children and the staff will recognize the distinction at a glance.

Classification may follow the customary lines so far as the stock requires, but the catalogue, although similar in physical form to that in the adult library, should eschew all but the very simplest scientific and technical terms and be reduced to the level of the untutored mind. Thus Ornithology may possibly be used in a science library to denote books of the 598·2 class, but Birds simply *must* be chosen for such works in the junior library.

A MANUAL OF LIBRARY ROUTINE

APPLICATIONS FOR MEMBERSHIP

A point of difference between adult and juvenile library routine occurs in the treatment of applications for membership. Every library welcomes the co-operation of teachers and should do its utmost to cultivate good relations with them. Their recommendations are gladly accepted without liability in so far as scholars at their schools are concerned. By arrangement, supplies of application vouchers should be sent to every school within the library area, and this stock should be maintained. The school stamp, implemented by the initials of the teacher, should be regarded as adequate authority for issuing tickets, and few teachers will hesitate to display at their schools a neatly executed poster inviting children to apply to their teacher or parents for a form of application. For the rest, the methods of registration are so like those already described as to call for no further mention.

As the little folk take out their first tickets they should be conducted to the shelves and shown how the books are arranged, so that they may know in future where to look for them. They should also be introduced to the catalogue—best in card form—so that they may know how to use it, and if simple little handbooks or leaflets of instruction in the use of the library and the correct manner of handling books are provided, each newcomer should be presented with a copy and instructed to read it carefully.

CHILDREN'S AND BRANCH LIBRARIES

Book charging

Charging is performed precisely as in the adult library, but the procedure in respect of overdues is dissimilar, for some libraries do not charge fines in this department, and others do not enforce them except in special cases, preferring to advise head-teachers or parents when books are otherwise irrecoverable. Persistent offenders should be noted in the "black list," and if it be thought desirable the defaulter's ticket may be suspended for a time. This is a drastic and usually effective punishment.

Reference books and reading-rooms

No large stock of purely reference books is usually provided, but suitable encyclopaedias, dictionaries, atlases, and similar works should be placed upon open-shelves, and at discretion other works may be borrowed for consultation from the general reference or lending department. Possibly children may be at a loss with regard to the best way of using such unaccustomed tools, and if aid is wanted it should not be withheld. Some youthful readers will be in search of information for general purposes, but the majority will desire reference books for school work, for many children do their lessons here. Forms of application are not called for, since the books are accessible, and the count of books used can only be approximate.

If the reading-room is separated, whether by wall, screen, or other partition, from the lending section, tickets of admission may perhaps be required; but they are issued upon easy terms and are shown as passes, serving as checks upon indiscriminate admission. The presence of this quieter room of reference books makes some such method desirable, and especially so where the room is not under immediate supervision. In busy libraries some desks should be reserved for reference work, but if that cannot be done the children engaged in school tasks must take their chance with other readers. Magazines and periodicals specially produced for young folk should invariably be provided with protective covers, and weekly and other illustrated papers which have done duty in the general reading department will find plenty of patrons here, both for reading and, ultimately, for cutting up for the collection of pictures.

One of the peculiar features of children's library work is that children are keen to serve as volunteer assistants, and with a little coaching and kindly oversight they do remarkably well. They will stamp and label books, keep the shelves and table in order, and usually prove competent to do the book charging. It is unsafe to allow them to undertake any form of ledger work or to deal with defaults, or even—because of impetuosity—to be invested with authority to preserve order among the readers; but for mechanical tasks they are often excellent, and are generally willing to adhere to time-table arrangements. It is not unusual to have a rota of candidates for this honorary work, and as soon as any of them become lax their services should be

CHILDREN'S AND BRANCH LIBRARIES

dispensed with—for a time at least. Any little favours offered by way of acknowledgment of their services are highly appreciated.

BRANCH LIBRARY WORK

To a considerable extent the routine at branch libraries is the same as at the central library. The classification must be uniform throughout if interchange of stock is not to be rendered impracticable; the charging system shows no variation, nor could it differ without great inconvenience if there is to be interchange of staff—to say nothing of the fact that borrowers' tickets are available for use throughout the library system as their holders may prefer at any time; and statistical returns must conform to the standard pattern or comparative and aggregate tabulation would be hopeless.

So far as the public are concerned, the chief and perhaps the only perceptible difference is that branch libraries are usually smaller than the main ones and may not have so many departments. The stock of books in the lending library will be more limited, and as the provision of costly or special works of reference would be justified neither by use nor possible for financial reasons the books supplied for consultation only are generally confined to works of ready reference; but, of course, the non-fictional stock in the lending department is also available. It is the exception rather than the rule to find special reference-rooms at branch libraries, but there is often a reading-room distinct from the newspaper-room, and there the reference books are used. Borrowers in the lending section present applications and receive and use their tickets in exactly the same manner as at a central library, and they are subject to the same conditions throughout. The public service is standardized, and departures from uniformity can be justified only by special circumstances.

Administratively, however, there are variations, and the staff work is not, or is not invariably, quite like that at a central library; but the difference is largely in degree, and is due to centralization in the interests of economy, efficiency, and uniformity. Book stock is generally ordered from, and delivered to, the central library. There all newly acquired books are checked, classified, accessioned, and catalogued, and more or less of the preparation of books for circulation is also performed. Applications for membership are (or may be) remitted to the central library where the master-registers are kept, and enquiries which a branch library cannot satisfy are similarly referred. All this makes for economy of effort, and it reduces the labours of the branch staff, which is thus freed for other duties; but centralization should not be pressed too far or local initiative may be unfortunately restrained.

Branch libraries in populous cities are often larger and more active than single libraries in the smaller towns, and it is not unusual for their librarians to be invested with a large amount of plenary powers. They may be subject to some restrictions and super-

CHILDREN'S AND BRANCH LIBRARIES

vision, but their authority sometimes extends to the selection and ordering new stock within specified financial limits. Where this is done, a full advice, specifying the cost incurred and the name of the bookseller, must in every instance be forwarded to the central administrative department, which, in turn, may have to advise the financial officer of the local council or other authority. All sorts of statistical returns have to be certified by the branch librarian and sent to the central office, where a complete service of book-keeping is maintained. The more usual procedure is for the local librarian to specify his requirements, and to these suggestions such sympathetic consideration will be extended as funds and a fair distribution will permit, for the branch librarian is in close touch with local needs and his recommendations are recognized as having special value. He will examine readers' suggestions, annotate them, and before passing them on to headquarters will state his opinion as to the desirability of purchase in view of the local provision of similar works and of the local demand.

Book reception

Normally, then, fresh book stock will arrive at a branch library in a forward state of preparation. They will be accompanied by a list, which should be checked, signed, and returned. If unlabelled or unstamped, these processes must be performed: probably the book-cards will have to be written and their pockets pasted into the covers, and the date-sheet and similar details may also demand attention before the books are placed upon the public shelves.

With the books will come the full complement of cards—or leaves if the catalogue is in sheaf form—and these should be checked with the books to which they severally relate, so that any shortages may be rectified. The cards (or pages) for the shelf-list will also be received, and these, too, must be examined for errors and omissions. When this is done, all that remains is to intercalate these items, in the former instance into the catalogue, and in the latter case into their file or volumes, carefully observing that each one is correctly placed. This process affords an excellent opportunity for detecting soiled or imperfect entries, which should be withdrawn for replacement.

APPLICATIONS FOR TICKETS

As application vouchers are handed in they should be scanned for obvious defects, which should be rectified before being accepted. They should then be filed and sent to the central library for detailed investigation. A record of the number sent should always be made in a special register, and it may be thought well to enter the names and addresses as likely to be useful in tracing any which by mischance may be wrongly delivered. A memorandum of the number forwarded should accompany the batches of vouchers, but whether or not a receipt is given for these depends upon local custom.

CHILDREN'S AND BRANCH LIBRARIES

This method suffers from the inherent defect of involving some delay, but if a delivery system is in operation this need be but a matter of hours. Otherwise the hiatus may cover two or even three days, but the convenience of readers can be met by the issue of temporary tickets which are restricted to a single issue.

The advantages of remitting all applications to the central department are: (1) that the registers and checks are centralized in the hands of experts who have all the requisite information at command; (2) that it is an effective check upon attempts by borrowers to obtain more tickets than they are entitled to hold; (3) that it prevents borrowers who default at one library from obtaining tickets at another until their names are removed from the "black list"; and (4) that a complete master-register is thus obtained. As the new tickets are written the details are recorded and the vouchers filed; tickets are then packeted and placed with a delivery note upon the shelf reserved for each separate library to await delivery. Rejected applications, marked with the reason for non-acceptance, are similarly returned. At the branch library the tickets should be examined, signed for, and filed. Rejected forms are filed, and when the applicant calls the difficulty should be explained and a new voucher proffered.

Mention has been made of defaulters who have sometimes to be "black-listed" for non-compliance with the rules. Whenever this occurs the details should be forwarded to the central office, where they

A MANUAL OF LIBRARY ROUTINE

will be copied into the defaulters' register, and all the branches should be advised as a matter of information. Weekly, monthly, annual, and occasional returns will have to be prepared as the local administration requires, and the result of the yearly stocktaking will also have to be reported.

REFERENCE AND READING-ROOM ROUTINE

Whatever other provision is made at a branch library, there will be, in addition to the lending department, a reading-room, and frequently a magazine-room also. The special reference stock is sometimes exhibited in glazed cases, but sometimes it is shelved in a detached portion of the lending library. The books are issued, in conformity with the usual reference procedure, by signed forms of application inserted in the positions vacated by the books as they are issued. Issue records are entered in the register day by day, and these statistics form one feature of the returns which have to be supplied systematically to the central administrative department.

Reading-room routine complies with the practice as described in Chapter XI. Papers must be checked immediately upon receipt; supplies must be kept up to time; the periodicals must be prepared for display, placed upon their tables, stands, or racks, and the file of old issues maintained in order. Disposal of obsolete newspapers and periodicals is almost always left to the branch librarian, but the central library will often require that certain publi-

CHILDREN'S AND BRANCH LIBRARIES

cations shall at stated intervals be sent to headquarters so that the best preserved copies may be selected for binding up when the volumes are required for reference stock. Newsagents' accounts are checked by the librarians of the particular libraries to which the papers have been supplied, and when certified correct as to delivery and price they should be sent to the central library, where they will be counter-checked as to prices and casting up and prepared for submission to the committee.

INTERCHANGE SERVICE

Borrowers' tickets are almost invariably made available for use at any of the libraries comprehended within the library system, and their holders use them at whichever library they may choose from time to time. If tickets are prepared at the central library only, they will most probably be numbered in one sequence; but if made out locally, each should bear the name of the library, and its number should be preceded by some mark, colour, or symbol as a supplementary indication of the library to which it pertains. Some libraries stipulate that borrowers shall return their books to the library from which they were obtained, but others allow returns to be made at whichever library the borrowers may find most convenient. This latter course entails redelivery by the library staff and the clearance of records at the library of issue, as the tickets must be recovered for insertion in the charging system. Meanwhile a temporary ticket is employed, the return of a library book affording sufficient evidence of qualification.

Another aspect of interchange is found in inter-library loans of books. Branch librarians pay visits of inspection to other libraries at stated times and select works of which they would like to have the use for a limited period. The central library may have a reserve stock of books acquired on favourable terms and held for this purpose and for replacing books withdrawn from circulation. Libraries which thus lend books must list the titles, record the branch to which they have been lent, and note the date of the loan and the date when due back. The branches receiving such loans should sign the inventory lists which accompany the books, and should file a duplicate copy by which the volumes must be checked when they have to be sent back. Probably the local date-sheet will have to be affixed over the more permanent one, and it will be found desirable that as the time of their return approaches these loaned books shall be withdrawn, or they will not be to hand when they are due back at the library to which they belong. It is perhaps best to place these books on special shelves where they will readily attract attention, but whether this be done or not, a list should be drawn up and displayed. They need not be further catalogued, but the library from which they are drawn may think it advisable to remove their cards from the catalogue; if filed apart they will serve as an inventory to which quick reference can be made in case of enquiry.

CHILDREN'S AND BRANCH LIBRARIES

BOOK DELIVERY SYSTEM

Another form of interchange is a method of delivery by which books asked for at one library may be procured from other libraries upon request. As these local applications are received they should be entered upon a schedule, the date, name and address of the applicant, author and title, with space for remarks, being required. A brief summary list, denoting only the works desired, is then circulated among the allied libraries. If a motor-car or a box-carrier tricycle travels round to the branches every morning and afternoon, or even if but once a day, it may collect these requests at one call, and deliver such books as are available at the next journey. Books not procurable are marked in the spare column of the register, and may be asked for again if the borrower wishes. Those entries which relate to books received may be cancelled. Libraries thus lending from their stock should charge the books to the library to which they are sent; the messenger gives a receipt, and the receiving branch becomes responsible for the loans. Whether it preserves any special record or not, it should charge the books in the card trays, for this course will automatically declare overdues. The issue is counted in at the point of service, for there the borrower's ticket will be. As the volumes are received back from readers they should be promptly returned to the libraries from which they were obtained, and an acquittance should be received.

A MANUAL OF LIBRARY ROUTINE

In order to facilitate inter-loans of books, specialization of stock at the different branches is sometimes attempted, and the staff acquire familiarity with the books and obtain fresh interests and reliefs if they are occasionally moved from one library to another. The telephone may be utilized for enquiries, but this should be done as a matter of grace rather than rule, for at busy periods the telephone may consume no little time, and it is unfair that the many shall be kept waiting for the advantage of the few.

General branch library routine

Except that returns of statistical and other information peculiar to branches have to be prepared and forwarded, and that the petty cash must be remitted to the central library at stated times, the routine presents few other variations from that of main libraries. The registration of borrowers has been dealt with. Stocktaking offers no special methods. Bookbinding and book repairs are largely left to the discretion of the local librarian, but he is expected to obtain authority before dispatching large consignments to a bindery, and to inform the central office when they are sent, with an estimate of the cost, for the administrative department must know what liability is being incurred.

Branch superintendents

If there is a branch superintendent or inspector he may desire to examine books before they are sent for binding. Branch libraries, and especially those of old standing, are apt to suffer from inadequate shelf room, and when the demand for any book declines it becomes unnecessary to retain copies of the same work at all libraries. Hence the necessity for thinning out, and the branch superintendent, with his comprehensive knowledge of the whole of the book stocks, is able to make the reduction in collaboration with the local librarians. He can also see that expenditure is not incurred upon re-binding books which are no longer required; he examines the administrative records, checks (and probably collects) the petty cash, sees that the supplies of printed forms and stationery are adequate, and that the library is being properly conducted. He is, in fact, the eyes and ears of the chief librarian, to whom he reports such matters as may need official attention.

Delivery and deposit stations

Delivery stations are conducted in the way just described in connection with branch libraries, but at delivery stations, as distinguished from libraries, there is no stock of books maintained for choice. Applications are received and filed pending the systematic call of the library collector, and books are accepted from borrowers, who leave lists from which one or other of the works they want may be selected. A shop or office, or any room in a factory or other works, with someone to be in attendance at stipulated times, is all the provision required at any one point. The attendant sees that the lists carry the names of the borrowers who hand them in, and, as a reserve in case of accident, he should retain a copy of the list which accompanies the books that he receives for distribution. The official charging is performed at the central library, and that department attends to overdues and the recovery of fines and the payment of assessed amounts for any damage done to books by borrowers.

Deposit stations differ from the foregoing inasmuch as they are supplied with a small stock of books, and this necessitates local charging. The main supply of books will, however, be borrowed from the central or one or other of the branch libraries, and the method is like that employed by branch libraries as described on page 200. A shop, with a subsidized assistant, on the lines of a local post office, is eminently suitable for this work, but every process should be simplified to the last degree. The deposited stock is changed occasionally, and an inventory is supplied and signed for, a copy being filed at the central office. The charging may be by the simple sheet system of which particulars may be found in Chapter VIII, for card charging sometimes offers unexpected difficulties to these assistants. Fines must, of course, be taken here, but the supply of official receipts must be nicely adjusted to probable requirements, and the shopkeeper or other person locally in charge must regard these as the local post office regards stamps, for which he must account in cash. Applications for tickets are referred to the central library as branch libraries do, and a pretty close system of oversight will generally be required. All book preparation and the tabulation of statistics, and as much clerical work as possible, should be done at headquarters. These stations are only found in operation in areas where the normal branch library would be out of place, and they are supervised by the nearest branch librarian or the branch superintendent, or, failing these, a member of the central staff.

Another way of exploiting the use of library books is by depositing an agreed number of chosen books for a given period in institutes, works, or colleges. A general guarantee or undertaking for responsibility is first obtained, and all that is then necessary is to enter in an appropriate record the particulars of the books sent, and to see that the books are returned when the loan period expires, when another selection may be forwarded. All the detail work is left to the option of the person to whom the books are sent, and a copy of the inventory should go with each parcel and must be signed by or on behalf of the person responsible for their return.

SELECTED REFERENCES

Children's Libraries

AMERICAN LIB. ASSN. Children's Library Year-Book. 1927 to date.

BAKER (E. A.). The Public Library. 1924. (Children's Libraries, pp. 63–74.)

BALLINGER (*Sir* J.). Work with Children. 1917. (In *Public Libraries; their Development and Future.*) 1917.

BOSTWICK (A. E.). The American Public Library. 4th edn., revised. 1929. (Ch. vi—The Library and the Child.)
BROWN (J. D.). Manual of Library Economy. 4th edn. 1931. (Chs. xxxii and xxxiii.)
GREEN (E.). School Libraries. (In *Lib. Assn. Record*, xii, 1910, pp. 227–41.)
HALBERT (J. F.). Libraries and Children: a Survey of Modern Practice. (In *Lib. Assn. Record*, 3rd ser., 1932, pp. 305–9.)
HUNT (C. W.). Library Work with Children. (A.L.A. Manual, 29.) 1929.
JAST (L. S.). The Child as Reader. 1927.
—— Library Work with Children. (In *Lib. Assn. Record*, xxi, 1919, pp. 90–102.)
MCCOLVIN (L. R.). Library Extension Work. 1927. (Ch. iv—Work with children.)
POWER (EFFIE L.). Library Service for Children. 1930.
REES (GWENDOLEN). Libraries for Children. 1924.
SAYERS (W. C. BERWICK). Manual of Children's Libraries. 1932.
—— Children's Library Work. (In *Primer of Librarianship*, ch. ix.) 1931.

Branch Libraries, Deposit Stations, etc.

BALLINGER (*Sir* J.). Municipal Library and its Public: Lending Libraries and Branches. (In *The Library*, new ser., 1907, pp. 309–22.)
BOSTWICK (A. E.). American Public Library, *as above*. Ch. xix—Branches and Stations.)
BROWN (J. D.). Manual, *as above*. (Sections 445–54.)
EASTMAN (L. A.). Branch Libraries and Other Distributing Agencies. (A.L.A. Manual, 15, revised edn., 1923.)
HAWKES (A. J.). Function of a Central Library and the Problem of Branches. (In *The Lib. Assistant*, 1909, pp. 371–5 and 394–401.)
SAVAGE (E. A.). Delivery Stations and Town Travelling Libraries. (In *Lib. Assn. Record*, vi, 1904, pp. 134–68.)

CHAPTER XI

MAGAZINE AND READING ROOMS

Newspaper reading-rooms in rate-supported libraries are sometimes combined with magazine-rooms, but where accommodation permits they are usually separated, for, whilst the former are subject to the noise and commotion which are inseparable from constant traffic, the latter frequently contain material of a technical, scientific, or other serious nature which demands a certain amount of quietude for mental application.

Newspaper reading-rooms are provided with sloping desks which are either affixed to the walls or are used as independent stands to which the papers are attached by close-fitting rods or spring bars which hold them in position. Almost invariably there are also tables upon which smaller periodicals are placed, with racks for those which the tables will not accommodate. These departments are generally placed near to the main entrance where they may be away from central supervision, and unless the stands are so arranged as not to obstruct oversight the difficulty of supervision will be increased. Yet it is here that the greatest risk of depredation occurs, for papers are available for all and sundry, and the temptation to mutilate them is one which, as every librarian knows, is not always resisted. If the staff includes a janitor it is usually part of his duty to patrol the rooms with more or less regularity, both for the preservation of order among the readers and the restoration of periodicals to their proper racks or tables. Failing this, some other member of the staff should be deputed for this work, and some indirect surveillance may be possible from an adjoining department.

SELECTION AND COST OF PERIODICALS

Each library has its own methods of selecting papers and periodicals and of adjusting the supply from time to time, but the dominant factor is always the amount of the yearly vote for such supply. This fixed sum will determine the extent of literature provided, and the problem is one of selection. Choice is determined by the same principle as that which obtains with regard to books, *viz.* the satisfaction of local requirements, and the same careful consideration should be accorded to papers as to books. Bearing in mind the fact that the list will have to be submitted to the committee for approval, it should be drawn up in such a way that any information then called for may readily be given. In any case the list, which will remain more or less intact throughout the year, should be classified, first by kind, then by subject, and finally by titles. The daily papers should be divided into morning and evening issues, grouped into local, London, provincial, and foreign sections—assuming that all these varieties are desired. The number of copies of each publication and the published price in every instance

MAGAZINE AND READING ROOMS

should be stated. Distribution among departments or branches may be usefully indicated by columnar markings, and the cost carried out in £ s. d. columns. Weeklies should be divided according to their kind, *e.g.* electrical, illustrated, religious, literary, etc., and the disposition and cost carried out as just described. Monthlies and quarterlies, if sufficiently numerous, may be similarly treated, but where they are few in number such sub-division is unnecessary. If this course is followed the cost of each subsection is easily ascertained; but a more important result is that the expenditure for each branch is shown, and these totals when added together reveal the aggregate cost. The approved estimate for this purpose must not be exceeded, and if the list proves to be too large adjustment must be made. It must not be overlooked that special "extras" and Christmas numbers will be required, and allowance must be made for these; and for various reasons it will be advisable to leave a margin for contingencies. New publications may have to be added during the year, and suggestions by readers may have to be satisfied, although those which are to hand at the time when the yearly list is drawn up will be considered then. Publications which have not justified retention may now be dropped, but since readers become accustomed to the details of supply, and arrangements for the display of periodicals are not easy to revise, the list once approved usually remains in force until the next annual revision.

A MANUAL OF LIBRARY ROUTINE

TERMS OF SUPPLY

The municipal year commences on April 1st, but the financial estimates must be considered by the local council well in advance of that date, and the library committee will have to make its recommendations earlier still: January or early in February is therefore the time when the prospective apportionments are dealt with.

As soon as the list has received official approval tenders for the supply should be obtained. The details for inclusion in the contract forms should include particulars of all the items required, the required editions of evening papers, the libraries at which delivery is to be made, the terms of discount to be allowed, and a guarantee of prompt delivery. Special arrangements may have to be made for provincial and foreign papers, for it is often cheaper and more satisfactory to procure these supplies either direct from the publishing offices or through an importing agent. In recognition of the advertising value of well-used libraries some proprietors offer to present their issues, but discrimination must be exercised in this matter or unwanted and little used papers will destroy the balance, cumber the racks and tables, and an assortment of proselytizing journals will accrue. Such papers as are accepted are often written into the registers in red ink, and those purchased are entered in black for purposes of differentiation. For general supplies the agent should not only be local, but,

MAGAZINE AND READING ROOMS

in a system which embraces branch libraries, he should be conveniently near to each library or irregularities may be tardily remedied.

Checking deliveries

Check-lists vary very much in style, but in essentials they are alike. Some libraries prefer to rely upon registers in book form, others on sheets or cards, and some use the book form for daily papers and cards for everything else.

If the book method is adopted there should be separate books, or portions of one general register, for dailies, weeklies, and monthly and other issues. Each title should have its own line of entry, and for daily publications there must be sufficient columns to cover the working days of each month or larger period. Alphabetical order is all that is here required unless the morning and evening papers are kept apart. As supplies are received the appropriate columns are marked with a tick to denote delivery. A page thus presents a bird's-eye view of no inconsiderable section of the supply, and unticked items indicate issues not delivered.

Weekly publications are often entered in one alphabetical sequence with columns which are dated or numbered according to the week of the year; but a good alternative method is to enter them alphabetically in sections according to the day of the week when they are due. Magazines issued at monthly or longer intervals are entered in their respective groups, but here the approximate date when delivery is expected may usefully be added, and enquiries should be made whenever these dates are exceeded. Unless the period for which any subscriptions have been paid coincides with that of the general supply, a red stroke should be marked two months in advance of the date when the subscription expires, to draw attention to the fact and enable arrangements to be made for continuance without a break. In every instance the price of each publication should be recorded, and in other columns the name of the respective suppliers and the terms of supply are indicated.

Sheets conform to the details of book-checks. They are preferably of loose-leaf form and are bound in adjustable covers.

Card check-lists, usually of the standard (5 in. × 3 in.) size, although sometimes much larger, exhibit diversity of detail, but their purpose and method are alike. When much data is demanded it can all appear upon one face of a large card, but if small cards are employed one side is occupied by the actual check-lists and the other by the supplementary information. Again, weekly, monthly, quarterly, and other infrequent publications are kept in groups, often distinguished by tints, and, as before, the groups are alphabetically arranged. At the top of each side of the card (assuming that both sides are used) the title occurs in very bold letters, and the name of the agent. The published price, terms of supply, date when subscription is renewable, where placed for public use, whether to be bound for

MAGAZINE AND READING ROOMS

stock, whether sold or not when done with, and other details also figure in the check-lists of various libraries. The other side of the card is ruled off into squares, twelve to a line for weeklies and monthlies, and the name of the month is written at the head of each column. A tick placed in each corner of the appropriate square, and one in the centre when there are five weekly publishing days in the calendar month, shows that deliveries have been duly made: absent ticks declare overdues. For monthly magazines the date of reception may be stamped or written in the squares successively. Unless indicating clips or "signals" are used to draw attention to undelivered items, these lists must be examined from day to day, until delivery of overdue issues has been completed.

Annuals are likely to be a source of trouble because of the uncertainty of publication. Societies which are supposed to issue a volume yearly are often in arrears, and the only thing to do is to maintain an accurate check upon deliveries, and make occasional enquiries of the publisher or secretary, otherwise the annual subscription may be paid for years without receiving anything in return.

To make the card check-list completely effective the use of indicating clips is recommended. These are tiny tabs of metal with a fork-like base which slide upon the upper edge of each card, and are moved one square to the right as new numbers are received. If the supplies are up to date these tabs form a regular line upon successive cards, and any deviation automatically calls attention to overdues. By a development of this card system two distinctively coloured "signals" are sometimes used for alternate years in the case of annual publications, four for quarterlies, and twelve for monthly issues, but the crowding of clips will be confusing unless large cards are employed.

It is by the check-list that newsagents' accounts are checked both as to delivery and price, each item on the bill being compared with the record and marked by ticks where found correct. A point to observe here is that no charge is passed for bank holidays or other occasions when the department may happen to have been closed, and the agent should be advised in good time of any such dates so that he may countermand his standing order with publishers or wholesalers.

DISPLAY METHODS

When checked off and found to be in order newspapers and other periodicals should with the utmost promptitude be made accessible to readers. Daily papers will, because of their size, be affixed to sloping stands beneath the facia tablets which boldly advertise their titles. Most of the weekly and monthly periodicals will either be placed upon the tables or within racks in the newspaper or magazine reading-room. In either event they will require to be protected by covers, and sometimes these covers are fastened to particular tables. Racks may be vertical with narrow ledges and protective brass

MAGAZINE AND READING ROOMS

rails, rising tier above tier to a reasonable height, or may be sloping shelves of sufficient depth to accommodate large-size journals. If the former method is adopted the titles should appear in large type near the top of the cover, for only this portion will be visible in the rack, but the position is reversed when sloping shelves are used, and the title should be displayed near the bottom of each cover.

The great drawback to racks of any style is misplacement, for comparatively few readers attempt to restore periodicals to racks after use, and still fewer replace them correctly. It is for this reason, and to obviate the recurrent labour of clearing the table and rearranging the racks, that many libraries attach the covers of periodicals to the tables to which they have been allotted. This is accomplished by using a thin chain or a piece of wire flex encased in leather or rubber which tethers them to their fixed location and prevents confusion through removal. Incidentally it puts an effective stop to the habit of greedy readers who collect journals from the racks and hide them underneath the paper they are reading, or even sit upon them, regardless of the convenience of persons who may be searching for them in vain. The tables have a strip of wood along their full length, and on either side of this central division the titles of the periodicals are displayed, whilst a framed list hung upon the wall near the end of each table indicates the issues there placed. In addition there should always be a complete list of the publications exhibited in the depart-

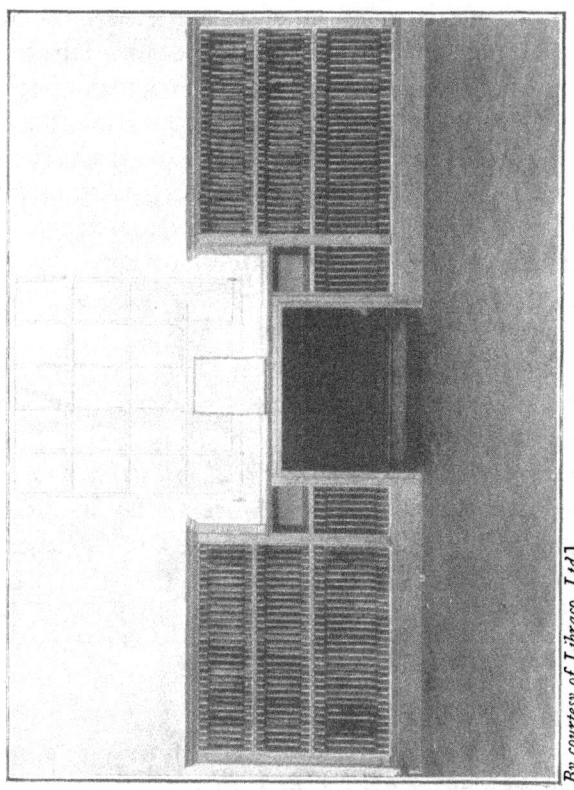

By courtesy of Libraco, Ltd.]

DISPLAY RACK FOR MAGAZINES AS USED AT
THE HENDON PUBLIC LIBRARY

ment, and the location of each paper or magazine should be indicated thereon.

Another method of displaying magazines is the case-rack fastened to a wall in the reading-room. The rack itself is a series of narrow divisions in which the publications, encased in covers labelled down their back, are placed, and each recess carries the title of the periodical which should be found there unless in use. The advantages of this system are economy of room, a clear indication of the range of supply, and its open invitation for assistance in correct replacement. Unfortunately there are always persons who are careless about replacement, and the tables become congested and confused.

Before publications are displayed they should be cut (if necessary) and stamped, and competition coupons should be obliterated. Betting and racing results are (or have been) occasionally "blacked out" or covered over to render them useless for undesirable readers, but refusal to display the latest evening editions goes some way to achieve this end, and most libraries are content to ignore this nuisance unless it assumes large proportions.

Magazines in reference-rooms

Among the magazines there will probably be some which when bound will pass into reference stock, and to place these comparatively expensive publications in the general reading-room would be to court unnecessary wear and tear by idle handling. To protect them from this risk they are often placed

MAGAZINE AND READING ROOMS

in a rack in the reference department. Failing this, and with the object of maintaining quietness and order in that room, such magazines as are destined for binding are sometimes filled underneath the counter or upon shelves and are produced only upon demand.

FILING BACK NUMBERS

Most of the periodicals will probably be filed in a special part of the general store, and this task should devolve upon one assistant who will be responsible for seeing that back numbers are promptly filed, preserved, and are easily accessible whenever required. Racks of special construction should be used, and the papers should be placed in their labelled sections in chronological order with a thick board on the top to hold them down and keep them clean. There is a considerable demand for these old issues, and except perhaps in the largest libraries, requests for them are preferred in the reference department. It is essential that the file should be properly kept, and if the store is near the point of issue so much the better. Recent numbers of *The Times* and of local journals should, at all events, be kept within easy reach, even although special arrangements have to be made to that end, and public and staff convenience will be served if a selection of periodicals is preserved in wide-backed covers provided with tapes or cords to hold successive issues. Half a year's numbers of *Notes and Queries*, constituting one volume when bound up,

A MANUAL OF LIBRARY ROUTINE

may thus be available for use, and a special shelf may be provided for their accommodation in the reference department or the magazine room. Stamping should always be performed with an eye to the fact that these parts are intended for permanent stock as bound volumes.

In reading-rooms shelves with drop-lids, or cupboards with sliding-doors, duly labelled, may occasionally be found as supports for display racks. In them are filed for a time a selection of periodicals removed from current display. It is better if these items are kept in separate boxes, but it will be necessary to examine this publicly accessible file systematically and to correct misplacements every day, or disorder will nullify their use.

Whenever back numbers have to be brought from the store-file a note should be made and filed at the issuing desk, and a stout manilla card should be inserted in the rack to signify removal. A memorandum affixed by a drawing-pin to the fore-edge of the file shelf will indicate the same fact, but this is a less desirable method as it tends to deface the shelf. The assistant in charge of the file should note these indications and see that the papers are restored, when the cards may be withdrawn or the memoranda destroyed. The check-list at the issue desk should be cleared every day, and when ticked and initialled as having been attended to, it should be restored to the reference assistant as evidence that the file is again complete. Under no circumstance should the daily task of filing be deferred. The

MAGAZINE AND READING ROOMS

mortality among such delayed papers is great; it is only by punctual attention that this can be averted and the convenience of readers be met.

BINDING PERIODICALS FOR STOCK

So far as lending departments are concerned few, if any, bound volumes of magazines will be required, but the reference library will certainly be in a different position. Archaeological, scientific, and other periodical publications will figure liberally among these desiderata, and the parts must be collected, collated, examined as to condition, and supplied with the title-pages and indexes (which are prudently extracted upon arrival, and are filed in a special box or drawer). Branch library copies may be called in to the central library for inspection so that the best copies may be selected. The local papers and *The Times* are usually bound up, and here again the branch copies may have to be drawn upon to make up satisfactory volumes. This is a task which should not be allowed to slide, for it may well happen that new copies of certain issues have to be purchased, and these have a tendency to fall out of print and to be difficult and expensive to obtain. When the volumes are completed they should be classified and accessioned, and when they are bound the catalogue should be adjusted, unless the entry has been made in a form which renders adjustment superfluous.

In some lending departments a selection of magazines is received as they become superseded by new issues, and they are circulated in covers. The cloth sides of these covers should be waterproof, and their backs should display the title, which must be visible, inasmuch as they are shelved and issued like books. As the interest in these old parts is short-lived the loan period is brief, extending from three days to one week. Each cover has a date-sheet and the charging is precisely as in the case of books. Three or four back numbers almost invariably suffice to meet the current demand, and as new issues come in the oldest ones are withdrawn and go upon the stock file. It is a question whether magazines destined for permanent stock when bound should be subject to this form of use, and this should not be allowed without authority.

Clearing the File

The withdrawal of parts for binding into volumes will to some extent relieve the file, but the bulk of this obsolete material will accumulate until the storage capacity is exhausted and drastic reduction become inevitable. When this happens the more recent issues should be retained and the older ones disposed of. It may be that, by local arrangement, some of the duplicate or unfiled papers and periodicals are given to hospitals, unions, settlements, etc., and in this case they will be collected day by day. Many of the illustrated papers and magazines may be passed on for the selection of the children's librarian, and when other uses have been satisfied the pictures may be cut out for their pictorial col-

MAGAZINE AND READING ROOMS

lections. The residuum may be sold to waste-paper merchants or given to the Salvation or Church Army in return for removal. For such useless lumber to lie about in heaps until a lorry load is ready simply harbours dirt and breeds vermin. It is better to dispose of it at frequent intervals even if nothing is obtained in return.

SPECIAL FEATURES

Few libraries now record attendances of readers, but where this is done actual counts are made, either during a whole day or covering different hours on different days until a complete working day has been compassed, and the result is assumed as the average attendance until a fresh census yields new figures. In at least one large library system an actual count throughout a week is taken twice a year. In practice reading-room attendances are often ignored, or an approximate estimate is made.

Advertisements of situations vacant are frequently cut from extra copies of daily papers, and are displayed either within or outside the library building at an early hour every morning. Special stands are occasionally provided in areas which have no branch libraries within easy distance, and the prompt display of the pages containing these advertisements is undertaken by a local newsagent who is paid for his labour by agreement.

Only one other feature remains for description—the use of reading-rooms for advertising library activities. This is sometimes done by displaying

A MANUAL OF LIBRARY ROUTINE

announcements of the facilities offered in other departments; occasionally special notices or forms of application for membership are placed in shallow boxes with an invitation to "take one," whilst another, and probably a more useful service, is performed by pasting within the covers of periodicals a select list of reference and lending library books on the subjects with which the various periodicals especially deal.

SELECTED REFERENCES

BAKER (E. A.). The Public Library. 1924. (Newsrooms and Magazine Rooms, pp. 55–63.)

BOLTON (G. R.). The Newsroom as a Department of the Public Library. (In *Lib. Assn. Record*, xii, 1910, pp. 335–43.)

BOSTWICK (A. E.). The American Public Library. 4th edn. 1929. (Ch. v—Reading and Reference Rooms.)

BROWN (J. D.). A Manual of Library Economy. 4th edn. 1931. (Ch. xxxi—Reading-room Methods.)

EVANS (J. L.). Reading-Room Methods. (In *Library World*, xii, 1910, pp. 375–8.)

GLENISTER (E. E.). The Filing of Periodicals. (In *Library World*, x, pp. 350–1.)

RAE (W. S. C.). Public Library Administration. 1913. (Reading-Rooms, pp. 19–33.)

ROEBUCK (G. E.) and THORNE (W. B.). A Primer of Library Practice. 1914. (Periodicals and Check Lists, pp. 73–82.)

CHAPTER XII

UNIVERSITY, COLLEGIATE, AND SCHOOL LIBRARIES

Routine work in university and other scholastic libraries varies in many respects from that in municipal libraries, and there is even less of uniformity in the former than in the latter, but, within limits, the differences are more superficial than fundamental. In other words, the major principles are constant, but they will, and must, be adapted to local and special requirements. There are, however, many processes which are common to all categories of libraries. Books must be selected and purchased; donations must be acknowledged and recorded; accessioning in one form or another is essential; classification and cataloguing cannot be omitted; books must be prepared for library use, and they must be maintained in good condition; stocktaking must be carried out at intervals, and the supply of books must be kept up to date by addition and withdrawal. Basic principles will dominate all these operations. Variations will largely be matters of degree rather than kind; but in collegiate libraries the book stock will be specialized: readers will consist of professors, teachers, or students; the sources of income and the administration will be totally different; the registration of borrowers and methods of book charging will have little resemblance to those found in municipal libraries, and it is more particularly with points of difference rather than of resemblance that this chapter must treat.

Scholastic libraries differ from public libraries in many primary respects. Briefly put, the former are special in their appeal and restricted as to their readers, while the latter are general in scope and are open to public use. The book stocks will accordingly exhibit wide divergencies, for while current fiction will find no place in the one, no enormous range of British and foreign periodicals will be permanently bound up for stock in the other. Collegiate libraries must cater in special ways for students; rate-supported libraries have to provide for all sections of the community. It follows, therefore, that the book stock of a collegiate library is confined to works of reference or books (other than ordinary textbooks, which students are expected to provide for themselves), supplied for purposes of general study or for advanced research.

BOOK STOCK

A feature peculiar to university and college libraries is the prevalence of seminar and other special collections, while (apart from bibliographical rarities) the book stock is acquired for educational use. Under these conditions the teaching staff, as a body of experts in their especial subjects, may suggest or even demand the acquisition of books for the benefit of their students. The departmental principal

UNIVERSITY LIBRARIES

is sometimes the nominal arbiter within the amount of the department's yearly vote for books; but more and more as trained librarians are being appointed the problem of book selection is being fined down to a method of practical co-operation between the professorial and library staffs, the former acting as experts in their particular subjects, and the latter preparing the more general lists and doing their best to preserve a proper equipoise, while a library committee or a faculty sub-committee may give the official decision. To the librarian will fall, of course, the tasks of ordering the books and preparing them for circulation, and the principles underlying these processes will to a considerable extent be the same as those described throughout this *Manual*.

CLASSIFICATION AND CATALOGUING

Systematic classification of books is now accepted as a necessity in collegiate libraries, and, indeed, it is an inevitable corollary to open access. But there is no uniformity as to the code of classification adopted: it may be the Brussels expansion of the Dewey decimal system, or that of the Library of Congress, or it may be locally devised. Sometimes for the convenience of students theoretical and practical books are placed together, thus (for example), blending the Dewey classes 5 and 6. Choice of code is a matter of administration; from the routine point of view the scheme locally in force must be thoroughly learned and its methods applied with exactitude.

There is a corresponding variation with regard to cataloguing. The mobility of cards is generally recognized and card catalogues predominate, but the plan of compilation differs in various libraries. In some only author lists are provided, for it is assumed that if the stock is classified no further subject guidance will be necessary; but elsewhere there are author and subject catalogues as separate entities. Printed catalogues are comparatively rare, but typewritten or manuscript lists are by no means uncommon, sometimes for general use, sometimes for the teaching staff alone. Usually these last catalogues are restricted to author entries. They are best done in loose-leaf form since the continued interpolation dislocates the sequence, and, whether additional entries are written or pasted in, the effect tends to disorder. The re-writing of catalogue pages becomes a recurrent task of routine.

SEMINAR LIBRARIES

Seminar (or special) libraries consist of books on special subjects which are selected from the general stock by professors and are placed in study rooms for the exclusive use of students in the classes concerned. Senior students are provided with keys so that they may have access to them at any time either for quiet consultation or in connection with discussions. Occasionally a class may be held there so that the teacher may give a practical demonstration in the right method of using books. The books may, or may not, as local regulations pre-

UNIVERSITY LIBRARIES

scribe, be available for home reading, but when that privilege is permitted a student librarian exercises general oversight of the collection.

The volumes thus withdrawn from general circulation must be charged up against the class concerned, and the general library card catalogue should be marked to account for the absence of the books and to show where they have been placed. In the absence of any uniform practice it may be suggested that two inventories of these deposits should be made out in addition to the record filed in the main library office. One copy of the list may be used as a check-list to be signed for by, or on behalf of, the professor, and the other retained as a detailed inventory showing what books have to be returned. Occasionally this duplicate copy is exhibited as a shelf-list in the study room, but more generally a card catalogue, sometimes on cards of a distinctive colour, is prepared by the library staff and remains in the room throughout the period of the loan. The routine work includes the recording of these deposits—author, title, date, and the name of the receiving department—the preparation of the inventories and the catalogue, and of clearing the records when the books are returned. It sometimes also provides for the examination of the books, for instances of misuse are not entirely unknown.

Departmental libraries

Somewhat similar to the foregoing is the departmental library composed of books on specific class subjects for the use of the professional staff and students in different faculties or divisions. Seminar libraries are invariably formed of books selected from the shelves of the university library, but departmental libraries are composed of entirely distinct book stock. The contents of seminar collections are (or should be) entered in the main catalogue, but those of departmental libraries are excluded since they are entirely independent.

CHARGING METHODS AND OVERDUES

Methods of book charging in collegiate libraries differ materially from those in kindred institutions. Card charging, as practised in municipal libraries, is little used, and the time factor ceases to be dominant. Scholastic libraries require to know at least two things, (1) where any book is at any time, and (2) what books any student has in his possession. Many librarians consider it advisable to have a time-check also for the purpose of discovering overdues, and thus three separate records are maintained.

Whenever a student is enrolled as a borrower a flapless envelope is made out for him, and his name (boldly recorded at the top), address, collegiate year, references, and possibly his faculty (or college if the ticket is for use in the main university library), are written thereon, and the envelopes are filed in name order. If a personal ticket is issued it is for identification only and not for charging purposes. A somewhat similar envelope is prepared for each library book, and, like the book card in a card-charging system, it carries particulars about the book to which it applies, and in which it is preserved when the volume is not in circulation. Each volume has a sheet in which the date of issue (or that when the book is due for return) is entered.

When a reader takes out a book he fills up two voucher forms (and a third if a date file is used), by means of carbon sheets, and either drops them into a box, or hands them to the assistant at the counter. In either instance they will be sorted out and filed in separate trays. One form will be inserted in the book envelope and another in that for borrowers; they are both printed upon white paper, and will be arranged, the one in classified order, the latter alphabetically by borrowers' names. The third voucher is generally printed upon tinted paper and it is placed in the date file, first arranged by date and then by readers' names. The vouchers so received state the name and address of the borrower, particulars of the volumes taken, and the date of issue. Often a space is left for the date of return, and as the books come back the forms are cancelled and handed to the readers as a discharge from further responsibility. Each file is adequately guided, and it is from these vouchers that statistics of use are compiled.

The period allowed for home reading of books varies, but a time limit of some kind is imposed, and the date-paper in each volume facilitates discharging from the time file just as the other details enable the readers' and book files to be cleared.

Overdues are intimated to resident students by notes sent to the common-room, or by personal reminder. Non-resident borrowers are communicated with by post in much the same fashion as in rate-supported libraries, the home address being ascertained from the college calendar or the office. A systematic record of overdues and applications for return should be kept, and in default of recovery and of the payment of the fines incurred, the matter may be reported for the decision of the library committee.

UNIVERSITY LIBRARIES

A feature characteristic of, and peculiar to, universities is that, whilst the affiliated colleges have libraries of their own they also have a literary *alma mater* in a general university library which in many instances is enriched with the heritage of centuries of valuable gifts and purchases. A yet more special feature is that under the provisions of the Copyright Act the Universities of Oxford and Cambridge—like the British Museum and the National Libraries of Scotland, Wales, and the Irish Free State—enjoy the statutory right to receive, without charge, copies of all new publications issued within the British Isles. The copies for the British Museum must be delivered by the various publishers without request; the other privileged libraries have to make written application for them within a period of one year of publication; but as this work is performed by agents, the only effect upon library routine of these "compulsory gifts" is that there are many more books

UNIVERSITY LIBRARIES

than usual to be accessioned and otherwise prepared for stock. The use of main university libraries is open to all members of the university. These are required to establish their right by filling up a form of application stating their name, college, and address. The signature of a professor or other college authority may suffice, or sometimes that of any two members of college is acceptable.

Universities, like that of London, which consist of scattered colleges, each possessing its own library for internal students, have, in addition, independent students who may reside in any part of the kingdom and take the external degree. These also enjoy the privilege of using the main library of their university, which, on its part, endeavours to supplement rather than repeat the stock of its college libraries. Here the most advanced of specialist literature and the collection of bibliographical rarities will be found. The main library is the reserve upon which registered students may draw when the resources of their college libraries are exhausted.

Periodicals

To the municipal librarian the term "periodicals" usually means merely the issues of those weekly or other publications which are displayed upon the racks or tables of reading-rooms and are supplied by newsagents. But university librarians understand the word otherwise, and, in addition to such specially substantial journals as are comprehended within the trade meaning, it includes for their purposes the journals of many learned societies and the periodical publications of government departments. Thus it happens that in collegiate libraries the provision of these intermittent issues assumes proportions quite beyond the scope of general libraries. Most of the Scottish universities spend almost as much upon these serial productions as upon books; several English universities spend even more, and in all cases this particular expenditure is proportionately considerable: it is an instance of demand and supply. In one way or another the treatment of these varied periodicals forms no insignificant part of university library routine.

A union catalogue of all the periodicals in the university and college libraries of Great Britain and Ireland is maintained at the National Central Library, London, and communications respecting these —and applications by university libraries for the loan of books—should be forwarded to the Enquiry Office at that address.

CHECKING METHODS

Checking the receipt of these issues is done by cards in the manner already described,[1] but college libraries generally prefer to use cards of a larger size than those at municipal libraries, 8 in. × 5 in. being quite common dimensions. On the top at the left-hand side the name of the publication appears, and the initials W., M., Q., or I. are printed at the right-hand corner to denote weeklies, monthlies,

[1] See Chapter XI.

quarterly and irregular publications. Below this the source is specified. If purchased, the agent's name is given; if presented, the donor's name appears, together with his address. The remainder of this side of the card is ruled off for check-receipt marks, and the date of arrival usually written or stamped there instead of being ticked. The reverse side may be ruled for the date of the subscription, the price, and the fund to which each item is to be charged, space being left for remarks. Data sometimes added include the approximate time when due, the number of parts to a volume, the date of the commencement of volumes, and the ultimate disposition of the work. Classification symbols or location marks are sometimes added, and coloured date-tabs (see p. 213) may usefully be added as automatic clues to overdues.

CATALOGUING PERIODICALS

The cataloguing of these journals is performed in the accustomed manner,[1] but there are one or two outstanding difficulties peculiar to periodicals which, in view of the prevalence of these publications in university libraries, may be alluded to in passing. One of these is the, unfortunately, not uncommon change of title occasioned by combination with another kindred periodical, or alteration of scope, or some less obvious reason, the volume enumeration remaining continuous. The common plan is to connect the titles by giving a cross-refer-

[1] See Chapter VI.

ence from the later to the original form, thus bringing the entries together in the catalogue just as the books are ranged together upon the shelves, and an exactly similar course should be followed when societies change their name. Another troublesome matter is the order of arranging cards or slips in the catalogue. Is strict alphabetical sequence to be observed, and, if so, are the first preliminary flourishes to govern the placing, or is there to be some transposition; and how is one to deal with foreign words which occur with different spellings? These are administrative questions, and they are ably discussed by Dr. Bradford and by Mr. Wilkes in separate papers in the *Library Association Record*, n.s., viii, pp. 178–93. All that need be said here is that the cataloguer must acquaint himself with his library rules and faithfully carry them out.

Books appearing at irregular intervals

A problem which confronts university as well as other libraries is that of maintaining an adequate check upon books which appear in successive instalments at irregular intervals. Probably they will be supplied promptly upon publication, but there is a possibility of oversight, and the contingency must be provided for by means of an effective check. For this purpose the cards of these publications should be filed precisely as in the case of periodicals,[1] either as a distinct section or intermixed

---
[1] See pp. 211–14.

UNIVERSITY LIBRARIES

in the periodicals check-list. In the latter case the cards should be distinctively tinted. They will thus come under observation whenever the file is consulted. If the date of receipt is entered upon the card as fresh volumes or parts are received, a time-clue is afforded, and if the interval is longer than usual, enquiries should be made. If the publication is issued in the ordinary way of trade (*e.g.* the Cambridge Ancient History) the trade lists will declare the fact: otherwise a communication should be sent to the society or other publisher or to the library bookseller with whom the order was placed. Even if no subscription has been paid in advance it will be well to have a check of this kind as an indication of sets in danger of becoming incomplete.

UNIVERSITY LIBRARY CO-OPERATION

The literary resources of scholastic libraries are reinforced in two ways, firstly by mutual loans of rare books, and secondly by utilizing the invaluable services of the National Central Library. The system of inter-loans, originated by the Association of University Teachers and fostered by the Joint Standing Committee on Library Co-operation, has assumed large proportions, and most of the university libraries of Great Britain—with the outstanding exceptions of Oxford and Cambridge—are comprehended within its operations. A detailed account of the working methods of this scheme is given by Colonel Luxmore Newcombe in his chapter on "University Libraries," in Dr. E. A. Baker's *Use of Libraries*.[1] The chief conditions are that loans shall be between library and library; that publications borrowed shall not be used outside the borrowing library without the special permission of the lending library; that the loans shall be restricted to a specified period; and that certain works, either because of rarity or cheapness or local demand, shall be exempt from inter-loaning. As Colonel Newcombe points out, "perhaps the most valuable side of the work is the locating of books which could not otherwise be traced." Records of outgoing and incoming loans must be kept, and the method employed by municipal libraries in connection with the National Central Library[2] will prove adequate, although local variations may sometimes be preferred.

EXCHANGE OF BOOKS

Exchanges of surplus books are a growing feature of collegiate libraries, but the practice is not extensive and no sort of uniformity has been evolved. Sometimes it is based upon a value for value scheme, and sometimes it is simply book for book. Lists of books available for this purpose are cyclostyled and circulated, and occasionally lists of desiderata accompany them. The routine consists of assembling and shelving these works, preparing the lists and issuing them, of accessioning acquisitions and recording details of those disposed of, and preparing for cir-

---

[1] *The Use of Libraries*, edited by E. A. Baker. Rev. edn., 1930, pp. 996–8.   [2] See pp. 266–7.

UNIVERSITY LIBRARIES

culation in the ordinary manner the volumes so received.

School and smaller college libraries

In colleges and schools which are fortunate enough to command the services of an expert librarian the methods of routine as explained in the various chapters of this book may be adopted or adapted as circumstances warrant, but where there is no professionally trained librarian all processes should be simplified as much as possible. A separate room should always be reserved for library use if possible, but, failing this, the books may be shelved in wall-cases in a study-room. The disadvantage of this alternative is that the quietness of the room may be disturbed by book borrowers, but if (as usually happens) the library is only open during two or three evenings in a week, the distraction may not be serious. Where the library room cannot be locked up it will be advisable to protect the books by wired or glazed doors, or the task of maintaining order and recovering works improperly borrowed will be wellnigh impossible. For economy of space the shelves should be adjustable in height, and they should be labelled for the guidance of readers.

As in the case of universities and larger colleges the teaching staff will suggest such books as they desire, but the book fund is generally inadequate, and a committee consisting of the principal and representatives of the staff and senior scholars will have to adjust supplies to resources. The rules should be few and explicit, and should be written out and displayed in the room, or printed upon the back of application forms. Borrowers should be allowed to choose their own books from the shelves, and the librarian should be competent to advise readers to sources of information. In larger libraries this advisory work often assumes large proportions, teachers and scholars alike requiring information bearing upon class work. It follows that the librarian must be well acquainted with the insides as well as the outsides of the books, and this duty here forms a more common aspect of routine than it normally does in other libraries.

Many of the registers considered essential for municipal libraries may here be dispensed with, but an accession register or stock book, in which the acquisition of fresh books is recorded, is fundamental. These registers, printed and ruled, may be purchased for a few shillings in a suitably strong binding, but where necessary one may be made by ruling the pages of a large exercise book. Columnar rulings are as follows: (1) for the running number line by line; (2) author's name; (3) title; (4) source—bookseller or donor; (5) its class number or location mark; and (6) the cost. The last factor may be required for insurance purposes; the others are for purposes of identification, and the accession number, as given in the first column, should be entered in each volume as the individual number of each book. This number serves as a clue whenever details of a book are wanted, and also as the item number for "charging" when the book is issued. The register forms a complete inventory of the book stock, and if additional narrow columns are provided it may also function as the record by which the stock is checked. Stocktaking should be done at least once a year. Many school libraries perform this operation once a term; but if done annually it should immediately precede the Long Vacation. If any books are then found to be missing without any tracing record, a list should be posted up in the room, and each form master should be asked to draw attention to it and to press for immediate return to the library. All books should be marked with the library book-stamp, and each should have a date-paper pasted in facing the front or back cover so that the date of issue (or that when the book is due back) may be marked thereon. Where the number of scholars is not large the boys or girls will all be known, and no recommendation or other evidence of *bona-fides* will be necessary; but in larger institutions the signature of a master appended to a voucher form filled up by the applicant will be sufficient. These vouchers should be of the standard 5 in. by 3 in. size, for this size is standardized for numerous library purposes, and it is advantageous to adhere to the standard so that filing may be economically performed. The voucher cards should be filed alphabetically as tickets are issued.

Charging Methods

Books may be "charged" or entered to borrowers in various ways. Card charging, as already described,[1] is the best method to employ in libraries where there is a special librarian. The university and university college plan of duplicate or triplicate forms filled in by borrowers is sometimes adopted, but its success is dependent upon the due and accurate filling up of the forms, and, unless the bookcases are locked up, or the shelves are under constant supervision, there is a real risk of confusion and disorder which will be aggravated into a breakdown if the forms are occasionally omitted. School libraries in which the scholars are permitted to help themselves to books should avoid this method of charging unless the borrowers are well drilled in this matter and faithfully carry out the regulations. The sheet or ledger system, in which the columns are dated and the book number and that of the borrower's ticket are entered upon lines progressively numbered, is simple and effective, and since these may be merely exercise books (with stiff covers for protection) ruled off to pattern, with the date-headings written in, their cost is negligible. This method is perfectly easy to work. The first blank page is ruled into columns for: (1) the day's progressive number; (2) the book number; (3) the borrower's ticket number; and (4) the actual date of return. Some libraries omit this last column and

---

[1] See Chapter VIII.

simply run an entry through to cancel it. A volume is selected from the shelves and is brought to the desk, and the borrower will produce his ticket or state its number. (In some libraries the boy's school register number is used.) If the book happens to be, for example, the tenth to be entered on any day the book's call number and the borrower's number would be recorded on the tenth line of that day's page; the date and the issue number—in this instance number ten—would be marked upon the date-sheet within the book, and the transaction is completed. When the book is returned the date is ascertained by reference to the date-sheet, the issue number is similarly declared, and the page and line are thus discovered. The entry can then be crossed out or cancelled by entering the date of return in the fourth column. Overdues are represented by uncancelled entries, and the borrowers should be notified.

Classification and catalogues

In small libraries classification is better "broad" than "fine." Main groups such as botany, geology, biography, geography, etc., will be more readily understood than any scheme worked out into minute sub-divisions; but as the stock increases it may become desirable to undertake some further splitting up of subjects, and this sub-division will increase as the library expands. Poetry, fiction, and essays are best arranged alphabetically by authors. When the books are arranged in classified order a subject-list may perhaps be dispensed with, but a shelf-list arranged in precisely the same order as the books upon the shelves is an extremely useful check, and is generally used for stocktaking purposes. The shelves as well as the bookcases should be "guided" with the names of the subjects there accommodated.

If the books are displayed in classed sequence an author list is all that is essential by way of catalogue. The mobility of cards (of the standard 5 in. × 3 in. size) makes the card catalogue pre-eminently suitable, for fresh cards can be inserted or obsolete ones withdrawn at any time, thus making the catalogue accurate and up to date in a manner which is troublesome or impossible in alternative methods. Author, title, edition, and date of publication, together with the location or call number, are the particulars required for a simple catalogue, and the two latter facts may be omitted in the case of fiction, poetry, and pure literature of all kinds. The cards can be kept in wooden or metal drawers or trays obtainable at reasonable prices from library furniture makers, or, in case of sheer necessity, in cardboard boxes reinforced with cloth. An excellent alternative form of catalogue is that known as the "loose-leaf" book. If pages are restricted to single items they are as mobile as cards, but that course is uneconomical, and several entries usually appear even upon a narrow page. The pages can be released for replacement by new ones as often as required, and corrections or additions are easily made. Loose leaves held in spring binders are occasionally used, but this plan is not recommended as the pages have a tendency to burst out if in constant use. If nothing better can be attempted a catalogue may be written in a book with thumb-indexes, but this is a miserable makeshift, and the loose-leaf method, with its perforated pages and strong fastening devices is altogether superior for general use.

Of the *minutiae* of school library routine it is needful to mention here only a few points of peculiar applicability, for much of the general library routine worthy of consideration by the school librarian will be found described elsewhere in this *Manual*. Works of reference will probably be few and of a general character, and they should be accessible at all times in the study-room. If there is a discussion class or a debating club the librarian can stimulate intelligent interest by drawing up and displaying book lists on the topics in question from time to time. Obsolete books and dirty volumes must be withdrawn from circulation, but before being disposed of it may be worth while to let the scholars cut out, mount, and classify their illustrations, and if this is done systematically a number of educational exhibitions may result. Light repairs, such as pasting-in loose leaves or mending torn pages, as described on p. 294, may be undertaken, and the books may be numbered on the back of their bindings for shelving purposes. Alternative methods of numbering books are discussed in Chapter III, and the electric stylus may be recommended if there is no likelihood of the worker placing the live point of the stylus in his mouth. Labels if used should be damped on both sides before being applied to the covers: they will then adhere so closely as to defy removal. It should never be forgotten that behind the book stock of the collegiate library are the vast reserves of the National Central Library, nor should practical co-operation with the local public library be overlooked.

SELECTED REFERENCES

BAKER (E. A.). The Public Library. 1924. (See index for numerous references to library co-operation with schools.)

BOARD OF EDUCN. Full-Time Studies. (Adult Educn. Report.)

—— Memorandum on Libraries in State-Aided Secondary Schools in England. 1927.

—— Universities of the United Kingdom: a Handbook compiled by the Universities Bureau of the British Empire. 1918.

BROWN (J. D.). Manual of Library Economy. 4th edn. 1931. (Ch. xxxiii—The library and the school.)

BUSHNELL (G. H.). University Librarianship. 1930.

FEGAN (E. S.). School Libraries: Practical Hints and Management. 1928.

KING (W. A.). The Elementary School Library. 1929.

LIBRARY ASSN. Public and Secondary School Libraries. 1929.

NEWCOMBE (L.). University Libraries. (In *Uses of Libraries*, ed. by E. A. Baker. New and revised edn.) 1930.

OFFOR (R.). University Libraries. (In *A Primer of Librarianship*.) 1931.

UNIVERSITY LIBRARIES

PEACOCK (B. M.). School and Club Librarian's Handbook. 1920.
PLUM (D. A.). Bibliography of American College Library Administration. 1899–1926.
SAYERS (W. C. BERWICK). Manual of Children's Libraries. 1932. (Chs. xviii and xix—School libraries, general and municipal.)
WILSON (M.). School Library Management. 1919.
WORKS (G. A.). College and University Library Problems. (A.L.A. *Gratis.*)
WYER (J. I.). The College and University Library. (A.L.A. Manual, 4.) 1928.
—— Reference Work. 1930. (Ch. xiii—Ref. work in school libraries.)

CHAPTER XIII

CO-OPERATIVE LIBRARY WORK

COUNTY AND RURAL LIBRARIES, REGIONAL CO-OPERATION, THE NATIONAL CENTRAL LIBRARY

The connecting-link between these three modern forms of library activity is that of co-operative effort for the advancement of library service throughout the country, and, as each agency is more or less dependent upon the other two for complementary assistance, it will be convenient to treat of them together.

COUNTY AND RURAL LIBRARIES

The main object of county and rural libraries, which we owe so largely to the statesmanlike guidance and support of the Carnegie United Kingdom Trustees, is to provide a book service for readers in districts other than urban, and even in urban districts where no public library exists. When, in 1915, Prof. Adams submitted to the Carnegie Trustees his *Report on Library Provision and Policy*, he estimated that "only 2·5 per cent. of the population in rural areas enjoyed library privileges." To-day the position is almost precisely reversed, for only some 3 per cent. of the population

CO-OPERATIVE LIBRARY WORK

remains without these intellectual and recreational facilities.

The various Acts, ranging from 1918 to 1929 under which these libraries have been established in England, Scotland, Wales, Northern Ireland, and the Irish Free State are recounted and explained by Mr. Minto in his *History of the Public Library Movement*.[1] Here all that it is needful to state is that county councils are now the constituted authorities "in respect of the administrative area lying outside an existing library area as defined in Section 10 of the Public Libraries Act, 1919." The county council must refer its library business to its education committee, which in turn may delegate its library powers to a sub-committee. "Within the prescribed financial limits the library sub-committee is in theory, so long as the delegation continues, independent of the education committee, though the actual amount of independence which is exercised varies in different areas."[2]

In a system so recent as this it is hardly to be expected that the practical methods of administration and routine will have become crystallized, but, although experiments and developments are proceeding apace, a considerable amount of common agreement has been reached, and at least the foundations of county library technique have been

[1] *Library Assn. Series*, vol. iv.
[2] The passages within quotation marks are taken from the *Report of the Public Libraries Committee* (Cmd. 2868). 1927. See also Mr. Cowley's articles on "The Organization of County Branch Libraries" in the *Library Assn. Record*, 1931.

well and truly laid and the superstructure is well advanced.

Headquarters library work

The heart of the system is the headquarters library, which is not necessarily in the county town. Here is the county librarian's office; here is the main store of books; here the administrative—and as much as possible of the detail—work is done. It is the clearing-house for books, the feeder of the local distributing centres, and the direct supplier of special books to students. Occasionally it doubles the part by also serving as a local library, but usually it functions only as the central reservoir for the supply of books to its branches. So far as book selection, acquisition, accessioning, and the preparation of books for stock are concerned the procedure conforms to the normal method of libraries, and to a large extent the same may be said of such other matters as cataloguing, the preparation and publication of catalogues or other lists of books, the tabulation of statistics—which here may assume large proportions—binding, store-keeping, and many other details.

The fundamental difference between county and ordinary urban public (rate-supported) libraries is that whereas the latter provide books for such borrowers, within a restricted area, who come to fetch them, the county library, with an immensely larger district to cover, sends its books to hundreds of deposit stations throughout the shire, and the col-

CO-OPERATIVE LIBRARY WORK

lections thus sent are in whole or part constantly being exchanged for fresh supplies.

The local centres to which the books are sent for circulation draw upon the headquarters' stock at stated intervals, which may be anything from three months to a year. Four months is a common period for small village centres, where the whole collection is changed, but in larger libraries, where there may be a practically permanent basic stock, and which may receive two thousand volumes on loan, a longer period is allowed for the reason that the stock is not so rapidly exhausted. Some three weeks before the collections are changed each centre is advised from headquarters, and local librarians, either independently or in concert with their committee, forward lists of books desired for inclusion in the forthcoming delivery. Unless such requests are forwarded the county librarian will select the books with due regard to local tastes and requirements, of which he maintains a record. Meanwhile, the three weeks' notification affords opportunity for books to be stopped, and when the new selection arrives the old one should be ready to be taken back.

The number of books sent to a centre varies in accordance with the size of the population to be served, or the number of registered borrowers, and they are conveyed in boxes so constructed as to do duty for storage and display in default of shelving accommodation. As the books stand upon their shelves at the main library each volume carries three cards. One is the ordinary white 5 in. by 3 in. catalogue card upon which a brief author and title entry is accompanied by the classification and accession numbers. Another is the book-card, which may be precisely like that used in ordinary card charging, for which purpose it is intended. The third is generally smaller and distinctively tinted, containing the same details as the catalogue card. The first two cards go with the book to its destination, but the tinted card is retained at headquarters, where it is filed in the issue trays behind a guide card bearing the name of the centre to which it has been dispatched, with a date-guide or other memorandum recording the date when sent. Thus, arranged in classified order, the cards disclose what each local library has on loan, and the whereabouts of each volume is declared at any time. When checked the books are packed, together with such sundries as stationery, printed forms, inkpads, etc., as may have been requisitioned. These sundries, too, are booked out from the stores to the library which receives them. Many counties have library motor lorries which transport the boxes in a series of zonal journeys, and, as it would be highly inconvenient for the exchanges to be made throughout the county at the same time, the work of changing deposits is more or less continuous.

When boxes are received back at headquarters the books are checked off by any written records which may be kept, the cards are withdrawn from the charging file and are restored to the books,

CO-OPERATIVE LIBRARY WORK

which are examined for binding or other defects before being put back into stock. If all the books sent are now returned the file is, of course, cleared; but it frequently happens that readers are dilatory, and the cards of unreturned volumes are treated in the normal way of overdues. They may be transferred to overdue trays, dated and guided by the name of the centre to which the books were forwarded, or they may simply be moved to the end of the tray and be similarly guided. It is the duty of the local library to make application to borrowers for the return of such books, and printed postcards, in which the appropriate details are locally filled up, are supplied to branches for this purpose. The presence of overdue cards at the main library acts as a reminder, and the headquarters' staff will take up the matter if the local librarian is unable to effect recovery.

The books sent out on deposit are usually of a popular character, for it would be wasteful to provide stocks of special works for which there might be little, if any, local demand. Provision is, therefore, made at the central library for the needs of students and other special readers, who are encouraged to make their requirements known. Printed forms are handed to these applicants who either specify particular books wanted or state as precisely as possible the subject of their study. The borrower signs his name and gives the address to which the books are to be forwarded. If the book or books (for usually more than one volume may be supplied to a reader) are selected from the library catalogue the classification number should be given, but if not the staff will search the shelves, issue the books, charging them up against the borrower personally by the ordinary method of card charging, and dispatching them by post. In some counties the library defrays the cost of postage; in others this charge has to be repaid by the reader, but in either instance the recipient is expected to acknowledge the receipt of the loan, and the acknowledgment is filed pending the return of the books. If any books thus applied for are stocked, but are not immediately available, the applicant is advised that he has been put on the waiting list, or an additional copy may be purchased. If the book cannot thus be supplied, it may perhaps be obtained as a loan under the scheme of regional co-operation, or failing this the county library may procure it from the National Central Library. If either of the two latter courses are followed it will become necessary to preserve a record of the loan, and a special form of time-charge must be made in order that the requirements of the owning library may be met. Headquarters libraries have official forms upon which these applications are made, and the books are sent direct to the address of the individual readers. Applications for extension of the time allowed for reading are not uncommon. If the books belong to the county library little difficulty will arise, the charge will require to be adjusted and the borrower advised; but if the book has been lent by an outside library

CO-OPERATIVE LIBRARY WORK

the permission of that library must be sought and the borrower must be informed that he must return the book forthwith if sanction for renewal is withheld.

LOCAL CENTRES

Of the organization of these distributing agencies nothing need be said here save that they are usually small, often open for only an hour or so during each week, and are worked by volunteer librarians. The routine is therefore made as easy and simple as possible. As consignments of books are received they are checked off, the catalogue cards are either filed for official use or made available for borrowers, and the books are arranged for inspection by readers. Forms of application for membership are distributed or handed to applicants upon request, and tickets are usually made out and registered without delay. Charging methods vary. If the centre is of any size the orthodox system of card charging is adopted, but in very small places, where no rush of borrowers is anticipated, some simple form of ledger entry may be preferred. However this may be, the local record must show who has each book lent and when it was issued. A classified analysis of the issues is compiled at the close of the day, and the figures are incorporated in a schedule which accompanies the collection when it goes back to headquarters at the end of the loan period. It is from these returns that the statistics for the annual report are compiled. When intimation is received (three weeks in advance of the time) of exchange of stock, books are issued upon condition that they shall be received back by a date which will allow time for the preparation of issue statistics and packing. The catalogue cards should also be checked and returned, and in anticipation of the fresh delivery the local librarian should furnish headquarters with particulars of any special loans desired. If everything is in order the boxes of books, with the statistical returns, will be ready for the county van, and as the new stock comes the old stock goes.

Regional branch libraries

Regional branch libraries are an interesting and important development of the county library system. Designed to supersede ordinary local centres and to act as sub-headquarters for districts in large and populous counties, they are specially housed, equipped with adequate stocks of books, are provided with study-rooms which are in effect reference departments, and enjoy the advantage of a professional staff. Ticket-holders registered anywhere within the county may avail themselves of its facilities at any time, and neighbouring village libraries draw upon their resources both for their periodically changing collections and by vitalizing their stocks through exchanging books for which they have no local demand. School libraries are fed either from this source or from the headquarters' library, and exhibitions of books, prints, etc., are occasionally

CO-OPERATIVE LIBRARY WORK

held. In addition to its own stock are the larger resources of the main library, upon which it draws for bulk and individual loans from time to time, and thus special requirements are met. The routine involved is a combination of headquarters and local centre work, with normal library practice for local issue purposes. The extension of this valuable and economic process of devolution, implying the appointment of trained assistants, should be a matter of practical interest to young librarians.

LIBRARY DELIVERY VANS

Tiny villages and scattered hamlets which cannot support a library centre for themselves have their book needs met by a library van which visits them at stated times. The vans are fitted with shelves upon which a fresh selection of books is displayed at each successive journey. A few days in advance of the visit all the registered borrowers are advised, and upon arrival one side is let down and the books become available. A member of the headquarters' staff attends to the charging, which must be kept distinctively for each place, but the vehicle is driven by a chauffeur. Before the van sets out the volumes are inventoried, and upon its return the books are checked off together with those which have been brought back from their borrowers; the issues are recorded and the charges adjusted in the records. Where the van delivery system is not in operation readers may procure books either from headquarters by post or by visiting the nearest local centre.

A MANUAL OF LIBRARY ROUTINE

OTHER ACTIVITIES

In some counties persons who are neither resident, employed, nor studying within the shire are allowed as a matter of convenience to use a local library upon payment of a subscription. They are registered in the accustomed manner, and a time record is kept in order that their subscriptions may be duly renewed. Reading-rooms are occasionally provided, and where this occurs the routine of ordering, checking, and displaying will follow the usual library practice as described in Chapter XI. Study circles and educational agencies, such as the Workers' Educational Association and evening schools, are catered for, and miscellaneous collections or multiple copies of books are provided by arrangement for generous periods. These loans are, of course, entered to the body supplied, either in the same way as loans to ordinary library centres or by such other method as may locally be preferred; and upon return the books are checked off and examined for defects before being replaced upon the library shelves again. Children, as well as adults, are included within the county library service, but their books are generally sent to schools where they are under the charge of a teacher, the actual work of issuing them being done as a rule by one of the elder scholars. The routine is as at local centres, but as children's books are often unsubstantially produced and are liable to heavy usage it is desirable that upon their return to headquarters they should

CO-OPERATIVE LIBRARY WORK

be examined with particular care. There is a fair amount of publicity work to be done, and the preparation of leaflets for distribution and advertising posters at flower shows and local meetings is a recurrent aspect of routine work. It will be obvious that there will be a large amount of correspondence devolving upon the county librarian and his assistants, and perhaps more than the usual amount of statistical returns for tabulation, but in general the office routine very much resembles that of other libraries.

REGIONAL CO-OPERATION

Regional co-operation, the latest development in library economy, is the voluntary federation of libraries of various kinds—urban, county, university, and institutional or special—within a wide geographical area to systematize and facilitate the interchange of books for the benefit of individual readers. County libraries provide deposit collections for the distributing centres within their respective boundaries, but the regional scheme pools the non-fictional literary resources of each co-operating library, and lends, upon request, such separate works as the affiliated libraries require but cannot supply from their own stock. The economy of such a method is sufficiently obvious, for the book service of each library is thus considerably widened, and, as the necessity for purchasing expensive and rarely used books is correspondingly reduced, it enables book votes to be used for works which are in more general demand.

Presaged by the pioneer effort established in Cornwall in 1927, by which libraries of that county only lend books between themselves, the first fully organized library regional system was that of the Northern Counties covering Cumberland, Durham, Northumberland, and Westmorland, with Middlesbrough on the Yorkshire boundary as an auxiliary. It was opened at the beginning of 1931 with the Library of the Literary and Philosophical Society as its headquarters or central bureau and clearing-house for enquiries. That of the West Midland Region, embracing the counties of Hereford, Shropshire, Stafford, Warwick, and Worcestershire, quickly followed, with its central bureau at the Birmingham Public Library; and the National Library at Aberystwyth performs a similar function for Wales.

GENERAL PROCEDURE

When a borrower applies at any library within the scheme for a book which it cannot supply, the details are recorded in a card (or other) special register. The date, name and address of the borrower, perhaps his ticket number, and full particulars of the book required are entered. From this record a form is filled up and sent to the regional bureau, where a union catalogue of the library stocks reveals whether or not the books are contained within the area, and, if so, where. The compilation

CO-OPERATIVE LIBRARY WORK

ROLLAND

ROLLAND, John

Ane treatise callit the Court of Venus, devidit into four buikis, compylit in 1575; ed. by W. Gregor. 1884. (Scottish Text Society).

Reduced facsimile (original 8 × 4 in.) of Union Catalogue Entry
By permission of the Northern Regional Library Bureau

of these master-catalogues is performed by a special staff, and the catalogues are in sheaf form, the lower half of each leaf being ruled off into numbered squares, each number indicating a particular library, and an asterisk or other mark placed there indicates that the library in question possesses the work.

This information having been discovered, the form is sent to a library possessing the work, and if available the volume will be dispatched immediately to the library which issued the original application. The request form will be dated, the cost of postage incurred will be filled in, and the form filed until the book comes back. The actual book-charge is made against the borrowing library, for it is an integral part of the scheme that libraries which receive loans shall be responsible for their safe and due return and for the necessary postal expenses. The record of outgoing books therefore includes date entry, identity details of each volume lent, the name and address of the library to which books are forwarded, a note of any known defects, the postal charge, and perhaps the date when due back. As the possibility of detention beyond the time allowed is ever present, the contingency must be provided for by some sort of time-check, and this may be done by charging the books in the ordinary files against the borrowing library or, if open access is not in operation, by examination of the return dates in the register of inter-library loans. The file of applications may be so arranged as to serve as a

CO-OPERATIVE LIBRARY WORK

supplementary check, but in any case these forms are cancelled when the volumes return, and are sent to the borrowing library as acquittance of responsibility. As the books are entered and charged they should be packed with ample protection in the way of paper or cardboard; indeed, a range of suitable cardboard cases of standard sizes seems to be desirable for inter-library loans of all descriptions, and a memorandum of the postage, or a request for payment to the amount as shown by stamps, should accompany the package.

If requested works cannot for any reason be lent, the bureau should be informed so that it may make application elsewhere. If they can be lent only under restrictive conditions, the library asking for them should be advised. Whenever the postal charge would materially exceed the normal amount, the instructions of the applicant library should be obtained before dispatching the package. Similarly, if a book is in circulation at the time of request, a stop-card should be inserted in the charge in the issue tray and the register will reveal the destination of the book is still required. If it be found from the union catalogue that a book is not locally obtainable, the bureau will forward the application to the National Central Library, which, either from its own stock or from one or other of its auxiliaries, will almost certainly be able to supply it.

Libraries receiving books should promptly acknowledge their arrival, and printed forms for this purpose are provided. The loans should then be entered in the appropriate columns of the inter-loan register or in a complementary record. The details for entry will include the date of receipt, columns for ticks or other marks indicating that acknowledgement of arrival and advice to the applicant have been forwarded, cost of postage, and provision for denoting the date of return, and that the charge for outward postage has been refunded. Loan books should be laid aside in an appointed place, and a card sent to inform the applicant that the volume awaits him. Finally, the book will be charged in the ordinary way to the borrower, and the loan must be applied for promptly if not returned within the limit of time. Unless the borrower's library itself defrays the cost of carriage the due amount must be recovered from the reader, to whom a formal receipt must be given; and when the book is sent back to the library from which it was obtained, the amount of outward postage should be refunded. The local record must be adjusted, and when the cancelled application form comes back, denoting that the volume has completed its travels, the transaction is completed.

Receipt of reference books which are restricted to use within the library will require to be acknowledged to the owning library; they must be entered in the register so far as is requisite, probably with symbols indicating their character, and the applicant will have to be advised in the usual way. As these books are often rare and valuable, special precautions should be taken for their protection by

CO-OPERATIVE LIBRARY WORK

adequate packing, and they may have to be conveyed by registered post.

LOCAL LIBRARY CO-OPERATION

The benefits of this form of co-operation are so manifold that, in some districts where there is no regional library system, libraries arrange between themselves for inter-loans of books other than fiction. By specializing their stock, particularly in the interests of local manufactures, the necessity for purchasing certain costly books at each library is reduced, thus enabling a larger number of works in more general demand to be obtained. The towns of Newark, Mansfield, and Worksop, in Nottinghamshire, may be cited as an instance of this arrangement, and as a union catalogue exists at each library it is easy to trace and procure such books as are included in the stocks so pooled. The method of working such a scheme is a simplified form of regional library routine. Requests and books are sent by post, and the issue and return of the books may be traced by ordinary charging or by special registration. Larger libraries rarely or never refuse without adequate reason to lend research or special works from their resources, and the National Central Library is ever in reserve.

THE NATIONAL CENTRAL LIBRARY

Behind all schemes of library co-operation stands the National Central Library (formerly the Central

Library for Students), which has not only a great and growing stock of its own, largely of works of an expensive or special character, but by reason of its "outlier" and other auxiliaries is enabled to place some four and a half millions of books, other than prose fiction, at the disposal of readers without charge save that of postage.

As summarized in *A Primer of Librarianship,* by Colonel Newcombe, its Principal Executive Officer and Librarian, its chief objects are: "(*a*) to lend otherwise unobtainable books to libraries in Great Britain and Ireland; (*b*) to lend books to organized groups of adult students; (*c*) to act as a clearing-house for the loan of books in the libraries associated with it (known as Outlier Libraries); (*d*) to act as a liaison department between the various Regional Bureaux; (*e*) to form a union catalogue of the books in the Outlier Libraries; (*f*) to trace the whereabouts of copies of scarce books; (*g*) to supply bibliographical information; and (*h*) to act as the National Centre for Bibliographical Information in Great Britain, in association with similar centres which have been, or are being, established in other countries."

As a clearing-house and liaison department it is in operative touch with books which are released for use through any library with which a reader may be connected. Novels, school textbooks, and volumes published at less than 8s. each lie entirely outside its scope, but on the other hand expensive treatises in the latest editions are either stocked by the Central Library or are generously purchased

CO-OPERATIVE LIBRARY WORK

to meet demands, and the more important standard works, sets of periodicals of all descriptions, and special and rare works are supplied through auxiliary libraries. English libraries which are included within a regional library area are supplied so far as possible through their own regional bureau, which will apply to the Central Library at London only in the event of necessity. Those which are outside regional areas send their enquiries direct to London, and the books when traced will be supplied direct to the libraries preferring the requests. County libraries are specially treated, and, for topographical reasons, books applied for by headquarter libraries may be posted direct to the borrowers. Scottish requests pass through the Scottish Central Library for Students, at Dunfermline; those from Wales through the National Library of Wales; and the Central Library for Students, at Dublin, either satisfies Irish readers from its own shelves or forwards the applications on to London.

The procedure in so far as regional areas are concerned has already been indicated, and the routine elsewhere is in many respects very similar. When applications are received at local libraries they must be dated and registered, applicants being first informed that some slight delay may occur, and that the cost of transit both ways will fall upon them. A form of application is then prepared by filling in the name of the library, details of the book required, and the address to which it is to be sent unless delivery at the library is required. If the book is supplied from the Central Library's own stock it will be accompanied by a receipt form which must be signed and returned without delay, and note must be taken of the postal charge as indicated thereon. The reader is then advised exactly as in the case of books received from a regional library. At intervals the Central Library will render an account of the postal charges it has defrayed on behalf of the library, and this must be checked by the record, the amount is remitted, and a receipt obtained and preserved, the disbursement being duly entered in the cash-book. An alternative charging method sometimes adopted where these borrowings are not numerous is simply to file the application forms in a clip together with the borrower's ticket. As the books are brought back and the postal charge is paid, the form is cancelled and taken from the file, those remaining being subject to a weekly scrutiny, overdues being written for.

"Outliers" will from time to time be called upon to issue books to unknown borrowers as well as other libraries, at the request of the National Central Library, and the requests will be received upon official forms which state all necessary particulars about the wanted books, the name and address of the person to whom they should be sent direct, and notifying whether the cost of postage should be charged to the borrower or to the Central Library. Record of these issues may be kept by filing the forms with the book-cards, as just described, or by entry in a register and including the charge in

CO-OPERATIVE LIBRARY WORK

the issue trays for the date when lent. In any case prompt recovery and return is essential for smooth working, and overdues must be closely followed up. Loans from the Central Library should be returned there, but books lent by outlier libraries must be sent back direct. The Central Library will periodically refund its postal debt, and individual borrowers from whom refund amounts are due, and who have been advised at the time when the books were lent to them, will discharge their liability when returning the volumes which they borrowed. Formal receipts must, of course, be given for these amounts, and in the unlikely event of default in payment the National Central Library should be advised.

If and when it happens that the Central Library finds itself unable to meet demands, it will advise the applying library by means of a printed schedule upon which variant reasons appear, the one pertinent to the request being specially marked. The book desired may be rare and there may be difficulty in locating it; it may have to be imported, and the Library wishes to know whether the applicant is willing to wait; no copy may be immediately available, and the applicant has been placed upon the waiting list; certain books as specified upon this reply form are suggested as substitutes and will be sent upon request; or the books are not within the scope of the library, or for other reasons are unsupplyable. The germane reason should be recorded and the applicant informed, when the

A MANUAL OF LIBRARY ROUTINE

request will be confirmed or withdrawn as the reader may decide.

SELECTED REFERENCES

BAKER (E. A.). The Public Library. 1924. (Ch. iv—Rural libraries.)

BOSTWICK (A. E.). The American Public Library. 4th edn. 1929. (Ch. xx—County libraries.)

BROWN (J. D.). Manual of Library Economy. 4th edn. 1931. (Ch. xxxv—County, or rural, libraries.)

CARNEGIE UNITED KINGDOM TRUST. County Library Conferences, 1924 and 1926: Reports of the Proceedings. 1925–27. And all other publications of the Trust bearing on this subject.

COWLEY (J. D.). Organization of County Branch Libraries. (In *Lib. Assn. Record*, 3rd ser., i, 1931, pp. 113–21; 185–91, 225–30.)

DAVIES (E. SALTER). Future of County Libraries. (In *Lib. Assn. Record*, 3rd ser., i, 1931, pp. 397–407.)

GRAY (D.). County Library System. 1922.

GREEN (E.). Regional Library Bureaux. (In *Library World*, 1929, pp. 38–9.)

LIBRARY ASSN. Regional Libraries in England. 1928.

—— Small Municipal Libraries. 1931. (Ch. vi—Co-operation of stock.)

MACLEOD (R. D.). County Rural Libraries: Their Policy and Organization. 1923.

NATIONAL CENTRAL LIBRARY. Regional Library Bureaux: Procedure for Borrowing Books. 1931.

OSBORNE (E.). Decentralization in County Library Work. (In *Lib. Assn. Record*, 3rd ser., ii, pp. 169–76.)

Primer of Librarianship: ed. by W. E. DOUBLEDAY. 1931. (Chs. xiii—County libraries, and xiv—Library co-operation and the Natl. Centl. Library.)

CHAPTER XIV

STOCKTAKING, WITHDRAWALS, AND REPLACEMENTS

The primary object of stocktaking in libraries is to ascertain if all the books that have been stocked can be accounted for; but there are other matters which require to be looked into as the work proceeds, *e.g.* the state of the books, the recovery of misplaced volumes, the cleaning of the shelves, and the laying aside of books for examination as to their need of repairs, replacement, or withdrawal. Except, perhaps, in libraries with indicators, it is no longer usual to close the department for this purpose, and the work has therefore to be performed whilst the normal library service is in progress. To enable this to be done the work of taking stock is more or less continuous; one section is taken at a time, and, at least in lending libraries, the whole of the stock should thus be covered annually. As the official year ends in March the work should be completed by that date so that the result may be embodied in the annual report.

The actual checking is achieved by comparing the book stock with the shelf-register or such other form of inventory as may be preferred. In open-access libraries the shelf-list is commonly used, but in closed libraries a stock book is often employed.

The shelf-list is a register of the books arranged

in the classified order in which the volumes stand upon the shelves. If it is in card form this order can always be maintained with precision, for as new books are added or old ones withdrawn the cards can be intercalated or abstracted as desired. If it takes the form of a loose-leaf register approximate accuracy can be achieved by re-writing the sheets as necessity demands. In the older style of stock book, in which fresh acquisitions are entered chronologically, the only order attempted is that of main classes, and either a separate register is devoted to each main class or the smaller classes are grouped together into composite books.

Card shelf-lists may be specially written or may be compiled from the process cards which were described in Chapter III.[1] If they are specially written (or, better still, typed) only condensed particulars need be attempted. All that is really required are particulars sufficient for easy identification. Details are sometimes pared down to the author's surname (only) and the "binder's short title," but the classification marks should appear at one topmost corner, for guiding use, and the accession number on the opposite corner to direct to the source of fuller information respecting each item. The rest of the card may be left clear for stocktaking marks, and a rubber stamp, such as is used for marking the date-papers in volumes, can be used, each impression denoting that the book in question was accounted for on the date so speci-

---

[1] See pages 49–51.

STOCKTAKING, REPLACEMENTS, ETC.

fied. Where process cards are pressed into service the front side will have been filled up, but the back will be available for stamping. Loose-leaf registers and bound stock books give the same details as described for cards, but they have dated columns in which ticks are made instead of date marks.

Taking stock

The *modus operandi* is one of those processes of which the simplicity may allure to carelessness. One assistant has the register, another calls out the author's name and title of each book as it stands upon the shelf, and every entry in the check-list is marked accordingly. If the books are marked with individual call numbers these should not be solely relied upon; it is better to announce the author and title also. Where there is more than a single copy of any volume the accession number must be ascertained, and it is the duty of the assistant who is marking the register to enquire which copy is referred to, for the registers inform him as to duplicates, whereas he who is examining the shelves has no knowledge of the number of copies stocked. If the lines or columns of registers are closely ruled it will be easy to put the tick in the wrong place, and, so far as this occurs, the object of stocktaking is defeated. Similarly, if a card list is being used the right card must be marked, and cards have a most distracting way of adhering to each other! Whether shelf cleaning has now to be done or not, it is advisable that each volume should be removed from the shelf as it is reached, for frequency of use may now well be tested, the condition of each book may be examined, and removal may disclose books hidden in unsuspected places.

At this stage there will inevitably be a large number of unmarked items, but the charging trays will account for many of these blanks. It has already been mentioned that only one class is checked at a time, and once again the differing colours of the classed book-cards afford a valuable clue, for only the cards of the colour representing the class under treatment need to be examined as they stand in the charging file. Obviously the best time for this interference with the charging trays is when the department is closed to the public, and early morning is therefore most suitable. The cards are dealt with in exactly the same way as the books upon the shelves, the appropriate details of each are read out and the list is duly marked.

Unless the section under treatment is temporarily withdrawn from circulation—an undesirable and difficult thing to do where the public are admitted to the shelves—it may perhaps be considered inadvisable to re-issue the books belonging to that section until they have been checked by the stock-taking record. This ought not to be necessary, for the charging trays should have yielded all the information thus obtained, but it is a double check which is occasionally thought worth while. If this course is followed the staff should be advised by a posted notice or otherwise, and as the books come

STOCKTAKING, REPLACEMENTS, ETC.

in they should be laid aside, marked off promptly, and returned to the shelves with as little delay as possible.

Even now there will be numerous gaps representing volumes not accounted for, and the withdrawal and binding books must be investigated and all items taken out of stock or sent for repair checked off. Probably there will be a cupboard or some shelves for the reception of books awaiting staff attention, either for light repair, relabelling, or because they are soiled or damaged or otherwise require examination for withdrawal or replacement. All these books must be turned out and checked. The "black list" and the register of books lost and paid for by borrowers will also disclose items which cannot otherwise be accounted for, and any record of special loans must be inspected and the books thus traced must be ticked in the inventory, for the object is to account for all the books and not alone those which are in sight. As it is a common practice to allow lending library books (other than fiction) to be used in the reference department, it may be that some of these loans have not been returned to their shelves, and this loophole of escape must be watched. To obviate trouble in this direction the books so lent should be recorded either in the charging trays or by filed memoranda, but even so the reference librarian should be supplied with lists of missing books as each section of stocktaking is completed, and search of the reference shelves may bring some of the truants to light.

Before assuming, when all these steps have been taken, that books remaining unmarked are untraceable, the bookshelves should be re-examined occasionally, for mysterious reappearances are by no means unknown. Indeed, they sometimes crop up long after the volumes have been written off as lost, and one, or sometimes two, years may be allowed to elapse before hope of recovery is officially abandoned. In the final event the check-list is examined, and a detailed record of the items remaining unmarked is made out and filed. It will be well to compare this list with the shelves now and again in the hope of reducing the number of blanks, but when all these processes have been exhausted the residuum must be reckoned as actually or potentially lost, and the facts and figures must be reported to the committee and will appear in the annual report.

Where indicators are in use one member of the staff will check the shelves, another the register, and a third will note that the book-number-blocks correspond, and will correct the indicator when errors are found. Otherwise the routine is practically the same as in open-access libraries.

Shelf orderliness

Decisions respecting the withdrawal of books from stock and as to their replacement or discarding are matters of administration, but the preliminary stages fall well within the compass of ordinary staff routine.

STOCKTAKING, REPLACEMENTS, ETC.

One of the constant duties of assistants is to see that the shelves are kept in proper order. When this work is in progress any books of doubtful appearance should be removed. They may have loose maps or plates, torn leaves, "started" sections, or shabby covers, and it may be observed that some have overstayed their welcome and are cumbering the shelves. Here is an opportunity for the staff to display its keenness. If the work is well done the shelves will show it, and the difference between active intelligence and the perfunctory discharge of duty will be so apparent that the assistants will be noticed accordingly. There will be a place reserved for the accommodation of the books which are intercepted for examination, but the decision in each instance will probably lie with a senior assistant. Those with which the staff can deal will be winnowed out for their attention; those for binding will go to the assistant in charge of that work; the remainder will require expert consideration, and will be sorted into groups to await inspection.

Reserve stock

One of these groups will consist of books which are not often in demand, but are of such established reputation that they cannot very well be discarded. If a binding is faded or has otherwise become unattractive, the book may have a new lease of life if put into a fresh cover, for a good book in a dingy binding competes at a disadvantage with less worthy volumes in braver array. If retained upon the public shelves they tend to deaden the general effect, and, moreover, where accommodation is restricted they are uselessly occupying valuable space. Under such circumstances they are generally relegated to a private part of the building, where they can be stored in classified order and will be available upon demand. To prevent persons from assuming that such volumes are not in stock because they no longer appear upon the shelves, and to obviate futile references to the catalogue, the card or sheaf entries should be stamped, under every heading in which they appear, with a notice that the books are stored away, but are available upon request. Unless the cards or pages carry on the front or back the class symbols of all the added entries it will be difficult to be certain that all the affected entries are duly marked, and the same difficulty would arise in adjusting the catalogue when books are discarded or replaced.

Withdrawals from Stock

Another of the groups will comprise books suspected of obsolescence or of being altogether out of date. It is of real importance that superseded works of a scientific, technological, sociological, or other educational nature should not be allowed to circulate, but it is often a matter of extreme difficulty to discover a satisfactory line of demarcation between the valuable and the valueless and misleading ones. Considerable assistance in this dilemma may be obtained by a careful study of Mr. Sayers's

STOCKTAKING, REPLACEMENTS, ETC.

Revision of the Stock of a Public Library,[1] but, when all is said, the solution in almost every individual case will call for discrimination fortified by knowledge and patient investigation. Clearly, this is no work for juniors; but notes of physical imperfections, or particulars of later editions, especially if accompanied by extracts from, or references to, critical reviews, may with advantage be slipped into the books by any member of the staff, and will be useful not only to the adjudicator, but also, in an educational way, to the assistant concerned.

Soiled or mutilated copies offer little difficulty. They should be intercepted anywhere at any time, for nothing gives a worse impression of a library than the circulation of books in a disreputable condition. A casual inspection will often disclose their undesirability: it is with borderline cases that problems occur. Whenever doubt arises the book should be laid aside for judgment.

As a rule the librarian is vested with authority to withdraw books from stock, but occasionally committees reserve the right to inspect the books before they are discarded. When a decision has been reached, those which have been rejected from further use must be entered in a withdrawal register. The form of this register varies in detail; its entries may be condensed or expanded, but whatever the style may be the record, if separately kept, is chronologically made. The shorter form has columns for

[1] Published in 1929. Appears in condensed form in Brown's *Manual*, 4th edn., pp. 188-92.

the progressive entry number, accession number, the baldest details of author and title, reason for withdrawal, and—sometimes—one for the record of disposal. Provision may also be made for the accession number of any replacing copy, and for initials or ticks to show that catalogue entries and stock cards have been withdrawn. Fuller forms give the date of publication, publisher, class analysis, and other particulars, but there is a distinct trend towards simplicity. The date of withdrawal is, of course, common to all entries in withdrawal records.

The registers thus affected (*e.g.* the accession register, invoice book, etc.) must be adjusted by the insertion of the serial number in the withdrawal register. If accommodation for it has been provided by a special column it will be entered there, but otherwise it may go in the remarks column. Small libraries may perhaps dispense with a separate register and find it sufficient to count off these withdrawals or replacements in the accession register. Where this is done it will assist if the markings therein are made in inks of different colours, but in any case great care must be taken to make sure that the adjusted entries are all counted.

In withdrawing books from the stock of a library where the shelf-list is in card form the card in each instance must be abstracted and cancelled, possibly to be filed until the end of the year as a current record of withdrawals; but if the list be in loose-leaf or bound-book form the entry in question should be struck out and the withdrawal number

STOCKTAKING, REPLACEMENTS, ETC.

inserted; otherwise the books will have to be laboriously traced at stocktaking. Similarly, if the catalogue be in card form *all* the cards relating to each book must be removed, and the entries in sheaf or book catalogues deleted. Where printed catalogues are in use the copies reserved for staff and library use may have these entries obliterated, but this is a clumsy device; it is better to compile a card list of all the books withdrawn and to keep it at the desk for reference. When all these entries and adjustments have been made the books are ready for disposal, and it will be advisable to stamp each volume boldly with the word "Withdrawn," since such books, after being given to charitable institutions or sold to be pulped, have occasionally been discovered on book-stalls and seized by the police, or have been found and returned by private persons, when the library's property stamp has not been cancelled.

Replacements

Some of the books withdrawn will doubtless be discarded as no longer desirable in any edition, but others will have to be replaced. These should be listed, and as the list is of a temporary character cards seem to be pre-eminently suitable. If the main-entry card taken from the catalogue is not wanted for other purposes it will serve here after being marked with the date (or number) of withdrawal, or the process card, if free, will do equally well. Particulars of alternative editions, or of better books on the same subject, may be added as opportunity permits, and the information is thus at hand when the bookseller's order is being made out.

As new copies are supplied they will require to be checked off in the manner previously described, and after collation, etc., they will be ready for entering in the permanent replacement register. Accessioning may have to be repeated,[1] and as full details of author, title, publisher, price, supplier, etc., will there be recorded, it will be unnecessary to duplicate all that minutiae here. Serial number, date, accession number, and short author and title particulars are all that are really essential, but if the cost as well as the number of volumes replaced within any given period are likely to be wanted, price columns should also be included. Where yearly estimates stipulate a maximum expenditure upon these purchases some effective progressive record of cost must be maintained, or the vote may be unconsciously exceeded.

Discard registers are occasionally undertaken, but the information they disclose is generally ascertainable from the withdrawal record. Their object is to show the number and cost of books withdrawn and not replaced.

[1] Whether replacements should be treated as new arrivals and entered as such in accession registers, or should be carried in to the original number, thus enabling successive copies of particular works to bear the same accession numbers, is a moot point. Brown's *Manual* (pp. 182-3) advocates the latter plan, but Dr. Bostwick vigorously rebuts that policy. See his *American Public Library*, 4th edn., p. 200.

STOCKTAKING, REPLACEMENTS, ETC.

SELECTED REFERENCES

ALDRED (T.). Stocktaking. (In *Lib. Assn. Record,* viii, 1906, pp. 244–7, 277–9.)

AMERICAN LIB. ASSN. Survey of Libraries in the United States. (Vol. iv, ch. 2—Inventory-stocktaking.)

BOSTWICK (A. E.). American Public Library. 4th edn. 1929. (pp. 200–4, Shelf lists and stocktaking; p. 157 and p. 267, Withdrawals and replacements.)

BROWN (J. D.). Manual of Library Economy. 4th edn. 1931. (Sections 240, 280, 366.)

DRURY (F. K. W.). Order Work for Libraries. (Ch. vii—Replacements and withdrawals.)

HATCHER (A. F.). Stocktaking methods. (In *Library Assistant,* v, pp. 43–6.)

RATHBONE (J. A.). Shelf Department. (A.L.A. Manual, 20). 1918.

STEWART (J. D.), *and others.* Open-Access Libraries. 1915. (Ch. viii—Stocktaking, pp. 194–8, by H. T. Coutts.)

WILLCOCK (W. J.). Recording, Replacing, and Disposal of Worn-out Books. (In *Library World,* iv, pp. 91–3.)

CHAPTER XV

BOOKBINDING: SPECIFICATIONS AND RECORDS

The wear and tear of books in busy libraries is always great, and it is particularly heavy when the original binding or the paper is poor in quality. For this reason it is usually uneconomical to buy the cheapest editions, for, although something may thus be saved in the first cost, it is more than counterbalanced by charges for subsequent repairs, and the physical life of such books is short. The cloth cases in which British and American publishers almost invariably bind their books are scarcely fitted for constant use, and if reinforced editions are available they should be preferred. It is the same with the paper upon which books are printed. Spongy "featherweight" papers, used for bulking purposes, are "a delusion and a snare": they suck up dirt like a sponge, and are most difficult to bind inasmuch as they are too soft to hold stitches and do not take kindly to glueing-up. Cheap plate-paper, loaded with clay or other minerals and presenting a very glossy surface for the display of process illustrations, are also awkward to bind: they are apt to smear wherever touched with moisture, and the thickest sorts will sometimes crack like delicately thin china. Wire-stitched volumes should be avoided because their metal corrodes and rots the paper which the stitches are intended to hold.

But the best produced books will in time yield to the strain of constant handling. Pages may break away and be lost; some amount of rough and occasionally violent treatment will be recurrent; damage will be done by carelessness and accident; normal usage will take its toll, and dirt and atmospheric conditions are leather's ever-active foes. It is with the treatment of these volumes that this chapter deals from the administrative point of view; but, although the art and craft of binding lies beyond the scope of library routine, its technique must be thoroughly understood, for every librarian must be able to decide with expert knowledge the nature of the repairs to be done to each volume, and he must be competent to judge whether the work has been properly performed.

Adapting binding repairs to books

As a general principle it may be laid down that bindings should always be adapted to the physical qualities of books and to the reasonable expectation of their life and use. To this dictum it may be added that "books should be bound as well as they can be; as cheaply as they can be done well, and as well as they can be done cheaply." Again, it has to be remembered that the lowest price is not necessarily the cheapest; indeed, it would probably prove to be quite the reverse in the long run, and, without the least disrespect to general binders, it may be suggested that the best and cheapest work will be done by firms which cater especially for library work. The binding of library books needs to be particularly durable, neat in appearance, of great strength, and low in price: in other words, library binding and book repairs demand abnormal treatment.

Shabby-looking volumes should not be allowed to remain in circulation, and this not alone for aesthetic effect, but also in the interests of economy, for when a binding once commences to "go" its deterioration is rapid, and defects capable of easy correction if dealt with in time will soon require rebinding if left untended. The safe rule is to withdraw such books at sight and to remove them to the place appointed for the reception of books for examination.

Only a proportion of these books will need to be sent to the bindery. Some will be discarded or replaced by new copies; others, with slight defects, may be repaired by the staff. Those sorted out for the binder will be carefully examined for their requirements, and treatment will differ, and much money can be squandered by ignoring the advice just given. Every book should be judged upon its merits. If the leaves are disfigured or dirty, it should be laid aside for replacement or discarding. If it is found to have exhausted its demand, it is not worth repairing. Even those which are to be rebound will probably not all be treated with the same material. It would be extravagant to bind in leather such volumes as are rarely in request, for unless a really good skin, tanned without the employment of acids, is used the leather would become dry, crack at the joints, and crumble at the back. Russian leather, and pigskin if not in constant use, are the worst offenders, but sheepskins run them close in this respect. Books showing premonitory signs of soiling may be put into a cheap cloth, and runs of volumes which must be preserved, albeit little used, may be bound in linen buckram or other durable covering. Large sized, and smaller books if heavy with plate-paper, must have a stronger binding than slighter ones, and the number of tapes, as well as the quality of the binding material, must be sufficient for the strain imposed upon them.

The term "leather" covers a multitude of skins, some of which are purely artificial. Commercial calf, roan, skivers, and other fancy varieties of split leathers are of no practical use for library books. A well-dressed Niger morocco is the ideal material for this use if its slight extra cost can be managed; but there is available a clever imitation having a textile body with a surface so like that of a fine-grained morocco as to evade all but expert examination. It is free from odour and wears well, but it does not take to gold tooling quite so sympathetically as leather. In 1914 the American Library Association issued the following recommendations:

(1) Always use leather for books which are to receive bad usage.
(2) Never use leather for books which will be seldom used.
(3) In case of doubt use cloth.

Subject to the foregoing conditions, and provided that the leather is free from acid, and the cloth strong and waterproof, this advice is sound.

Library binderies

Only the largest of libraries can support a bindery of their own with any prospect of success. The necessary plant is costly, material cannot be purchased upon the same advantageous terms as are conceded to firms with an enormous output; quality of workmanship must be high; the wage-bill will be a matter of concern; with a limited staff delivery will necessarily be slow, and it has been asserted that unless a minimum of 15,000 volumes a year are bound a bindery cannot pay its way. It is not surprising, therefore, that, with few exceptions, libraries send out their work to specializing firms.

Binding specifications

Contracts for bookbinding and repairs are usually entered into yearly or triennially, and they embody specifications to which the contractor has to work. The general conditions stipulate that the materials used shall be of the character and quality as specified; that the workmanship shall be of the best; that the books shall be collected and returned free of charge; that all volumes shall be collated and defects reported before receiving treatment; that lettering and numbering shall be done with the best English gold-leaf; that the best unbleached linen thread be used for sewing (unless hempen

BOOKBINDING

thread is specified by preference); that plates and maps shall be mounted on strong linen guards and securely fastened, etc. In fact the details involved in forwarding and finishing are all provided for, as also is the time allowed for re-delivery of the books. Mr. Douglas Cockerell, in his *Bookbinding and the Care of Books*, surveys this subject from the library point of view, and offers expert suggestions for the technical points which should be comprehended in a specification. Book sizes are scheduled and repairs are charged accordingly.

BINDING SHEETS AND RECORDS

When books have been examined and the nature of the repairs in each case determined, they are entered, an item to each line, in the binding book, and an order-sheet or binder's list must be prepared.

In form and detail these vary, but the examination of a large number of examples reveals that the following particulars commonly appear in the binding book: class number, author, title, size, number of volumes or copies of each work, instructions, and date returned. At the top of each page appears the order number, the name of the binder, and the date. The binder's list is almost identical, but it is headed with the name of the library to which the books are to be returned, the order number and the date, and is provided with £ s. d. columns so that (like book order-forms) the sheets may serve as invoices. If a carbon copy can be made as the books are entered in the order-book the labour of transcribing and checking can be avoided; but under any circumstances the books must be carefully compared with the record, and the entries counted up and checked by the books.

In the "instructions" column such directions as are requisite are given in condensed form, *e.g.* hf. cf. for half calf; mor. for the kind of morocco stipulated for in the contract; cl. for cloth, etc. Special bindings should be accompanied by slips pasted in the covers, and, in fact, some libraries insert individual slips of instruction in every volume sent. A rather elaborate style has ruled spaces for the lettering on the back, library block, name or initials; author, title, filleting, bottom lettering or numbering, and a section for special notes. By the side, in columnar form, are printed the names of binding materials and forms of treatment, those required being underlined by the librarian. Some libraries adopt small forms upon which the style of binding or nature of other repairs is set out and the precise lettering indicated. Elsewhere slips of distinctive colours for binding, re-backing, recasing, or other repairs are in use. General or particular directions are appended as required. These are "tipped" into the books, and sometimes the binder is required to "tip" them in the covers of the volumes when they are returned.

As binders' sheets are completed they should be checked and signed, and the cost estimated. Branch librarians are expected to furnish this information to the central administrative department,

BOOKBINDING

for the extent of liabilities must be recorded as they are incurred, and the local regulations may require that the authority's finance officer should be seised of this information.

Checking off returns

When the books come back and the invoice is to hand the books should be arranged in order as invoiced, but if the leather of any binding is at all moist it will be well not to stand them "back up" for long, or the backs will have a tendency to sag and become unshapely. The volumes should be inspected as to material and workmanship, and also to see that the detailed instructions have been carried out, and that contract prices have been charged. Lettering and numbering are the most likely sources of error. As entries and books are found to correspond, the items in the binding book should be ticked in the "return" column with the date written into the first entry on each page. The invoice must also be ticked, and when the checking process is completed the long and cross tots must be examined, when the pages may be certified, and the invoice filed for preparation for payment.

It is possible that not all the volumes forwarded will be returned bound, for defects which had escaped detection at the library are sometimes discovered at the bindery. The library is almost invariably advised of deficiences thus disclosed, and contract forms provide that volumes which are in any way imperfect shall not be bound without the written instructions of the librarian. If pages are missing, publishers will sometimes supply the appropriate section at a nominal charge, or the library may retain imperfect copies of popular books in the hope that other imperfect copies may be completed therefrom. If a new copy has to be procured the discarded one should be registered in the withdrawal record, and the card for its replacement prepared and placed in the order file. The books themselves will require to be labelled afresh—unless this has been done by the binder—and if the local custom so prescribes the fact of binding must be entered in the accession register.

Some libraries make a special card-list of books withdrawn for repairs. Where that is done this file should be kept within the counter enclosure so that enquiries for missing books may be answered. A like purpose is served in libraries using the "book-card in tray" system of charging if the cards of books away for book repairs are stored in a binding-file behind a guide-card which records the date when sent and the binder to whom they were despatched. The contract provides for a time limit, and the date of the return of repaired books can thus be approximately declared.

Staff repairs to books

Although anything like a completely equipped bindery would usually be out of place in a library, there yet remains the constant necessity for executing minor repairs, and where accommodation is

BOOKBINDING

available a well-lighted and well-ventilated room or portion of a store should be set aside for this work. There is always book numbering to be done,[1] plates and leaves to be stuck in, dirt marks to be removed, maps to be mounted on linen, pamphlets to be affixed within provided (stock) covers, perhaps a little sewing or simple binding may be attempted —and certainly will if a working binder is employed; backs of books may be re-covered or re-lettered; cloth sides may be renewed, and volumes which have broken away from their (cased) covers may under certain circumstances be glued-up to prolong their life for awhile. Mr. Cockerell suggests that "leather-bound books with perished backs or broken joints can be re-backed with new leather covering the spine and slipped under the leather of the sides," and that battered and disreputable volumes which are not often in demand may have their original bindings covered with buckram. There is, he points out, a "range of American library buckrams that are nearly the colour of old calf bindings, and if the lettering is made to tone with the old volumes and there is some indication of the bands, re-covered volumes can take their place in sets without offence." The hint is worthy of consideration whether for home binderies or otherwise.

Whether torn pages are to be repaired or not is a matter for local choice. Some libraries encourage it in the interests of economy, but it cannot be denied that unless the work be skilfully done the

[1] For instructions, see pp. 54–9.

result will be somewhat unsightly. Perhaps the best way of doing it is to place a piece of clean paper underneath the torn page, and, after smoothing out any creases, to bring the frayed edges closely and accurately together. These should be touched with paste, either by the finger tip or by means of a camel-hair brush, and made true. A narrow strip of Japanese or other strong tissue-paper is then applied to both sides of the paper where torn, and it should neither be pasted nor rubbed over, but merely left to dry. When that stage is reached the unattached portion may be peeled off and a neat repair is achieved. Another way is to paste a strip of chiffon over the torn portion: in this case excess of paste and creases must be guarded against.

The removal of dirt and stain from pages will be governed by the nature of the paper and the character of the stains, and bad cases should not be attempted by library assistants. Soft rubber is best for pencil marks, and it must be lightly used. Normal dirt is more or less removable by rubbing stale bread with a circular motion over the page, but unless carefully done creases or tears will result. Stains are more difficult to dislodge since the correct treatment calls for the immersion of the pages in a bath of warm water to which a little powdered alum is added. The affected parts should be painted with this solution, well rinsed, and left to dry. Some grease stains may be cleared by covering them with blotting paper and pressing a hot iron over them, followed by washing with petrol, benzine, or ether, but these substances are dangerous because of their extreme inflammability, and should on no account be used where there are open fires or naked lights. Finger-marks and some grease stains may be removed by washing with a scalding-hot solution of white soap or soapflakes, a soft brush being used for the operation; or, alternatively, by rubbing white soap into the stained surface and allowing it to remain for half an hour before washing it off. If this is ineffective a light brushing of chlorine water, or benzine, should be tried, followed, of course, by washing-off. Inkstains may be removed by the application of a weak solution of chlorine followed by the application of water to which a modicum of hydrochloric acid has been added. A strong solution of permanganate of potash will remove inkstains and fox-marks, but it is necessary to leave the paper in the liquid until the page assumes a dark brown colour, when it must be well washed in water to which a little sulphuric acid has been added, but a third bath of hyposulphate of soda will be required as a corrective to any remaining acid.

Chemical treatment obviously demands exactitude, and liquid bleaching processes are expert work. For this reason "dry cleaning" is perhaps as much as most libraries will care to undertake. Books badly marked may be "scrapped," or, if too valuable to be thrown away, they should be sent to the professional bookbinder for treatment.

Inserting sections which have broken loose is a binder's task necessitating sewing plant and technical skill, but loose leaves may be "tipped" in by pasting the extreme margins of their inner edges, and neatly and truly inserting them in position, or by using a narrow strip of thin linen folded as a guard. The latter is the superior way for maps, plates, or thick papers. The plate or page is pasted for about an eighth of an inch and affixed to one side of this guard, the other side of which is pasted to the adjoining leaf. It has to be neatly done, and the paste must not be too thin. Missing pages may be reproduced by the photostat process if desired. No dark room or previous knowledge of photography is required for this operation, but the cost of the apparatus may in many cases be a difficulty. Some of the larger libraries, such as Birmingham, will under certain conditions undertake to make these reproductions of pages, manuscripts, or maps for libraries at a nominal cost.

SELECTED REFERENCES

AMERICAN LIBRARY ASSN. Care and Binding of Books and Magazines. 1928.
BRITISH MUSEUM. Binding Preservatives. (In *Lib. Assn. Record*, n.s., v, p. 27, and vi, pp. 46–7.)
Bookcraft: the Time-tested Method of Library Book Repairing. 1926. (A pamphlet. Agents, Woolston Book Co.)
COCKERELL (D.). Binding for Libraries. (In *A Primer of Librarianship*, ch. xix.) 1931.
—— Bookbinding and the Care of Books. 1901.
—— Bookbinding as a School Subject.
—— Some Notes on Modern Bookbinding. 1929.

BOOKBINDING

Coutts (H. T.) and Stephen (G. A.). Manual of Library Bookbinding. 1911.
Hewitt (Bates). Bookbinding for Schools. 1927.
Library Assn. Book Construction: chapters in Paper, Binding, and Leather for Bookbinding. 1931.
—— Report on the Durability of Paper. 1930.
—— Small Municipal Libraries. 1931. (Ch. x—Book repairing.)
Peacock (V. M.). School and Club Libraries. 1920. (Ch. vii—Preservation of books, and binding.)
Philip (A. J.). Business of Bookbinding. 1912.
Vaughan (A. J.). Modern Bookbinding. 1929.
Warner (J.). Modern Bookbinding Leathers. (In *Lib. Assn. Record*, n.s., vii, 1929, pp. 153–64.)

CHAPTER XVI

FINANCE, COMMITTEE WORK, AND OFFICE ROUTINE

Library committees are so rarely authorities for the payment of accounts that exceptions from the rule may be regarded as negligible. It follows that the official book-keeping is performed by the finance officer of the superior authority, whether that be a local council or a board; but, nevertheless, there is a fair amount of book-keeping to be done in libraries. The petty cash accounts, for example, fall well within the scope of library routine, as also do the checking of bills and certifying of accounts before they can be submitted for payment. Then, too, it is found to be desirable almost to the point of necessity that each library shall maintain an adequate record of liabilities and payments in order that expenditure recommendations may be kept within the limits of the estimates as approved for the official financial year.

ANNUAL ESTIMATES

In municipal circles the financial year commences on 1st of April and terminates on the following 31st of March, and the local rate is based upon the estimates of the various committees as they are finally approved. These departmental estimates have to be prepared well in advance of March. Usually

FINANCE AND COMMITTEE WORK

they are roughed out early in January, when the librarian is furnished by the treasurer with a statement of expenditure since the commencement of the official year and is requested to specify, in lump sums, under the various numbered votes, his estimates of expenditure for the remaining quarter. He will also be provided with a statement of income received, and will be expected to indicate the amounts likely to be obtained from fines, sales, and other similar sources. At the same time he will be asked to suggest amounts to be included in the estimates of income and expenditure for the ensuing financial year. The finance department will supply such items as loan charges, insurances, and other amounts of which he has the requisite information, and the librarian will propose for each separate vote such amounts as he is prepared to submit for the consideration of his committee. These individual votes will probably be divided into groups for: (*a*) buildings, repairs, and maintenance; (*b*) cleaning, heating, lighting, and water; (*c*) insurances; (*d*) salaries and wages; (*e*) books; (*f*) papers and magazines; (*g*) bookbinding and repairs; (*h*) printing, stationery, and advertising; (*i*) loan charges—principal and interest; (*j*) general fund establishment charges, and (*k*) postages, telephones, and miscellaneous. To these normal library items must be added special features, if any, *e.g.* exhibitions or museum charges. On the income side will be the estimates of receipts from fines, sales of catalogues, periodicals, and waste paper, and amounts expected to be derived from penalties for lost or damaged books. Sources of income from bequests, etc., will be dealt with by the treasurer.

Of the foregoing items those marked c, d, i, and j will be left for treatment by the finance department, but the other details must be filled in by the librarian, for he alone can supply them. The figures for the previous year may be taken as the main guide, subject to such special factors as may call for attention, and it will be essential that the librarian has at hand a trustworthy record of liabilities incurred or to be incurred during the period under consideration, or it will be impossible for him to estimate with any degree of accuracy what the expenditure is likely to be. When by reference to this record he has ascertained the extent of the commitments, and has carried into the schedule such further expenditures as he is prepared to defend in committee, the treasurer may wish to go over the figures with him, for that officer will have to pilot the business through the council's finance committee, and it is necessary that he should be seised of all the facts and considerations.

All this is, of course, administrative work, but it cannot be accomplished without the aid of routine book-keeping, and it is therefore necessary that records of expenditure be scrupulously maintained, and that all commitments be registered as they are sanctioned, so that the available balance is always known. Some libraries reduce this book-keeping to an almost invisible minimum, and refer to the

FINANCE AND COMMITTEE WORK

borough treasurer whenever the state of any financial vote is in question, but it is sometimes difficult to obtain the desired information immediately, and it may be urgently needed at short notice. The records should be kept under the headings of the respective votes progressively as the liability is incurred, or as the accounts are finally passed for payment, and if this be done the financial position is always ascertainable at the library.

Orders and Order Records

Many authorities insist upon a uniform system of ordering for all their departments, and for this purpose they provide oblong books with perforated page-sections from which parts are detached as they are filled up. The outermost portion takes the form of a trader's official invoice (generally used for statements of accounts when the entries are numerous); the middle section is an advice note which is forwarded to the treasurer when any order is issued, informing him that liability has been incurred to the extent indicated for goods to be supplied, or work done, by the firm mentioned, and that the amount is to be charged to the maintenance vote as specified. This procedure enables the treasurer's department to keep a record of outstanding liabilities. The remaining portion, which is bound into the covers of the book, is the library register of commitments. Each page (and each section of every page) is numbered, and the section retained in the book preserves the name of the supplier, the details of the order—in bulk when the details are extensive, but set out in full when possible—with the contract number if there be one, and the date and number of the order. Each section is signed by the librarian, the two first-mentioned parts are dispatched, and the third section remains as a record. As the order is filled the facts are recorded thereon, and the date when the account, duly checked and certified, was forwarded to the treasurer is stamped in, showing that the transaction has been cleared.

Under this system orders are recorded promiscuously as they are issued, and the pages not marked as cleared show outstanding items; but something more scientifically arranged is desirable if classified expenditure is to be registered as a sort of financial thermometer. A method often adopted is to record expenditures by gross amounts only upon a loose-leaf schedule ruled in twelve monthly columns, with an additional column in which the approved financial vote for the various categories is set out. It is part of the staff routine to see that these figures are correctly recorded, and thus the state of each vote is easily discoverable as the year progresses. Subject to local variations this system of recording payments is commonly met with in municipal libraries, and with little adaptation for the inclusion of special fund accounts it may serve equally well for others. The chief consideration here is to have the entries promptly, completely, and accurately made.

No accounts will be accepted by any financial

FINANCE AND COMMITTEE WORK

officer unless they are checked and certified in accordance with the local official practice. Usually all items have to be ticked to denote receipt, long and cross tots are similarly marked, the discount is deducted, the number of the contract (if any) entered for reference, the date and amount of the authorized expenditure are briefly recorded, and, finally, the librarian signs his name upon each statement of account by way of certifying correctness in every respect. Not until this has been done should accounts be forwarded to the treasurer who, on his part, will see the bills through all the remaining stages and will retain them when receipted.

PETTY CASH EXPENDITURE

The almost universal practice is for the treasurer to deposit a certain amount with the librarian by way of imprest, and to forward from time to time sums corresponding with disbursements to maintain that deposit at its original amount. As petty cash payments are made proper receipts must be obtained, for these will be required in the first instance by the treasurer, then by the committee (who may, however, be satisfied by the submission of the petty cash book certified by the librarian and the treasurer), and ultimately by the auditor. Each receipt must be posted up in the petty cash book, and month by month or quarter by quarter the book will be balanced up and the imprest adjusted. Branch petty cash books, checked and certified by the branch librarian, are forwarded, with the necessary receipts, to the central library at stated intervals. There they are checked and entered into the general petty cash book, and before these books are returned to their libraries they are usually laid before the committee so that opportunity occurs for personal examination.

PETTY CASH RECEIPTS

Fines, reserved-book cards, sales of magazines and periodicals, penalties for lost or damaged books, sales of catalogues and other publications, and miscellaneous sources, will in every case entail some form of official receipt being given, unless some kind of registering cash till, as approved by the auditor, supersedes voucher receipts for such sums as are paid at the library. The general custom is to have books of numbered vouchers for fines of each varying amount,[1] and for catalogues and other publications, and for these to be supplemented by counterfoil books with pages numbered in duplicate so that a carbon copy may be preserved therein for each amount received where the ordinary vouchers do not apply. These books are supplied by the treasurer, who alone has authority to have them printed; and, since each voucher represents money for which the library becomes responsible, they require careful handling and preservation. As amounts are received a numbered receipt is torn off from the perforated page and given to the payer, or a written receipt made out for special cases. Not

[1] Numbered roll-tickets are sometimes used.

FINANCE AND COMMITTEE WORK

only is each voucher consecutively numbered, but the margin of each page is also numbered, and thus it is easy to record there the value of the receipts removed from day to day. These amounts are then entered daily in an analytical register, the total being shown in the final column, and at the end of the month the register reveals the total amount received from the different sources. These registers vary in detail, but in every instance it is necessary to check the receipt books with the cash in the till; to mark off in the margins the number of the vouchers parted with during the day; to post up the figures in the receipt book, and to hand over the money to the officer appointed for that purpose. The sooner these takings are locked up in the safe the better. At intervals they will be remitted to the treasurer, who will forward a receipt for them. At the end of the month these intermediate receipts will be returned to him, together with any balance of cash, and the monthly statement set out in gross or detail, when the amounts will be credited to the library account. A receipt for the month's total should be received from the treasurer, and in due course a member of his staff will audit these accounts, examining the voucher books, checking the correctness of the entries in the cash books, and signing the book when all is found to be correct. At the annual audit, which is conducted by the government (or by a locally elected) auditor, all the receipt books and vouchers will be required at the town hall or other central administrative office, and as they may be absent for a day or two it will be requisite to take out such supply of vouchers as may be deemed requisite for current use. A note should be kept of these extractions, and unused receipts should be restored to the appropriate books immediately upon their return. Where branch libraries exist each one has its own supply of receipts; each maintains its own registers, and the summaries of each are carried into the general register at the central library for aggregating purposes.

Postage accounts

Supplies of postage stamps are obtained by requisition from the treasurer, and as they are received their value should be entered in the general post book in ledger form. As branches are supplied the values should be entered up against them. The central library and each branch will each require its own detailed post book in which the names of addressees and the cost of their respective letters are recorded under date. Some libraries require that the person actually posting letters shall initial the entry, and occasionally the time of posting is added. At such times as the books are made up they are sent to the central administrative department where they are checked and initialled, and the totals are carried into the general post book which, like ordinary petty cash books, are counterchecked by the finance officer before submission to the committee. All these books will be required for inspection by the auditor.

FINANCE AND COMMITTEE WORK

COMMITTEE WORK

Much of the routine work of preparing material for committee use has already been described, *e.g.* the submission of lists of books, accounts, statistical returns, etc. What remains to be explained is chiefly the method of procedure in committee. Occasionally a librarian is also the official clerk to the committee, but almost invariably the town clerk or the college secretary occupies that position, and he, or his representative, submits the business and records the minutes.

From time to time the librarian will have placed in his committee file notes of matters for inclusion in the agenda, both as individual items and for admission into his general monthly report. There will also be matters, such as certain contracts, the revision of supply of periodicals, financial estimates, and also the reconsideration of staff salaries, which are considered yearly in many libraries. These items should be placed behind date-guides in the committee file, or registered in the office diary or in any other way which will prevent omission by inadvertence at the proper time. In addition there will, of course, be the items which are common to all ordinary meetings—accounts, sundry requirements to be sanctioned, the librarian's monthly (or quarterly) report, and correspondence. Some time sufficiently in advance of the date of the meeting to allow for the preparation and circulation of the agenda the librarian will forward to the clerk particulars of such items as he desires to be included therein. The clerk may have other matters to add, and should such business in any way affect the librarian he is duly advised.

Agendas take various forms, and the arrangement of their items is sometimes regulated by the instruction of the local council. Some committees have considerable executive powers and report their decisions as things done; others have to make recommendations before their decisions can be effective. A fairly common form of agenda for a library committee may assume something like the following:

> Minutes of the previous meeting.
> Report of the Finance Sub-Committee.
> Report of the Book Sub-Committee.
> Librarian's monthly report.
> Special matters, separately set out, as occasion requires.
> List of sundry requirements.
> Correspondence.

The first item is a formal matter in which the librarian is not perhaps directly concerned. The report of the finance sub-committee will include the accounts submitted for approval, and a list of them is submitted by the treasurer. At the meeting of the sub-committee the accounts and petty cash and post books are placed upon the table for examination, sometimes half an hour prior to the meeting, for the detailed investigation of members; at the full committee the process may be repeated, but usually the findings of sub-committees are largely relied

FINANCE AND COMMITTEE WORK

upon. The proposal that the accounts be approved for payment must, however, be formally put and carried at each meeting, and thenceforth all that the librarian needs to do is to examine the printed list as submitted to the council on the off-chance of finding a misprint or other error—an unlikely contingency. The treasurer will submit the accounts as approved to the finance committee of the council and subsequently to the council itself, and the librarian will be supplied with a copy of the list of cheques for office use. This must be filed for reference. The report of the book sub-committee will embody the recommendations respecting supplies of books and periodicals, and may have to be treated in the same fashion as accounts, but most committees obtain powers to expend the year's book vote at discretion, subject to report by way of information only. The monthly report is a sort of "omnibus bill" in which the librarian inserts such details of information or recommendation as he thinks fit. Constant items are statistics of book issues in such detail as the committee may desire, and a succinct statement of petty cash receipt from fines, etc. Generally speaking only gross figures are required, possibly department by department, with the figures for the corresponding month in the previous year. Brief reports on lectures, and concise notes of any occurrences of especial interest are included, and the tactful librarian will find this report an excellent vehicle for suggesting developments or changes for the extension or improvement

A MANUAL OF LIBRARY ROUTINE

of the library service. The list of sundry requirements will embrace such items as fuel, binding, fittings, etc., not sufficiently important to appear upon the agenda for individual consideration and report. They are entered in a register under the date of meeting, and the contract number (if any) is recorded, with the actual or estimated cost in each case, and the total is carried out for report. The items may be read out *seriatim* or in groups, and the summary total will be "put" from the chair and voted upon. When the accounts are rendered it will be necessary to mark upon them the date of the committee's approval, and possibly the authorized amount, of these expenditures.

Although the official minutes will be taken by the clerk, the librarian will find it desirable to make for his own use a record of all decisions. For this purpose the agenda items may be copied into a register in which spaces are reserved for notes, or a copy of the agenda is cut up and the slips pasted in similarly spaced. The librarian's monthly report will have its items numbered, and these will be spaced out in the register. As the business proceeds the librarian (or his attendant clerk) will record all decisions and may make notes or take instructions respecting matters for which further information is desired, or are referred to sub-committees for consideration and report. At the close of the meeting these decisions should be compared with the official notes of the committee clerk to ensure accuracy, and before the report of the committee

FINANCE AND COMMITTEE WORK

is printed for submission to the council a draft will be sent to the librarian for his confirmation. Such decisions as are immediately effective will be carried out under the direction of the librarian without delay, but matters requiring the sanction of a council vote must be deferred until that approval has been given. If the librarian attends at council meetings he can mark his copy of the agenda in conformity with these final decisions; if not, he must await the receipt of the printed copy of the council minutes, which may be weeks later, or he can procure information from the town clerk. The manner of giving effect to official decisions has already been indicated.

OFFICE ROUTINE

The detail work connected with the financial matters just described forms part of the ordinary routine of the office staff. Where no such special staff exists it must be allocated to other assistants, and the same may be said of the various returns which are received at weekly or monthly intervals from each separate department of the library system for tabulation in separate or aggegated form. These statistics will be wanted for committee meetings and for the annual reports, and if printed schedules are not provided for them sheets must be ruled as required for use or cyclostyled for general supply. Branch libraries are usually provided with blank forms upon which they fill in their statistical returns which are forwarded to the central library at stipulated times; the central departmental books are always at hand, so that return forms are not required for them. The range thus covered is dependent upon the local administrative system, and sometimes it is very extensive. Separate schedules for petty cash receipts and expenditures, for issues of books and borrowers' tickets, attendances in reading-rooms and at lectures, may be required in differing degrees of fullness, filled up and certified by branch librarians, will have to be dealt with recurrently, and the results entered in master-records for use whenever required.

PREPARATION OF ACCOUNTS

To the central office will come all invoices, branch and central, which have been checked off and certified by the assistants who received deliveries. If goods are supplied under contract, the register of contracts must be referred to for verification of prices: in any case all charging out must be counter-checked; probably the date of authorization of expenditure and the number of the vote to which particular accounts are to be charged will now be carried in. When thus prepared the bills will be ready for examination and signature by the librarian, and so far as the library staff is concerned they will then only need to be remitted, with or without an inventory list, to the finance officer. Pending the completion of these processes the bills must be filed, and care must be exercised to prevent any from going astray. If errors are discovered the

FINANCE AND COMMITTEE WORK

bills are returned to their senders for correction. Where annual subscriptions are paid the date when they are due should be anticipated and a card sent to the publishing or other society asking for the account to be rendered in time for submission to the next meeting of the committee. Accounts passed forward for payment will be registered under their respective votes, as explained in the first section of this chapter.

Correspondence

Correspondence occupies a quite appreciable portion of time in an active library, both as to letters going out and letters coming in, and it must be dealt with methodically, or confusion and complaints will ensue. In writing or dictating letters brevity and clarity of expression should be cultivated. Nothing is gained, and trouble frequently arises from expansiveness, while ambiguous phrases are likely to lead to misapprehension, trouble, and delay. If the librarian has a shorthand clerk or secretary, much of the routine of this work will devolve upon her, but, failing any such officer, it will have to be performed either by the librarian personally or by a member of the ordinary staff, and the fewer who engage in it the less risk of confusion there will be. Shorthand is a desirable accomplishment in more than one department of library work; it is extremely useful, for example, in committee, where it is often necessary to take notes of matters under discussion. If the librarian

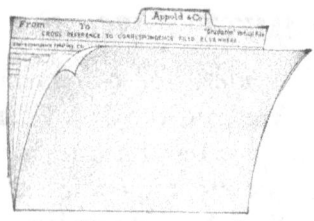
INDIVIDUAL FOLDER

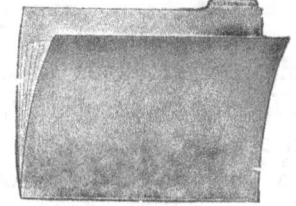
MISCELLANEOUS FOLDER

By courtesy of Libraco, Ltd.]

A VERTICAL FILE

happens to be also clerk to the committee (or to sub-committees, as more generally occurs), his secretary will be required to record these points so as to leave the librarian free to attend to the conduct of business.

LETTERS GOING OUT

Letters are dictated in detail or in substance according to their importance and the qualifications of the clerk, who should carefully read over the notes and have any obscure details cleared up before attempting to write them out. When completed they should be perused for literal or other errors, and only clean drafts should be handed in for signature. Omissions and wrong letters are the most common faults in typewriting, and figures should always be closely checked. If mistakes are found, it will be better to re-write a letter than to submit a corrected one. In every case a carbon copy should be made when letters are typed, for filing purposes; but should there be no typewriter, copying ink must be used, for in such case the letter will have to go through the old-fashioned copying press, where a thick ink and a nice precision in damping and pressing will be requisite to obtain a satisfactory result. If the ink is too faint or the pressure insufficient, the copy will be illegible; if, on the other hand, the ink is too thick or not sufficiently dried in, or the page is charged with too much moisture, there will be a blurred and more or less undecipherable impression in the book. Several

FINANCE AND COMMITTEE WORK

copies of a letter may be carboned by the single operation of typing, and in this instance the script will always be legible.

Somewhere near the top left-hand corner of the sheet the outgoing and incoming reference symbol and number should be given, and frequently the words "Our ref." and "Your ref." are printed in readiness to receive these clues. The library will probably allocate a tracing number for each correspondent, and this number will be indexed to render such reference easy. That is the number which, with any qualifying symbol, denotes a particular file or other arrangement, and is to be entered immediately after the words "Our ref." The correspondent may have a similar device, and, if so, his symbol and number should be carried into the line marked "Your ref." If this be done, these numbers serve as guides for filing, and all uncertainty as to the whereabouts of letters is avoided. Either at the head or foot of each sheet the name and address of the person to whom it is to be sent will be given on the left-hand side. If a copying press is used, the better position will be near the top, where the details will readily be seen; but if carbon copies are filed, it is immaterial where these particulars appear. Centred immediately above the first line of the text the subject of each letter should be tersely stated, and it may be that the initials of the typist or writer, and those of the person who dictated the letter, are also required to be given to trace responsibility. When all these details have been attended to, and the letters have been examined and found correct, they should be taken to the librarian in a basket marked "For post" for his perusal and signature. This done, they will be ready for stamping and entering in the post book. In many offices revolving detachable trays are clamped by the base of a central column to the table, and the groups of letters in any stage are thus easily distinguished.

All that remains to be done is to deal with the carbon copies of dispatched letters. The library's reference number is recorded on the letter received, and the reply being similarly numbered the two are filed together.

INCOMING LETTERS

The opening and sorting of letters, other than those marked personal, is usually done in large libraries by the librarian's clerk or secretary, but in smaller libraries the librarian may do it himself, and he personally attends to the correspondence. Incoming letters should be stamped with the date of receipt as soon as they are opened, and it may be advisable to make sure that whenever a letter is withdrawn from its envelope that nothing of a supplementary nature remains. They are next sorted into groups. Some will be requests for the renewal of books, or will relate to matters of routine performance for which the staff will require no instructions: they will be deposited in table-baskets or trays and removed to the departments concerned. Communications demanding instructions will form

FINANCE AND COMMITTEE WORK

another group and will be placed in a receptacle suitably labelled. The librarian will probably divide his mail into further groups: one for letters intended to receive immediate reply, another for those passed on to different departments, and a third for such as require consideration. These last should be acknowledged immediately by postcard stating that the matter will receive attention, and that a reply will be forwarded at the earliest opportunity; they will then probably be kept in the librarian's office file and will be dealt with in due course. The second section will be marked with the name of the officer or department concerned, and will be sent, with or without brief instructions, for treatment, while the others will be ready for treatment forthwith. The clerk will every morning take down replies or fresh letters at the dictation of the librarian, and may have to repeat the procedure with heads of departments to whom matters have been referred. When letters have been written they should be checked, then taken for the librarian's perusal and signature, stamped and entered in the post-book, and the carboned duplicate copy will be filed in the position indicated by its reference number. In small libraries the librarian may have to undertake much or all of these duties himself, but the general principles will nevertheless be followed.

LETTER FILING

Almost universally now letters, and sometimes cognate material, are preserved in vertical files consisting of metal drawers running on roller-bearings and nested in a metal frame. Each drawer is provided with a liberal supply of stout folders with tabs upon which the names of correspondents (or subjects) are written boldly in block letters, the surname coming first. Each correspondent, save casual ones, is allotted a tracing number, and this number may appear upon the tab either in addition to, or in substitution for, the writer's name. This is the number marked upon outgoing letters for filing and identity purposes, and the duplicates of letters dispatched, and such letters coming in as carry these numbers are preserved in their especial folder. Whether the order of arrangement shall be merely by these clue numbers, by names, or by subjects, is a matter of local determination; but practice suggests that while it is generally convenient to isolate each correspondent's letters in its own special folder, there may be occasions when it will be more convenient to group together communications relating to particular topics. If uniformity of treatment is preferred, subject-tracing can be made easy by a subject-index. Printed on the inside of each folder are lines and headings for cross-references, and correlated matters are thus readily traceable. The folders, being separate entities, can be manipulated as choice dictates; they enjoy all the mobility of cards and are capable of indefinite expansion.

Letters from occasional correspondents may safely be placed in a collective folder, labelled "miscel-

FINANCE AND COMMITTEE WORK

laneous," and preserved at the end of the file. If they are arranged according to the names of their writers, no difficulty will arise in finding them, for the number of the folder supplies all other necessary guidance. Should correspondence develop, the letters concerned can easily be provided with a distinctively numbered folder reserved for any individual correspondent.

When any folder is withdrawn for use an indicating sheet or card should attest the fact. This should be dated and initialled, and the assistant who removes material must be held responsible for its orderly replacement. Similarly, whenever an item is extracted from a folder which remains in the file, an indicating clue, marked in like fashion, should be left in the vacant place. Failure to restore folders or items to their correct positions is a certain way to trouble. File indexes are usually prepared in card form, and they are regarded as part of the office equipment.

Although the drawers of an average vertical file are capacious and a cabinet will accommodate an enormous quantity of letters, it will be necessary to go over it at intervals and thin out all material possessing no further value. Probably the librarian will like to undertake this task personally, but otherwise a responsible assistant will be required for its discharge. A small library may find that one drawer suffices for all current purposes, and it may relegate obsolescent papers to a lower drawer. Larger institutions sometimes have a battery of cabinets—

one for the current year, and others for letters which may perhaps retain business interest; but in any event a time for weeding-out will come. Only those papers which are clearly of no remaining value should be destroyed, the others should be classified by correspondents or subjects, as local custom may prescribe, and placed in labelled cardboard boxes for preservation in the office. After seven years these may be emptied and the letters destroyed, unless any be adjudged to possess historical interest to justify retention in the reference department.

Catalogues and other lists and samples, which are received in quantities at every library, are usually of temporary interest alone. The more important ones, including publishers' lists of announcements, may, after inspection, be preserved in labelled boxes, and samples should aways be dated and a reference should be given to relative quotations or communications, unless these are all filed together. Here again congestion will demand recurrent elimination, for much of this material soon becomes superseded, and the latest list is all that need be kept.

RECURRENT OFFICE ROUTINE

Throughout the year statistical returns of many kinds will be under compilation. Tables showing accessions to stock, the number of borrowers, and the issues of books, will be required for submission at committee meetings and for the annual report. The weekly or monthly returns will be made up

FINANCE AND COMMITTEE WORK

or checked at the central office, and the petty cash books are here examined and posted into the general books. Here official orders are issued for books and other supplies or works in accordance with the instructions of the librarian, and the book-order-file is housed in the office, where the checking-off is usually done. Bills are examined and statements of account checked before reaching the librarian for certification, and supplies of stationery, electric lamps, and general stores are ordered and booked out to the departments drawing upon them.

As these supplies are received they are checked off and inventoried in registers, the receipts being entered on one page and outgoings on the other. Small goods will probably be stored in locked cupboards, properly arranged by kind, and although the registers should accurately reflect the state of the stock at any time, it will be found prudent to maintain a limited reserve stock of all supplies which may suffice for current use in case of oversight in ordering or of delay in delivery. Books containing voucher receipts are often procurable only through the finance officer, but where librarians are vested with authority to order them direct from the printer, they must be most carefully guarded, since the vouchers represent cash for which the library is responsible.

Manifolding work

The introduction of rotary cyclostyles and similar manifolding machines has enabled libraries to effect a great economy in the printing bill, for with a typewriter and a cyclostyle copies of circulars, lists of books, agendas, reports, etc., may be struck off quickly and at little cost. The matter for reproduction is first typed upon a waxed sheet, which takes the place of the ordinary sheet of writing paper, and the stencilled sheet is then transferred to the cyclostyle. Great care must be taken that it is truly fastened into its frame on that machine, and that the waxed surface of the typed sheet is not cracked during the operation, or the crack will call for expert doctoring or demand an entirely fresh sheet. Apart from this the process is simplicity itself, the only requirements being that the rollers are properly inked and the register set to show the number of copies to be run off. If too much ink has been applied, the fault can be corrected by taking copies on waste paper until the desired effect is obtained; if the impression is not black enough, more ink should be added, but this should be done carefully, or the opposite effect will result. The first copies produced may not appear encouraging, but a few trial impressions will work the ink through the stencilled sheet satisfactorily, and with careful handling any number of copies can be produced.

FINANCE AND COMMITTEE WORK

SELECTED REFERENCES

BOSTWICK (A. E.). Administration of a Pub. Library. (A.L.A. Manual, 12.) 1928.
—— The American Public Library. 4th edn. 1929. (Ch. xxxi—Statistics, reports, etc.)
BROWN (J. D.). Manual of Lib. Economy. 4th edn. 1931. (Div. i—Committees, finance, statistics, reports, etc.)
DRURY (F. K. W.). Order Work for Libraries. 1930. (Ch. x—Office management; xi—Statistics and reports.)
FLEXNER (J. M.). Circulation Work in Public Libraries. 1927. (Ch. xii—Statistics and reports.)
LEFFINGWELL (W. H.). Office Management: Principles and Practice. 1925.
LIBRARY ASSN. Small Municipal Libraries. 1931. (Ch. ix—Records and statistics; xii—Model budgets.)
MITCHELL (J. M.). Library Budgets. (In *Lib. Assn. Record*, 3rd ser., ii, 1932, pp. 297–304.)
NOWELL (C.). Committee Work and Office Routine. (In *Primer of Librarianship*, ch. x.) 1931.
Public Libraries Committee Report. (Cmd. 2868.) 1927. (Pp. 49–57, and Appendix A.)
SAYERS (W. C. BERWICK). The Library Committee: its Character and Work. (Lib. Assts. Assn., ser. vi.) 1914.
—— Library Finance. (In *Lib. Assn. Record*, xix, 1917, pp. 17–29.)
WARREN (I.). Filing and Indexing with Business Procedure. 1924.
WILLCOCKS (W. J.). What should an Annual Report Contain? (In *Lib. Assn. Record*, 3rd ser., 11, 1932, pp. 297–304.)

CHAPTER XVII

SOME EXTENSION ACTIVITIES

LECTURES. PUBLICITY. BROADCASTING CO-OPERATIVE WORK. HOSPITAL LIBRARIES. BOOKS FOR THE BLIND

LECTURES

Library lectures, both for adults and juveniles, are a common feature of modern library work, but since the Acts make no provision for expenditure in connection therewith, the legality of defraying such charges out of rate money is not quite clear. Instances have been known where the Ministry of Health (or, previously, the Local Government Board) has sanctioned the raising of a loan for the erection of a library lecture hall, and its own official auditor had disallowed expenditure out of the library rate for its use when built! Elective auditors are rarely so stringent, but the law on this subject loudly calls for clarification. Some municipalities have solved the problem by operating under empowering local Acts; others attempt to do so by taking retiring collections at the doors, or by raising precarious voluntary contributions; and Mr. Hewitt states[1] that elsewhere this expenditure is met out of payments "received by way of fines or by the sale of books, etc." Charging for admission is dangerous, because it might bring the library into full rating. Libraries in the Irish Free State have plenary powers

[1] *A Summary of Public Library Law* (Library Assn., 1932), p. 31.

SOME EXTENSION ACTIVITIES

under the (Irish) Local Government Act, 1925, but until the recommendations of the Public Libraries Committee (1927)[1] have the force of law the problem will remain uncertain and difficult.

It happens, therefore, that comparatively few libraries are in a position to pay fees to lecturers, and that volunteers have usually to be procured. Many of them are excellent, but some are more willing than able, and one of the primary difficulties of a programme organizer is that of selection and exclusion. An interchange of confidential notes between libraries materially assists in this direction, and by taking advantage of the good offices of suitable societies,[2] organizations, and individual lecturers, local and other, a satisfactory list of lecturers may be obtained. It should be reviewed from year to year. Travelling expenses are paid where necessary, but if these are inflated the local auditor may object.

Lantern illustrations will often be required, especially when lectures are given to children. Fortunately it is not difficult to operate an ordinary lantern, and with a little practice this can be done by any member of the staff. Slides are generally brought by the lecturer, but if not they may be hired from firms which issue catalogues and supply selected slides at a fixed rate or up to a fixed maximum for an annual subscription. At some libraries

[1] *Public Libraries Committee Report* (Cmd. 2868), 1927, pp. 74–5.
[2] For a list of these agencies, see McColvin's *Library Extension Work*, pp. 91–5.

an assistant with a knowledge of photography makes slides, but unless this is done from the lecturer's own material, copyright trouble may arise unless permission to reproduce pictures is obtained. The epidiascope does away with the necessity of making slides, and gives an excellent projection directly from the objects to be illustrated, with the additional advantage of reproducing the natural colours of the original.

A cinematograph is always a popular adjunct to lectures, but if inflammable films are used (and some lecturers offer them), it will be necessary to comply most carefully with all the official conditions for the prevention of fire. The cinematograph must be confined within a fire-proof chamber, pails of sand must be at hand in readiness to extinguish flames there, and the instrument must be erected over a pit into which the apparatus is to be thrown if necessity arises. The local by-laws on the subject must be studied and all stipulations faithfully adhered to; oversight might well produce extremely serious trouble. Non-flam films are free of these severe conditions of use, but on the other hand the supply at present offers a limited choice of suitable subjects.

If lectures are provided for children in a building where steps have to be negotiated for access, it will be necessary to ensure the attendance of a sufficient number of adults to regulate the traffic, especially in the event of any panic. The conditions of the Children's Act should be studied in this respect.

SOME EXTENSION ACTIVITIES

Arrangements with lecturers should be made well in advance of the lecture season, and they should in each instance be confirmed before the programme is printed. The chief points for verification are date, title, the correct description of each lecturer, and whether the lecture is to be illustrated or not, and if so, how. The programme itself should be accompanied by a list of selected books relating to the subjects under notice. This will serve the double object of advertising the books—perhaps the chief justification of library lectures—and of securing the approval of any auditor if charged for as a list of books. A marked copy of the programme should, upon publication, be sent to each lecturer as an official reminder of his engagement, and a week or so before the lecture date a direct reminder should be sent, with instructions as to the best way of reaching the library unless the lecturer is a local resident. All lectures should be advertised by bills and posters displayed within and without the libraries, and at schools and other institutions by arrangement. Where possible, they should also be advertised in the ordinary way in the local papers, and reports of lectures should appear in the local press.

Courses of University Extension and similar lectures are delivered in many libraries, and where the latter are willing the choice of lecturer, subject, course fees, and advertising, together with financial liability, will be left to them. The two first items must be selected from the official list issued by the university; the latter are subject to mutual arrangement between the two authorities. No charge is exacted for heating, lighting, or attendance, but if advertising, printing, or other costs are incurred, it will be well to secure from the university a full indemnity in case of disallowance of such expenditure by the auditor. These lectures demand staff attendance, unless other arrangements are specially made. If there is a local University Extension Committee, it may undertake this responsibility. A lanternist may have to be provided; books for enrolled students will be supplied by the university or the library, or both, and will have to be issued, recorded, and their return secured. There will also be an examination at the end of each course, and the fees must be collected, entered up, and passed to the university together with a schedule of attendances. It will be seen that these courses entail a fair amount of labour, and before the hospitality of the library is extended to them all these factors should be worked out and the library responsibility fully ascertained.

Some libraries derive a considerable income from the letting of their lecture halls. Where this is done the booking engagements must be carefully recorded, and any special requirements should be noted at the time of booking. A special register may be required for this purpose, in which the date, time of the meeting, its nature, particular requirements, letting fee, and record of payment are entered. Where a library hall is let for revenue purposes, it almost

SOME EXTENSION ACTIVITIES

inevitably follows that the whole building will be brought into full rating.

PUBLICITY

No more than a business concern can a library afford to neglect the value of publicity, and the advertisement of its resources is undertaken in numerous ways. Journals or bulletins announcing recent acquisitions to stock, and supplemented by items of library news, are issued at regular intervals by many libraries. Lists of books on subjects of topical interest are drawn up and displayed from time to time, and some libraries attempt an almost daily list of books on some subject of particular interest in the newspapers. A similar object is achieved by an ever-changing display of books on matters engaging public attention, relating to library lectures, or of books recently published. All these methods involve the labour of selection, and, in the case of lists, of typing, and of multigraphing if intended for circulation among readers at the library or persons attending lectures. Outside educational and similar bodies will usually receive with gratitude cyclostyled lists of library books upon subjects in which they are interested, and Chambers of Commerce respond similarly to lists likely to interest their members. The local newspapers offer another and perhaps a wider publicity, and their co-operation should be assiduously cultivated. Many of these journals will readily insert library statistics, reports of lectures, lists of books recently added,

A MANUAL OF LIBRARY ROUTINE

details of gifts of value and notes which are likely to be of any interest to their readers. Some of them will "run off" any number of reprints of the lists of new books, at a nominal cost, for distribution in the library where the publication of a journal is financially impossible. Book and picture exhibitions are arranged at intervals, and whenever this is done the Press is usually willing to afford all reasonable publicity. Lists of books should be displayed or distributed in connection with these exhibits, possibly a special lecture may be arranged by way of inauguration, and descriptive handbooks may be published for sale. Local manufactures will always demand special library attention, not only by the provision of technical books, but also by the preparation of lists, revised from date to date, for display or distribution among the workers. Every local society should be cultivated in this way. Educational bureaux, supplied with prospectuses, handbills, and display matter; emigration and holiday bureaux, kept scrupulously up to date by fresh supplies from Government offices, railway, steamship, coach, and aeroplane companies, will always prove attractive to the public, but will require constant revision and care to ensure that obsolete material is not offered for use.

The list just given is by no means exclusive: every avenue of publicity should be explored and co-operative contact made with every possible agency. For this purpose the local directory may have to be studied and a record made of societies,

SOME EXTENSION ACTIVITIES

institutions, factories, etc. The library needs of each must be considered; fresh books must be obtained for them if necessary, personal acquaintance with their representatives should be made, and in every possible way their respective requirements should be satisfied. Finally, if a street-register of borrowers is maintained at the library it should be examined from time to time, and a circular letter descriptive of the activities of the library should be sent, with a form of application for membership, to those residents who are not already registered as borrowers.

BROADCASTING CO-OPERATIVE WORK

There can be no doubt that the series of educational talks offered by the British Broadcasting Corporation open out a new and profitable opportunity for library co-operation, and it is claimed that this service is best maintained by the establishment of reading circles within the library building. In his paper on *Broadcasting and Public Libraries* Mr. C. Nowell[1] ably describes how these groups of readers can be formed and the routine involved. Members may be recruited by announcements displayed in and about the library buildings or published in the library journal, or—perhaps more usefully—by securing the active support of local societies, which should be approached and invited to participate in the arrangement. A room for recurrent meetings and a good wireless set will be required,

[1] *Library Association Record*, new ser., viii (1930), pp. 81–92.

and "the B.B.C. engineers will advise regarding" the latter, and will "supply specifications of the most suitable sets, and instal and demonstrate the set, if required." Experience has shown that the success or failure of reading circles depends to a very large extent upon the suitability and enthusiasm of its leader. The day and hour of the meetings will depend upon the time when the chosen subject is broadcast, and the discussion should be suggestively but briefly opened by the leader. The library will find it beneficial to provide lists of appropriate books contained in the lending or reference departments, and may arrange for the issue of books to members either from a selection displayed in the room, or by inducing the members to enrol as library borrowers. For further particulars reference should be made to Mr. Nowell's article.

Where the establishment of reading circles within the library is not possible, the library can still assist in the formation and maintenance of circles elsewhere, and lists of books, or even displays of books, can be made, although in the latter event some security for return may have to be obtained. Failing any such service there yet remains opportunity for co-operation useful alike to the librarian, his readers, and the B.B.C., whose lists of talks are generously supplied to libraries. These brochures not only contain valuable outlines for study, but are accompanied by extremely useful lists of recommended books, drawn up jointly by the B.B.C., the various lecturers, and the Library Association. The lists

SOME EXTENSION ACTIVITIES

enable the librarian to prepare for coming demands and are useful bibliographies for other purposes. The programmes of talks should be publicly exhibited, for they engage and direct the attention of readers and promote the use of "worth-while" books, and develop the use of the educational side of the library.

Hospital libraries

Bibliotherapy, the use of books "to induce interest and cheerfulness in hospital and other patients, and possibly even their use to cure certain complaints," has been discussed by American hospital librarians and doctors, and there appears to be a wide acceptance of Sir B. Bruce-Porter's claim that "every hospital should have an adequate library and efficient distribution as part of its equipment." Permanent collections of books are, accordingly, now being established as part of the neuropsychiatric treatment of the sick, and the local stock of literature is reinforced by loans from the public library. Books so lent are, of course, kept absolutely apart from infected wards or cases, and they should be entered in a special register which may be something after the fashion of the system employed by county headquarters libraries when deposits are forwarded to local centres. If the hospitals are few in number, a book register may be found preferable. Particulars to be recorded embrace: (1) the name of the hospital to which they are sent; (2) a note of the duration of the loan; and (3) identity details of the books lent. It should be stipulated that any of the volumes must be returned at call if required by the library. The selection may be left to the librarian or may be made in conjunction with the hospital librarian, and, so far as fiction is concerned, morbid, and possibly tragic, works may be considered undesirable. Specially important books may be obtained from the National Central Library, in which case the transaction should be a matter between the hospital and that library. A list should accompany each loan delivery to serve as inventory and catalogue, and it should be made in duplicate so that a signed list may be filed at the library pending the return of the deposited books, when the library copy may be cancelled and returned, and the books checked off in the register and replaced into stock.

The hospital librarian is responsible for the receipt, circulation, and return of books so borrowed. In a more domestic way he may also purchase books from such funds as may be available, and it may also be part of his duty to solicit donations for this purpose, and to acknowledge gifts. Actual distribution is done in various ways. Nurses may choose and take books to bedridden patients, or selections may be displayed upon a "Watford" book-trolley which is paraded through the wards for the inspection of the readers. Convalescent patients may perhaps select their volumes from the library shelves, and in any case the librarian should always be ready to advise his borrowers, and for that purpose it will be necessary that she should herself be thoroughly

SOME EXTENSION ACTIVITIES

acquainted with the books, and should be competent to "prescribe" them according to the several necessities of the readers. In doubtful cases the assistance of the attendant nurse should be sought, and occasionally the doctor may have to be consulted. Where the circulation is small some simple method of sheet or ledger charging may serve, but where the issues are at all large the ordinary method of card charging will be more suitable. As an alternative to bulk loans particular books for individual patients should be available for issue to hospital patients upon the responsibility of the hospital librarian, through whom alone such applications should come.

BOOKS FOR THE BLIND

Another afflicted section of the community which systematically receives the benefits of library service consists of sightless readers for whom books printed in the embossed Braille or Moon types are provided. These volumes are expensive to purchase and extremely bulky to store, consisting of thick sheets of paper embossed upon one surface only. Few libraries, therefore, carry a permanent stock. An ever-changing supply is better obtained on loan by subscription from the National Library for the Blind, whose chief offices are in Great Smith Street, Westminster, S.W., or 5, St. John's Street, Manchester. Selection is governed by local demand; deposits should be registered as received, and issues are made in the ordinary way. A list of these special books should be kept within the staff enclosure for use in case of enquiries, and perhaps some blind reader will, as required, emboss a special card or other form of catalogue for the use of his fellow sufferers. Failing this, such a catalogue may be made by any Blind Institution to which the requisite details are sent. Under ordinary circumstances special collections are generally housed at the central library, but in this case the special disability of the readers makes it desirable that they should be put to as little inconvenience as possible. Their embossed books are accordingly supplied to some degree at the branch libraries, but in any case they should be enabled to obtain desired books from other libraries comprehended within the library system by means of a delivery system, and due record of these loans must be kept. Perhaps the best way of maintaining this record is for the lending library to book them to the issuing library, and for the latter to charge the books to the readers and make themselves responsible for their return.

In some towns the library makes a contribution to the local Institution for the Blind, and in return enjoys the right to refer readers there for supplies of books to read. Whichever plan be preferred, co-operation with such institutions is always worthy of consideration.

SOME EXTENSION ACTIVITIES

SELECTED REFERENCES

Lectures and Reading Circles

Baker (E. A.). The Public Library. 1924. (Lectures, pp. 100–14.)

Ballinger (Sir J.). Lectures and Extensions. (In *The Library*, x, 1909, pp. 188–200.)

Brown (J. D.). Manual of Library Economy. 4th edn. 1931. (Ch. xxxiv—The lecture-room.)

Gordon (R. J.). Library Lectures. (In *Lib. Assn. Record*, xvi, 1914, pp. 313–21.)

Harris (W. J.). Organization and Conduct of Reading Circles. (In *Lib. World*, xiii, pp. 289–94, and xvii, 69–72.)

Haxby (R.). History, Organization, and Educational Value of Municipal Library Lectures. (In *Lib. Assn. Record*, xiii, 1913, pp. 123–32.)

Jast (L. S.). A Note on Library Readings. (In *Lib. Assn. Record*, xviii, 1916, pp. 53–62.)

McColvin (L. R.). Library Extension Work and Publicity. 1927. (Chs. iii—Library lectures, and vi—Co-operation with societies and other organizations.)

Pomfret (J.). Reading Circles. (In *Lib. World*, xii, 1911, pp. 289–94.)

Rae (W. S. C.). Public Library Administration. 1913. (Lectures, reading circles, etc., pp. 89–92.)

Sayers (W. C. Berwick). Manual of Children's Libraries. 1932. (Chs. xiii to xviii—Children's lectures, story hours, readings, exhibitions, publicity, etc.)

Publicity

Bostwick (A. E.). The American Public Library. 4th edn. 1929.(Chs. xvii—The library as a producer of bulletins; xxvii—Publicity.)

Briscoe (W. A.). Library Advertising: Publicity Methods for Libraries. 1921.

CANNON (C. L.). Publicity for Small Libraries. (A.L.A. Manual, 31.) 1929.
FLEXNER (J. M.). Circulation Work in Public Libraries. 1927. (Ch. ix—Library aids and publicity.)
McCOLVIN (L. R.). Library Extension and Publicity. 1927. (Pt. iii—Direct publicity.)
WARD (G. O.). Publicity for Libraries. 1924.
WARNER (J.). Holiday Literature and Picture Exhibitions. (In *Lib. World*, xii, 1910, pp. 49–54.)
WHEELER (J. L.). The Library and the Community: increased Book Service through Library Publicity. 1924.

BROADCASTING CO-OPERATION

LIBRARY ASSN. Year Book. Vol. I. 1932. (Libraries and the B.B.C., pp. 187–8.)
NOWELL (C.). Broadcasting and Public Libraries. (In *Lib. Assn. Record*, new ser., viii, 1930, pp. 81–92.)

HOSPITAL LIBRARIES

BISHOP (W. J.). Hospital Libraries and Bibliotheraphy: a Bibliography. (In *Lib. Assn. Record*, 3rd ser., i, 1932, pp. 198–200, 231–2.)
GREEN (E.) and SCHWAB (S. I.). The Therapeutic Use of a Hospital Library. (In *The Hospital Soc. Serv. Quarterly*, 1919, pp. 147–57.)
JONES (E. K.). The Hospital Library. 1923.

BOOKS FOR THE BLIND

BOSTWICK (A. E.). The American Public Library. 4th edn. 1929. (Ch. xxiv—Libraries for the Blind.)
CHAMBERLAIN (M. C.). Library Work with the Blind. (A.L.A. Manual, 30.) 1930.
DRURY (F. K. W.). Book Selection. 1930. (Books for the Blind, pp. 41–4.)
ROEBUCK (G. E.). Public Library Service to the Blind. (In *Lib. Assn. Record*, xiii, 1911, pp. 455–60.)

APPENDIX

SOME EXAMINATION QUESTIONS[1]

A

The Library Association

B

University of London Diploma in Librarianship
(School of Librarianship)

Note.—The questions in these two groups are purposely varied so as to show without undue repetition the range and scope of library routine.

---

[1] *Reprinted by kind permission of the Library Association and of the University and the College, respectively. The "Year Book" of the Library Association contains all the questions set at its Examinations during the previous year, 5s. net (2s. 6d. to Members of the Association only).*

A
The Library Association

Describe a satisfactory system of registering and indexing borrowers, and give the ruling and letterpress of an application card.

Show what guides you would provide in a closely classified open-access library to facilitate the finding of books. Illustrate your answer.

Describe two charging systems in vogue in open-access libraries, and the various kinds of appliances used in connection with them. Give a diagram of a card-tray with guides.

What do you know of "Information Bureaux" in public libraries?

Describe a satisfactory charging system for use in a reference library, and give the ruling and wording of a reference library application form.

What aids would you provide in a closely classified reference library to facilitate the quick finding of a book, and to account for the absence of one from the shelves?

In forming a local collection what material would you consider of sufficient importance to merit inclusion? State the system of classification you would adopt, and the kind of catalogue you would prepare, to render the collection useful to readers.

State the principles you would observe in selecting books for branch libraries, and the advantages of centralizing all cataloguing, classification, etc. Describe also any system of interchanging among central and branch libraries known to you.

How would you record the day's issues in a lending or reference library under the various classes? Give rulings of an issue book or sheet.

Show in what directions collections of pictures may be helpful to readers, and briefly describe how you would collect and arrange the material.

A MANUAL OF LIBRARY ROUTINE

Describe a card-charging system suitable for the central office of a rural library system. Illustrate your answer.

Describe the aims and work of the National Central Library, and show how public libraries may co-operate advantageously with this institution.

Describe how you would organize a series of library lectures so as to avoid financial difficulties, and include a syllabus of six lectures suitable for adults and six for children.

What are University Extension Lectures? Show how public libraries may advantageously co-operate in their organization.

Enumerate the principal points you would include in a specification for bookbinding.

Describe the various processes a book withdrawn from circulation for binding goes through before its return to the shelves.

State what you consider to be the best methods of filing periodicals and newspapers, temporarily and permanently.

Set out the processes through which a book passes from the time of its receipt to its issue to a reader. Give the ruling and wording of a form denoting the various processes.

Describe some methods of conducting school libraries in connection with public libraries. Which do you consider the most satisfactory? Supply ruling and wording of the various labels, stock cards, etc., and show how issues are recorded.

Compile an annotated list of the principal routine duties of a lending-library staff.

Describe an adequate system of ordering, storing, and issuing stationery and other supplies.

In what ways can a library prove its value to the business community?

It is decided to purchase books recommended by the British Broadcasting Corporation. How would you display these to the best advantage?

SOME EXAMINATION QUESTIONS

B

UNIVERSITY OF LONDON DIPLOMA IN LIBRARIANSHIP
(School of Librarianship)

What tests would you apply to discover whether additional books for a library already established were desirable or not, having regard to finance, supply, and demand?

Describe how you would prepare a list of books proposed for purchase, and the routine treatment of the list in committee and subsequently (exclusive of ordering).

In what form would you issue an order for new books, and what steps would you take to ensure that the books are correctly supplied?

Describe the routine of stocktaking in any kind of library, and give rulings for the form of check-list which you would employ for this purpose.

Write a short essay, with particular reference to routine methods, upon any *one* of the following subjects:

(a) Commercial (or Technical) Libraries.
(b) The National Central Library and Regional Co-operation.
(c) Children's Libraries.

Explain (a) how overdue books are detected by any form of issue records, (b) what steps you would take to obtain the return of such books, and (c) a satisfactory system of receipts for fines.

Describe in detail the routine respecting (a) bespoke books, and (b) book renewing.

Briefly indicate the scope and purpose of a county library, and an effective charging system at the headquarters library.

Describe in detail a charging system suitable for a university or a school library.

Give a succinct account of office routine, with especial reference to the treatment of correspondence.

Describe two methods of checking the receipt of periodicals, one by means of cards, and the other by any alternate method.

Outline the object and principal routine methods of municipally maintained commercial and technical libraries.

Regarding the accessions register as the centre of your system of stock records, explain how the other stock records supplement it and link up with it.

What is involved in "the preparation of books for the shelves"? Comment on the importance of the different processes. How would you secure that no step was omitted?

Describe the process of "charging" books in (*a*) an open-access lending department, and (*b*) in a closed lending library with or without an indicator.

Discuss the relative values, for library binding purposes, of pigskin, skivers, sealskin, moroccos, basil, roan, and Persian leathers. Under what circumstances would you give preference to buckram or other cloth material as a covering for books?

Describe and discuss the following methods of sewing books: sewing two sheets on, overcasting, sawn-in sewing, and sewing all-along; and state under what circumstances you would approve overcasting.

How would you ensure, by means of administrative records:

(*a*) That every book purchased went into library stock?
(*b*) That no book was paid for more than once?
(*c*) That the yearly publications of Societies, and successive volumes of a work appearing at irregular intervals, are duly supplied and are charged for at the proper rate?

What means do librarians use to attract and maintain the interest of children?

How would you prepare the manuscript of a catalogue (or book list of any character) for publication? Give ten marks as used in the correction of printers' proofs, and state their meaning.

INDEX

Accession numbers, uses of, 72–3
Accession registers, 61, 68–75
Accessioning—
  definition of, 62
  redundancy in, 61
  variant methods in, 61, 74
Accessioning by lot, 74
Accounts—
  preparation of, 300–1, 310, 319
  submission of to committees, 306–7
  treatment of in committee, 307
Administrative records, 61–79
Admission—
  to lectures, 322
  to lending departments, 122–44
  to reference departments, 165
Agendas for committees, 306
Alphabetico-classed catalogues, 95
Alphabetization in catalogues, 100
American Library Association on bindings, 285–6
Analytical cataloguing, 114–15
Anglo-American cataloguing rules, 99
Application forms—
  in university libraries, 228–9
  lending department, 128–32, 197
  reference, 163–4
Approval, books on, 34–5
Attendance registers, public, 165
Attendances in reading-rooms, 211

Balance of stock, 26–8
Bibliographies, use of, 25–6
Binderies at libraries, 286
Binding, 282–95
  adaptation of, 283
  cased books, 17–18
  examination of books for, 284

Binding, leathers and other materials for, 285–6
  records relating to, 287–9
  specifications for, 286–7
  staff repairs, 290–4
  treatment of newly bound books, 18
"Black list" of defaulters, 137–8, 160
Blind, books for the, 333–4
Book carrying, 19
  charging cards, 147–50
  committee lists, 32–4
  numbering, 54–9
  ordering, 36–8
  purchasing considerations, 32
  selection, 23–41
  terms of supply, 39–40
  trade symbols, 44–5
  votes, 31–2
Book delivery system, 201
Bookcard-in-pocket system, 146–9
Bookcard-in-tray system, 148–50
Books—
  collation of, 45–8
  condition of used, 284
  displays of, 119, 327
  disposal of old, 279
  on approval, 34–5
  stamping, 49
Borrowers—
  application forms for, 129
  branch and centralized registration of, 134–6, 196–7
  change of address of, 141–2
  examination of applications of, 129–32
  issue of tickets to, 132–3
  lost tickets of, 140–1
  registers of, 133–8
  renewal of tickets of, 139
  varieties of, 122–8

343

Branch library routine, 193–205
  accounts, 310
  book stock, 193
  interchange service, 199–200
  reference and reading-rooms, 198–9
  registration of borrowers, 134–6, 196–7
  superintendents, 202–3
British Museum Catalogues, 25
Broadcasting co-operation, 329–31
Bulletins, library, 101, 327
Bureaux, library, 328
Burnishing, gold-leaf, 56–8
Business libraries, 181

Cannon's *Bibliography of Library Economy*, 20–1
Card accession registers, 75
Card catalogues, 112–16
Card-charging methods, 146–52
Card indexes to correspondence, 316
Cased bindings, 17–18, 282
Catalogues, 95–121
  alphabetico-classed, 95
  alphabetization in, 100
  analytical entries in, 114–15
  card and sheaf forms of, 112–18
  cyclostyled, 119–20
  dictionary form of, 100
  mechanical methods of preparing, 97, 100–12
  printed, 105–12
  reference, 164–5
  subject, 101, 111–12
  topical lists as, 118–19
  typewritten, 113
  union, 115, 259–60
Cataloguing—
  codes noticed, 99
  co-operative, 112–13
  cross-references in, 98
  errors in, 96–7
  essentials, 96–7

Cataloguing—*continued*
  rules, 98
  subject-headings in, 96–7
Centralization discussed, 135–6, 194, 197
Chambers of Commerce, 327
Changes of address, 141–2
Charging—
  county library methods of, 248–50
  sheet systems, 240–1
  term defined, 145
  university method of, 228–9
  variant methods of routine of, 144–60
Checking off deliveries, 42–4
Children's Act lecture requirements, 324
Children's libraries, 187–92
  attendance of children at lectures, 324
  book stock for, 89
  catalogues in, 111
  county forms of, 256
  lending-library tickets, 128–9
Cinematograph films at lectures, 324
Classification—
  and its practical applications, 80–94
  close classification discussed, 83–4
  codes of, 82–5, 92
  methods of, 80
  numbers and symbols in, 87–8, 90, 92
  pitfalls in, 85–7
  systems explained by their authors, 84
  theory of, 84
  value of, 80–1
Cloth bindings, 282, 285
Clue numbers, 75, 76
Codes—
  cataloguing, 99
  classification, 82–5, 92

INDEX

Collation of books, 45–8
College and school libraries, 237–44
College library work, 237–44
Commercial and technical libraries, 178–80
Committee work, 305–9
Co-operative work—
 broadcasting, 329–31
 cataloguing, 112–13
 library methods of, 246–68
 with educational agencies, 327
 with newspapers, 327
Copying letters, 312–13
Correspondence, treatment of, 311–18
County libraries, 246–56
 charging at headquarters, 249–50
 co-operative work by, 252
 development of, 246–8
 headquarters routine of, 248–53
 local centres, 249, 251–4
 other activities, 256
 regional branches of, 254–5
 van delivery system of, 255
Cross-references, use of, 97–8
Cutter author-marks, 90
Cutting leaves of books, 51–2
Cyclostyle work, 119–20, 319–20, 327

Date stamp setting, 146
Defaulters' register, 137–8, 160
Delivery notes, 42
Delivery stations, 203–4
Delivery vans, 255
Deposit stations, 203–4
Dewey Decimal System—
 abbreviated code of the, 92
 its problems for classifiers, 83
 reference of queries to its editor, 83
Dictionary catalogues, 100
Dirt, removal from pages, 292–3
Discarded books, treatment of, 280

Discharging books, 151–2
Donation records, 65–8
Drury's *Book Selection*, 26
Dusting of books, 20

Educational agencies, co-operation with, 327
Electric stylus, 58–9
Embossing book covers, 49
Emigration bureaux, 328
English Catalogue of Books, 30–1
Epidiascopes, 324
Errors in cataloguing, 96–7
Esdaile's *Manual of Bibliography*, 25
Estimates, financial, 31–2, 296–9
Exchange of book stock, 236–7

Fatigue in cataloguing, 97
Fees for lecturers, 323
Fiction, selection of, 31–2
Filing of correspondence, 315–18
Films at lectures, 324
Finance routine, 296–304
 annual estimates, 32, 296–8
 ordering and order records, 299–300
 petty cash accounts, 301–4
 postage accounts, 304
 preparation of accounts, 300–1
Fixed location, 89–90
Foreign book lists, 30
Forms for orders, 36–7

Gifts, treatment of, 66–8
Glaire, 57
Gold tooling work, 55–8
Guarantors for borrowers, 136–7, 140
Guides in card catalogues, 116

Handling of books, 17–18
Handwriting, 16–17, 113
Holiday bureaux, 328
Hospital library work, 331–2

345

A MANUAL OF LIBRARY ROUTINE

Indexes, correspondence, 316
Indexes to subject lists, 112
Indicators, 92
 how checked, 274
Infectious diseases, 142–4
Information desks, 181–3
Inkstains, removing, 293
Interchange of book stock, 200
Inter-library loans, 200
Invoice books and files, 45, 61, 63–5, 76
Invoices as accession records, 74

Jast, L. S., on classification, 84–5

Labelling of books, 52–4
Lantern slides, 323–4
Leathers discussed, 284–6
Lecturers—
 fees to, 323
 selection of, 323
Lectures—
 arrangements for, 325
 children's, 324
 expenses of, 322
 films at, 324
 lantern slides at, 323
 programmes and book lists for, 325
 reports of, 307, 327
 University Extension, 325–6
 voluntary lecturers for, 323
Ledger charging, 152–3
Leeds Public Library *Handbooks*, 26
Letters, treatment of, 311–18
Library journals, 29
Library of Congress—
 catalogue cards, 112–13
 classification of the, 84–5
Local centres. *See* County libraries
Local collections, 174–5
Local library co-operation, 263
Loose-leaf records, 73–4
Lost tickets, 140

Magazine-rooms, 207–22
Magazines for home reading, 219
Maintenance of stock, 28–31, 276–9, 284
Manifolding work, 319
Mansfield Library co-operation, 263
Manuscripts, accessioning, 73
Maps—
 treatment of, 177
 use of, 179–80
Master-catalogues, 115
Minto's *History of the Public Library Movement*, 247
Minute taking in committee, 308–9
Morocco leathers, 285

National Central Library—
 objects and methods of, 34–5, 183, 264–8
 "outlier" libraries of the, 266–7
 Scottish, Welsh and Irish Central Libraries, 265
 union catalogue of the, 264
Net book system, 39–40
New book displays and lists, 119, 327
Newark Library co-operation, 263
Newspaper co-operation, 327
Newspaper-rooms, 207–22
Nowell, C., on broadcasting co-operation, 329–30
Numbering book covers, methods of, 54–9

Office routine, 309–21
Open-access library classification, 80–1
Opening new books, 18
Orderliness on shelves, 274–5
Orders and order records, 32, 36–8, 299–301, 319
"Outlier" libraries, 266–7
Overdue books, 158–60, 230

INDEX

Pagination, 46–7
Pamphlets, treatment of, 175–6
Papers, physical qualities of, 282
Paste, recipe for making, 54
Periodicals—
  binding up for stock, 218
  commercial and technical, 179
  delivery checking, 211–14
  display methods, 214–17
  filing back numbers of, 217–20
  selection of, 208–9
  terms of supply, 210
  university provision of, 231–4
Petty cash accounts, 301–4
Photostat, use of the, 293
Pigskin bindings, 285
Placard catalogues, 118
Plate paper, 282
Pollard, A. C. F., on the Universal Decimal Classification, 85
Postage accounts, 304
Print collections, 73, 177–8
Printer's copy, preparation of, 101–4
Printing—
  catalogue specifications, 105
  marking for press, 103–9
  preparation of manuscript for, 100–5
  proof correcting, 105–12
  revises, 106–10
  terms used in, 46–8
Prints, accessioning of, 73
Privilege issue, 155, 171–2
Process records, 49–51
Programmes for lectures, 325
Proof marks and correction, 105–12
Publicity methods, 221–2, 256, 327–9
Purchase of books, 32

Qualities for success, 15–16

Ratepayer borrowers, 123–4

Reading-room routine, 207–22
Reference libraries, 162–78
  attendance registers, 165
  book-issue methods, 163–70
  catalogues, 164–5
  discharging, 166–7
  issue check-files, 169–70
  local collections in, 174–5
  maps in, 177
  open access in, 170–1
  pamphlets in, 175–6
  print collections in, 177–8
  regulations, observance of, 167
  shelf orderliness, 168
  special loans, 171–2
  students' rooms, 173–4
Regional co-operation, 256–62
  existing regions, 258
  routine methods of, 256–62
  scope of, 257–8
Registers, administrative, 61–79
Registration of borrowers, 122–44
Reinforced binding, 282
Renewal of books, 153–5
  of borrowers' tickets, 139
Repairing books, 290–4
Replacements—
  accessioning of, 70–2
  expenditure on, 31
  routine, 279–80
Reports to committees, 307
Reservation of books, 155–7
Reserve book stocks, 275–6
Reviews of books, use of, 29–30
Revision of book stock, 276–9
Routine defined, 9
Rules and regulations, 133
Russia leather bindings, 285

Sayer's *Revision of the Stock of a Public Library*, 277
  works on classification, 84, 94
School library methods, 237–44
Scientific literature, selection of, 29–30

A MANUAL OF LIBRARY ROUTINE

Scottish National Library for Students, 265
Second-hand books, 37, 42
Sections, a book term, 46–7
Sheaf catalogues, 112–18
Sheepskin leathers, 285
Sheet-charging methods, 152–3
Shelf—
 arrangement, 88–92
 guiding, 91–2
 orderliness, 18, 270–5
Shelf-lists—
 described, 269–70
 use of in taking stock, 271–4
 variant forms of, 270
Shorthand, use of, 311
Signatures, printing term, 47
Sizes of books, 46, 88
Specifications—
 binding, 286–7
 printing, 105
Stains in books, removing, 292–3
Statistical returns, 318
Statistics—
 in committee, 307, 309–10, 318
 summary, 76–7
Stencil work, 91–2
Stock books, 68
Stocktaking methods, 269–74
Students' rooms, 173–4
Stylus, electric, 58–9
Sub-committee work, 306–7
Subject—
 catalogues, 111–12
 headings, 97–8
 indexes, 112
Subscriptions, annual, 311
Suggestions by readers, 35–6
Summary statistics, 76–7
Sundry requirements, lists of, 306
Symbols, book trade, 44–5

Technical libraries, 178–80
Technical literature, selection of, 29–30

The Times Literary Supplement, reviews, 29
Tickets —
 children's library, 187–90
 lending library, 123, 132–3, 139–51, 196–7
Titles of books, vague, 85–6
Topical lists, 118–19, 327
Typewriting, 113, 119–20, 312

Uniformity, importance of in cataloguing, 97–9
Union catalogues, 115, 258–60
Universal Decimal Classification, 85
University Extension Lectures, 325–6
University libraries, 223–36
 book exchanges, 236–7
 book stock, 224–5
 charging methods and overdues, 228–30
 classification and cataloguing of, 225–6
 college libraries, 230–1
 co-operative work between, 235–6
 departmental libraries, 227–8
 general routine of, 223–4
 periodicals in, 232–4
 seminar libraries, 226–7

Van delivery system, 255
Vertical files, 315–18

Welsh National Central Library, 265
Wire stitching in books, 282
Withdrawal of books from stock, 117, 276–9
 records, 71, 91
Workers' Educational Association, 256
Works libraries, 181
Worksop Library, co-operation, 363

For Product Safety Concerns and Information please contact our EU representative GPSR@taylorandfrancis.com
Taylor & Francis Verlag GmbH, Kaufingerstraße 24, 80331 München, Germany

www.ingramcontent.com/pod-product-compliance
Lightning Source LLC
Chambersburg PA
CBHW071151300426
44113CB00009B/1172